Media Laboratories

FLASHPOINTS

The FlashPoints series is devoted to books that consider literature beyond strictly national and disciplinary frameworks, and that are distinguished both by their historical grounding and by their theoretical and conceptual strength. Our books engage theory without losing touch with history and work historically without falling into uncritical positivism. FlashPoints aims for a broad audience within the humanities and the social sciences concerned with moments of cultural emergence and transformation. In a Benjaminian mode, FlashPoints is interested in how literature contributes to forming new constellations of culture and history and in how such formations function critically and politically in the present. Series titles are available online at http://escholarship.org/uc/flashpoints.

A complete list of titles begins on page 235.

Media Laboratories

Late Modernist Authorship in South America

Sarah Ann Wells

NORTHWESTERN UNIVERSITY PRESS | EVANSTON, ILLINOIS

mLI the modern language initiative

THIS BOOK IS MADE POSSIBLE BY A COLLABORATIVE GRANT FROM THE ANDREW W. MELLON FOUNDATION.

Northwestern University Press
www.nupress.northwestern.edu

Printed in the United States of America

10 9 8 7 6 5 4 3 2 1

Library of Congress Cataloging-in-Publication Data

Names: Wells, Sarah Ann, 1979– author.
Title: Media laboratories : late modernist authorship in South America / Sarah Ann Wells.
Other titles: FlashPoints (Evanston, Ill.)
Description: Evanston, Illinois : Northwestern University Press, 2017. | Series: Flashpoints
Identifiers: LCCN 2016024107 | ISBN 9780810134546 (pbk. : alk. paper) | ISBN 9780810134553 (cloth : alk. paper) | ISBN 9780810134560 (e-book)
Subjects: LCSH: Latin American fiction—20th century—History and criticism. | Experimental fiction, Latin American—History and criticism. | Mass media in literature. | Senses and sensation in literature.
Classification: LCC PQ7552.E97 W45 2017 | DDC 863.6209112—dc23
LC record available at https://lccn.loc.gov/2016024107

♾ The paper used in this publication meets the minimum requirements of the American National Standard for Information Sciences—Permanence of Paper for Printed Library Materials, ANSI Z39.48-1992.

Contents

Acknowledgments

This book was written while shuttling back and forth among many cities, institutions, and homes. It was made possible by the people who helped transform these often transitory places into sites of connection.

I first became interested in late modernism as a graduate student in the Department of Comparative Literature at the University of California, Berkeley. I would like to thank Francine Masiello, Tony Cascardi, Miryam Sas, Carolyn Porter, and José Luiz Passos for their advice and influence, and for teaching me about Borges, Benjamin, *literatura do Nordeste*, and more. Francine and Zé Luiz deserve special thanks for continuing to support my career long after I had left the Bay Area for the Midwest.

Between Oakland, Iowa City, Buenos Aires, Rio de Janeiro, São Paulo, South Bend, Indiana, Chicago, and, finally, Madison, Wisconsin, I have been lucky to find outstanding interlocutors. The following people took the time to help me think through this project in various ways: Michelle Clayton, Steve Choe, Paul Saint-Amour, Jason Borge, Diana Klinger, Florencia Garramuño, Jennifer Buckley, María Inés de Torres, Paul Ramírez, Sylvia Sellers-García, Teresa Villa-Ignacio, Jaime Ginzburg, Guadalupe Salomon, Allison Schachter, Tom McEnaney, Rielle Navitski, Jillian Porter, and, last but not least, Gonzalo Aguilar, whose own work has taught me much. I would like to give a special thanks to Matt Karush and Jesús Costantino for generously offering to read and comment on parts of the book in its late stages.

Support for this research was generously provided by the University of Wisconsin–Madison Office of the Vice Chancellor for Research and Graduate Education with funding from the Wisconsin Alumni Research Foundation. Additional support was provided by the Modern Language Initiative of the Andrew W. Mellon Foundation. Earlier, an International Dissertation Research Fellowship from the Social Science Research Council was fundamental in exposing me to the little magazines and periodicals that are an important voice in this study. Additional support from the Latin American Institute at the University of California–Los Angeles and the Institute for Scholarship in the Liberal Arts at the University of Notre Dame allowed for follow-up trips to the archives. I would also like to thank all these institutions, along with the librarians and archivists who helped me, in particular those from the Instituto de Estudos Brasileiros, Centro de Documentación e Investigación de la Cultura de las Izquierdas en Argentina, the Biblioteca Nacional in Buenos Aires (especially Juan Pablo Canala), the Felisberto Hernández Special Collection at American University, and the University of Wisconsin–Madison. For their assistance in tracking down citations, I thank graduate students Ingrid Luna and Javier Mocarquer at Notre Dame and Alec Schumacher, Marin Laufenberg, and Joelle Tybon at UW–Madison. For furnishing me a screening copy of the Quay Brothers' *Unmistaken Hands: Ex-Voto F.H.*, I thank Edward Waisnis. Portions of Chapter 1 appeared in *Modernism/ Modernity* ("Late Modernism, Pulp History: Jorge Luis Borges' *A Universal History of* Infamy") and *Luso-Brazilian Review* ("Mass Culture and the Laboratory of Late Modernism in Patrícia Galvão's *Parque Industrial*"). I am grateful to Johns Hopkins University Press and the University of Wisconsin Press, respectively, for permission to publish these essays here in revised form.

I found a wonderfully supportive network at Notre Dame, where the bulk of this book was written, and wish to thank my colleagues in and beyond the Department of Romance Languages and Literatures, in particular Ted Cachey, Zyg Baranski, María Rosa Oliveira Williams, Diana Jorza, Anne García-Romero, Jennifer Jones, and, for their advice and support at critical junctures, Julia Douthwaite and Carlos Jáuregui. For accompanying me in the very last stages, I thank my new colleagues in the Department of Comparative Literature and Folklore Studies at the UW–Madison, in particular Jordan Rosenblum, for his advice and humor, and Mary Layoun, a mentor, colleague, and friend of extraordinary generosity. The modernist reading group I formed with Dean Krouk at Madison was a touchstone as I put the finishing touches on this manuscript.

I would like to give special thanks to those who read the entire manuscript: the two anonymous external reviewers and Edward Dimendberg, my series editor. Their suggestions from a variety of disciplines, including modernist studies, film and media studies, and Latin American literature, were illuminating. It was a pleasure to work Gianna Mosser and the Editorial Board and production staff of Northwestern University Press, and I would like to thank them, along with Tim Roberts at the Modern Language Initiative, for their support. Special thanks go to the Editorial Board of the FlashPoints series for believing in this project and ushering it into fruition.

Those people who not only read and commented on portions of this book in stages from the larval to the almost-there but also helped me beyond the page deserve a special category. They did double-duty as friends and readers; they made authorship feel collective: Brian Gollnick, Ayelet Ben-Yishai, Salomé Aguilera-Skivrsky, and especially Jennifer "Eagle Eye" Feeley and Hannah Freed-Thall, confidant and fellow traveler in the often circuitous routes of modernism and modernist studies.

As I was finishing this book the deaths of two amazing women, unrepentant avant-gardists to the very end, occurred. I like to think that the provocative presences of Rachel Perlmeter and Ruth Lee Wells made their way into the finished product. Special thanks are also due to two key figures in my life: Jessica Teal Perlmeter Cochrane, for her steadfast camaraderie in all pursuits artistic and intellectual, and Beth Baker, the first person to show (rather than tell) me that writing and editing could be at once craft, profession, vocation, and passion.

This book is dedicated to Víctor Goldgel Carballo, for his time, patience, and irony.

Preface: Alternative Circuits

"Starstruck" (El enamorado de una estrella, 1933), a short story by the Argentine author Nicolás Olivari, tells of an idiosyncratic home movie forged from stolen scraps. The unnamed protagonist finds a discarded filmstrip from a Joan Crawford picture on the streets of Buenos Aires. Bringing it back to his grim tenement, he repeatedly projects it, using a "modest apparatus," onto a sheet in his room. Animating the still frame as though he were a cinematographer or projectionist—"in moving the handle of my machine, the image acquires seventeen different gestures"—he repeatedly "chain[s] himself to the image." In this way, he develops an entire world around this remnant, "a bit larger than a fingernail."[1]

Recounting his experiences to an interlocutor in the lobby of a movie theater, the protagonist spins different stories from the animated scrap. He vernacularizes Crawford through the tango, *sainete* (popular theater), and other working-class local forms: she is the girl from the *arrabal* (the outskirts of town) who makes it big; he is a down-on-his-luck flâneur, prowling the streets of Buenos Aires. In the process, he also underscores the fragile materialities that undergird these stories: "I make the star travel thousands of kilometers and I capture her, now a little withered from her long journey, on the sheet of my domesticity. She has passed through all the world's cinematographs. She made her way to Buenos Aires a few years ago, and her story is engraved on the film canister that housed her as she made her way here, in the mountain range of bumps it has suffered" (165). "Starstruck" describes a process of reanimated residues, of corporealization, sacralization, and reimagined scripts, by which the detritus of mass culture becomes an alternative circuit. The entire experience is narrated, moreover, in the liminal space of a movie theater lobby. We are invited to query the strange symmetry of the tenement home projection and the multitude waiting to enter into the movie palace. The former runs alongside the latter, as its other face.

Fantasies of rerouting mass media circuits haunt fiction from Brazil, Argentina, and Uruguay during the late modernist period (1929–46). In fact, Olivari's brief narrative describes a series of procedures that appear with surprising frequency during this moment: a protagonist drags an automatized medium into a fictional, often explicitly peripheral site; once there, he or she takes it apart, before ultimately setting it up to operate in a mode that exceeds its original use. In the media laboratories of late modernism, hypodermic needles infect listeners with radio commercials and tinkling tangos, only to meet their match in abrupt home remedies; eccentric users create "touch chambers" to rival cinema palaces; a writer constructs a ventriloquist dummy jury-rigged with a phonograph to vie for the attentions of the clamoring masses; an all-encompassing virtual reality machine is interrupted by the sudden appearance of a wayward hand that quivers, uncannily. Throughout, these texts also foreground unresolved problems of access and agency from outside the centers of transnational capital.

Along with many of his contemporaries, Olivari thus presents us with a number of questions: How has a space repeatedly depicted as peripheral to global media networks produced some of modernist literature's most powerful accounts of media change, consolidation, and disenchantment? How do such accounts trouble our assumptions about how modern media function as they travel from their point of spatial and temporal emergence? How might literature confront the production, consumption, and circulation of media at a moment in which demiurgic fantasies of inventing new, world-making technologies no longer seem possible? Attending to these questions, I argue, shifts our narratives about modernism and modernity, and the role of media within them, narratives long premised on a familiar arc of origins, development, and obsolescence.

I call media laboratories the temporary sites—the way stations or itinerant camps of fiction—where authors test out the implications of changes in the production, circulation, and reception of media. The laboratory is where literature, and fiction in particular, produces an alternative circuit to the bureaucratization of formerly new media, especially cinema, the radio, and the typewriter, and also where writers navigate their shifting relationship to these. Media laboratories are phenomena that become prominent, I argue, during moments of perceived consolidation, as opposed to emergence, of extant media. They are responses to the sense that media have become increasingly out of reach—blackboxed or opaque—even as they grow increasingly ubiquitous. In light of asymmetries in global modern media networks, South American late modernist literature showcases multiple, at times perverse tactics.

Laboratories are also sites of labor, directed toward a result as yet unknown or unproven. They are places of making, doing, and using. The frequent appearance of the suffix *ship* throughout this book—authorship, usership, spectatorship, and what I call feelership—underscores this sense of work and craft but also that of rank and title that lends the author legitimation and which is particularly fraught in the South American context. To the earlier understanding of authorship as the creator of new worlds, late modernist authorship juxtaposed alternative figures, including the listener, tinkerer, viewer, or feeler. Late modernist authorship thus refers not only to the process of creating a work and tethering it to a signature but also to the self- and collective fashioning of the author himself or herself as a precarious and anachronistic figure in late modernity.

Media Laboratories is not structured around a specific medium, as is common in media studies, or around a single author or text, as tends to be the case in modernist studies. Nor is it linked by a set of direct affiliations or influences. It is true that several of the protagonists converge around a cosmopolitan Buenos Aires of the 1930s–1940s, above all around the figure of Jorge Luis Borges and the editor and patron Victoria Ocampo, who together promoted the works of their Uruguayan contemporary Felisberto Hernández (Chapter 4) and the Cuban writer-in-residence Virgilio Piñera (Chapter 2). They even, very briefly, encountered the Brazilian author and activist Patrícia Galvão, who brushed shoulders with both in the early 1930s (Chapters 1 and 2). In addition, during these same years, the Buenos Aires intellectual Benjamin de Garay was the first to translate Graciliano Ramos, the focus of Chapter 3.

My analysis, however, does not depend on such immediate encounters but on thinking through a set of questions that emerge when we read synchronically across interconnected but distinct contexts. Each chapter of this book explores a late modernist scene of reception that repositions authorship. In turn, each transformation of authorship entails specific sensorial dimensions, including the visual, the aural, the proprioceptive, and the haptic. As W. J. T. Mitchell reminds us, all media imply multiple sensory dimensions, even "the so-called visual media"; no media are "pure" in this sense, nor does pure perception exist.[2] For this reason, certain authors and texts return at different moments throughout the book—Jorge Luis Borges's scopophilic spectator in the first chapter is transformed into the user of imaginary media in the last; Patrícia Galvão's viewer of Soviet film in the first chapter becomes an ear tuning in to proletarian voices in the third. Throughout, I also incorporate archival material from little magazines, mainstream cultural periodicals, and film journals that flourished during the period. This rich archive, part of a boom in periodicals often overlooked in favor of their avant-garde predecessors, registers the polemic encounters between writers and the no-longer-new media that continued to inspire them.

The introduction establishes the central claims of this study: the concept of the media laboratory as a site in which authorship is transformed and the relevance of the periodizing term "late modernism." Subsequent chapters theorize different iterations of authorship in late modernism. In Chapter 1, "Conscripting Global Cinema," I adopt the structure of montage to compare two very different writers, Borges and Galvão, both grappling with the same problem: the imperative to reposition authorship as a form of cinematic viewership, part of a broader struggle over global film language taking place on both screens and pages. The second chapter, "Tuning In," moves among various short texts from Argentina, Brazil, and Uruguay like a radio dial, pausing to home in on different late modernist approaches to voice, in particular through the figure of the *acousmêtre*, or disembodied voice. Chapter 3, "Pounding Away at the Typewriter," compares the Brazilian novel *Anguish* (Graciliano Ramos, 1936) to its unlikely successor, Clarice Lispector's *The Hour of the Star* (1977), both of which posit the proletarianized typist and the rhythms of her repetitive labor as an extension of authorship. This chapter also opens the second half of the book, which focuses on usership, located in different labors of the hand and/or in the body's proprioceptive responses.

In Chapter 4, "The Residual Haptic," I show how Uruguayan writer Felisberto Hernández's fiction fashioned a place for the user through the residual sensory dimension of the haptic and its privileged role in silent film. Finally, Chapter 5, "Imaginary Media," invokes the *what if?* experiments that pit the anachronistic technology of writing against a fantastic apparatus in the 1940s works of Borges and his partner-in-crime, Adolfo Bioy Casares. As I argue in this chapter, the black boxes of media obscure their operations from potential users; in South American late modernist fiction, their presence allegorizes the unequal circulation of global media in the twentieth century. The shadow of underdevelopment that plagued much of earlier media history is called into question within the archaeology of imaginary media.

Like Olivari's "Starstruck," many of the works I analyze in this study are hinge-texts, difficult to locate in our traditional literary histories.[3] Although I examine a few canonical texts—namely, novellas by Clarice Lispector (*The Hour of the Star*) and Adolfo Bioy Casares (*The Invention of Morel*) and two very famous Borges stories—the majority are ephemeral and often overlooked, representing either minor works by major authors or texts by lesser-known figures. Not coincidentally, they also breach one or more periods and/or movements: the leftist Galvão's lateral relationship to Brazilian modernism; Felisberto Hernández's sideways glance at the French surrealists who deeply informed him; the way in which Borges, Virgilio Piñera, and Lispector whittle away at high/low distinctions, hinting at elements of what was very recently known as postmodernism; or, throughout, how the troubled status of the author during this period often evokes contemporary debates on "new" media.[4] The media laboratory interrupts and productively entangles our narratives of media change and development but also of literary history, periodization, and, beyond these, the broader, passionately desired, and endlessly contested narrative known as modernity.

Media Laboratories

Introduction

Media Laboratories

AUTHORSHIP IN THE MEDIA LABORATORY

In the first decades of the twentieth century, cinema, radio, and the typewriter held out the promise of radically new experiences for South American writers, as they would for their contemporaries in and beyond the continent.[1] Scholarship has tended to consecrate these media in similar terms: cinema epitomized modern life; radio was a fantastic, nearly otherworldly apparatus; the typewriter revolutionized writing. Beginning in the 1930s, however, a shift in perception occurred. Artists and intellectuals began to perceive these same media as consolidated and automatized. In South America and globally, an understanding of the anaesthetics of mass media—the sense that modern life has become hyperstimulated by technological and scientific modernity, including advertising, the assembly line, and the collective, quotidian experiences of cinema and radio—became increasingly entrenched.[2] While this process had antecedents, especially in vexed contexts like Weimar Germany, the conviction that there were fewer and fewer opportunities to tap into the latent utopian potential of these media had now become dominant.

As formerly new media were becoming massified, artists and intellectuals began to hear the clamor of a different sound: the emergent and slippery category known as the masses. A phenomenon rarely pursued by their avant-gardes predecessors, the figure of the masses is central to several accounts of the global 1930s. They are particularly charged in Latin America, when a nascent populism, the region's most prominent political idiom, appeared in Brazil during the regime of Getúlio Vargas (1930–45) and later in the regime of Juan Domingo Perón in Argentina.[3] For influential media theorist Jesús Martín-Barbero, this period witnesses a historical shift by which the working classes become incorporated into state politics through a negotiation with elites that takes place in and through the mass media.[4] The masses will become increasingly prominent in aesthetic, political, and economic discourses of the region; they will continue to shape South American art well into the twenty-first century.

Late modernist literature emerges partially in response to these dual phenomena: on one hand, writers' shifting relationship to the masses and, on the other, their shifting relationship to formerly new media. It is often characterized by a sense of disillusionment induced by what writers perceived as failures of innovation: of formerly new media like the cinema, radio, and typewriter, now domesticated and, to a certain extent, politically neutralized; and of the historical avant-gardes of the 1910s–1920s. The intensity of the avant-garde self was frequently recast as part of a larger, collaborative effort to produce and sustain new reading and viewing publics, and the status of the author as demiurge began to weaken. As this book argues, authors began to experiment with a series of alternative figures to understand their place in this fraught context. Rather than prescient seers and producers of new worlds, they became conduits of a dense, embodied reception of the troubled present, recasting themselves as spectators, listener, and users.

The stakes were high, for authorship had long held an especially prominent role in Latin America. According to Ángel Rama's influential argument, the prestige accorded to the *letrado*, the man of letters, indelibly shaped power regimes from the colonial period until the early twentieth century. Here, the ostensible demotion of writing arguably had starker implications, for the privilege of authorship had a lengthier and more pronounced history than it would in either Europe or the United States.[5] (This process occurred unevenly even within South America well into the twentieth century; the pronounced difference between Brazil and Argentina, neighbors if not friends, is but one example.)

For Rama, the historical avant-gardes of the 1910s and 1920s occupy a transitional moment, and one where his powerful narrative essentially ends. The figure of the *letrado* is eroded—or expanded so much as to undermine his elite privilege—through professionalization and specialization, liberalizing reforms in education, the emergence of the working classes, massive immigration, and a discourse of the national-popular.[6] In this context, the avant-garde artist constitutes the last gasp of the *letrado*: he or she simultaneously celebrates the eroding of his predecessor's power and laments the demise of this powerful figure of authorship.[7] He or she longs to smash institutions, yet is unable to relinquish the belief in the artist as a privileged minority who will inaugurate the region's ever-deferred modernity. In Brazil, for example, this period is alternatively described as the "heroic," "combative," or "euphoric" phase of modernism, reflecting language from the seminal Modern Art Week of 1922, Brazil's "vibrating" or "trembling" years.[8] The first issue of the seminal *Revista de Antropofagia* (1928) uses metaphors of the tabula rasa and biblical floods; writing of the modernist movement more broadly, its most important practitioner, Mário de Andrade, will write retrospectively, "We were really pure and free."[9]

During the 1930s, the lingering prestige of the author enters into crisis. (It will not disappear altogether but will reemerge periodically, most prominently in the demiurgic author figures of the Boom of the 1960s–1970s.) In "Literature and Underdevelopment," the Brazilian critic António Cândido argues that it is during the 1930s that a burgeoning understanding of Latin America's "underdevelopment" begins to replace the tacitly optimistic trope of the continent as virgin land, as a space ripe for hope and the inscription of futurity, which had remained powerful from Romanticism to the early twentieth century.[10] The privileged place of newness and its grammars of futurity—that "we were really pure and free"—are called into question, and with it the figure of the author as change agent.[11] As I show at the end of this chapter, this weakening of the author figure is most immediately visible in the perceived death of clearly defined movements, those "isms" whose performative utterances distinguished the avant-gardes, with their privileging of a temporal elite (local and global), from other intellectual and artistic currents. Under late modernism, in contrast, the author becomes "just one more," a body that might blur into the crowd, or fade into the repetitive rhythms of daily life under capitalism and its modern media.

The demotion of the specificity of literary language, and the role of the author as its producer, is one potent casualty of this shift. João Luíz Lafetá's formulation for the Brazilian context has resonance beyond this context: the 1930s "is witness to a near-forgetting of the essential aesthetic lesson of Modernism: the rupture of language."[12] Lafetá here echoes "the permanent right to aesthetic exploration," which one of the earlier avant-garde's most influential figures, Mário de Andrade, defined as modernism's gift to the world.[13] The archive of 1930s periodicals brims over with rejections of this earlier approach: style is now a luxury; the writer is a laborer; the orgy of aesthetic experimentation is over.

Yet to take seriously the continual rejection of form or style in 1930s modernism requires more than just recognizing its reactionary (in the most literal sense) dimensions. Late modernism is indeed a reaction to economic or political crises, from the dictatorships that sprung up across the continent during this period to the global economic depression that affected the material experiences of writers, including Jorge Luis Borges's new relationship to the rapid-fire production of mass journalism, Felisberto Hernández's struggle to make a living in a Paris evacuated of surrealist promise, and the alliances with the proletarian and precariat found in the novels of Graciliano Ramos and Patrícia Galvão. More immediately, late modernism is a reaction to its artistic predecessors: rupture, the avant-garde's mobilizing condition, had become a "sales pitch," as the autobiographical narrator of "Around the Time of Clemente Colling," a short story by Felisberto Hernández, puts it.[14] In this description, the new (*lo nuevo*) parades in front of the narrator's gaze, evacuated of content. In contrast to the earlier euphoric expressions of the avant-gardes, which had experimented with telegraphic writing and epiphanic moments in an impulse to break open older structures, this relentless temporality induces melancholy. "Our capacity for surprise is becoming exhausted" is a frequent commentary from the archive. "The world will soon become, or already is, a book that repeats the same page, down to the very last yawn."[15] Indeed, the rejection of the earlier avant-gardes becomes something of a cottage industry in the numerous literary and cultural journals that are founded during the period.

Yet this reactive moment also housed its own possibilities. What Rosalind Krauss called the "repressed" form of the copy in the avant-garde myth of originality began to constitute its own force field, along with the contiguous categories of the scrap, the residual, and the repetitive.[16] In addition, genres like the proletarian novel, regional novel, and "anti-manifesto," all of which make an appearance in this study, began to articulate alternatives to the avant-gardes. Authorship took on different guises, including feelership, listenership, spectatorship, and usership. These alternatives have often been overlooked by scholars in favor of the movements of the 1910s–1920s, whose "sales pitch" of the new continues to exercise its own seductions. The story of its aftermath, of the specific experiences that emerge in its wake, remains somewhat in the shadows.

In a late journalistic sketch (*crónica*) the Argentine author Roberto Arlt considers the present to be the era of Ecclesiastes: not the Book of Genesis and its birth of the world but a case of nothing new under the sun.[17] Significantly, Arlt's formulation occurs in a discussion on cinema, which in recent years had seen its status change from a new to a consolidated medium. The beginning of the twentieth century saw the first literary and journalistic texts that address cinema in South America, in the works of writers like Fray Mocho (Argentina) and João do Rio (Brazil). In "Cinematograph of Words" (1908), the latter described the cinema as perpetually renewing itself: "One does not tire or become worn out by it."[18] This journalistic sketch lies at the center of monographs on the medium in early twentieth-century Brazil and, as such, has become a shorthand for the experience of cinematic change, as in the familiar assertion that cinema is a metonymy for modernity, "the invention of modern life."[19] Late nineteenth- and early twentieth-century literature often expresses "awe and mystification" at the technological marvel of the new medium.[20] Cinema was an apparatus for producing ever-newer inventions and more intense experiences, with the genius-inventor at its helm. In the second decade of the twentieth century, the Argentine Horacio Quiroga's fables of the technological fantastic provide the most sustained early explorations of the power of cinema to reshape the texture of daily life and the social imagination, including literature; in his early production, cinema is characterized by its plasticity: the innumerable shapes it could take, the seemingly endless variations on desire it could index.[21] For its part, the avant-garde engagement with cinema during the 1920s paralleled Quiroga's fascination, during a moment that one film scholar has described as a transition between "utopian euphoria and subsequent systematization."[22]

For these writers, as well as for the scholars who will analyze them, the newness of cinema, radio, and the typewriter paralleled the newness to which avant-garde literature itself aspired. In this homology, new writing and new media were functional equivalents that shared an origin: modernity, with its libidinal charge. Thus, embracing cinema was a sign of avant-garde affiliation—Pearl White over Sarah Bernhardt, in the words of one of the opening speeches of Brazil's Modern

Art Week (1922). Cinema also epitomized enthusiasm for modernity in the first issues of Uruguay's only avant-garde journal, *La Pluma* (1927–31), and especially in Brazil's most important avant-garde little magazine, *Klaxon*, which reveled in the "cinematográficamente dinámico," a belief in these new technologies as aesthetic potential. (In the third issue of *Klaxon*, Mário de Andrade declares: "KLAXON is initiating the art of cinema criticism.")[23] Influenced by Louis Delluc and Jean Epstein's concept of *photogénie*, the cinematic equivalent of Viktor Shklovksy's defamiliarization, this first wave of modernists sought to render anew the poetry of daily life, to see with new eyes and through the metaphor of cinema, as in Fernand Léger's pithy quote: "Before the invention of the moving-picture no one knew the possibilities latent in a foot, a hand, a hat."[24] Inspired by cinema and cinema-centric writers like Blaise Cendrars, South American modernists also wrote their first cine-novels and cine-poetry.[25]

Yet by 1929, even Quiroga, that most eager chronicler of the cinema, had adopted the language of exhaustion and saturation. In a late *crónica*, he critiques the relentless drive for technological progress that symptomizes the automatization of cinema's resources: "The settings of the Far West, of Canada, of finance, sport, dancing—of all the strange countries that cinema invented—are spent."[26] Cinema was no longer a harbinger of the future but a ubiquitous component of daily life, sutured into capitalism through its industrialization and the heightened presence of advertising tie-ins and product placement, threatening to tip the balance between the "Siamese twins" of art and industry that Jean Epstein described in 1924 as constitutive of cinema.[27] In the words of the Brazilian writer (and film actor) Olympio Guilherme, the aura of the face, so important for reflections on silent film, had withered and transformed into the commodification of the mass-produced smile, which no amount of corrosive laughter seems able to interrupt or reroute.[28] If, in 1928, Brazil's most avant-garde writer, Oswald de Andrade, "envisioned the possibilities of revolutionary human behavior in Hollywood films," a decade later he would approach the medium as a stumbling block.[29]

Beginning in 1930, fewer avant-garde films were produced globally, while the abyss between commercial and avant-garde production had begun to crystallize; studios integrated vertically; national industries consolidated at the level of genre, production, distribution, and exhibition; genres become codified.[30] Adorno and Horkheimer would soon coin the phrase "culture industry," and the effects they describe were arguably more sharply inflected in Latin America, that "elsewhere" that figured prominently in the U.S. mass media's expansive networking of the world (Chapter 5).[31] Thus a Brazilian writer notes that this art-industry opposition—still present in Epstein's image of the two-headed figure—had, by 1931, collapsed upon itself in "our democratic era."[32] Writers now view this and other formerly new media with exhausted eyes. They hear their white noises, indistinguishable whines and murmurs, insidious undercurrents, and they feel their numbing repetitions.

In *The Technical Imagination: Argentine Culture's Modern Dreams*, Beatriz Sarlo defines the enthusiasm for new media and technologies of early twentieth-century cultural production as "the technical aura." Epitomized by Quiroga's early writings on cinema, the technical aura is the gap between concrete experiences with these technologies and the possibilities of what they might become. While indebted to Sarlo's pioneering study—itself indebted to Raymond Williams—this book expands her argument both in its historical frame and in its emphasis on rupture and on writers as "enthusiasts of the new."[33] Under late modernism, the horizon of expectation has shifted from the emergent to the dominant—and, in some cases, to the residual as well. Dominant media cannot be sublimated by technique. Rather than the bricoleur-inventor who protagonized *The Technical Imagination*, I focus on the receiver, the author as antenna of sensation in the era of media consolidation. These writers do not seek futurity but reuse. Abandoning their womb envy—the desire to create and master life—they immerse themselves in the media laboratory.[34]

Like scientific laboratories, media laboratories delineate a bounded site; they serve as a means to withdraw from the world.[35] This withdrawing seeks to momentarily or tactically bracket what Michel de Certeau defined as the strategies of media under a globalizing capitalism.[36] Media laboratories are transitory, in contrast to strategies; they are tactics, like the itineraries that walkers carve out through the dense and opaque grid that threatens to dwarf them. But these are not just any tactics: they embrace a DIY ethos that looks toward the eccentric, the peripheral, and the residual to fashion an alternative definition of both writing and authorship. De Certeau's own theories, it is worth recalling, are deeply informed by the South American, as well as by other postcolonial, encounters. His continual turn toward the Brazilian indigenous tribes who reelaborate Catholic practice or to Borges's "reading as poaching" underscores his assertion that tactics are thrown into relief by those who reveal what has been "unrecognizable at home."[37]

Media laboratories also grapple with geopolitics, often by reflexively foregrounding peripheral spaces: Olivari's tenement, Felisberto Hernández's tunnel (Chapter 4), Borges's basement (Chapter 5).[38] Yet the media laboratory displays more than the pernicious effects of the dominance of global capitalism and media networks, and more than negative classicism or a resistance to northern cultural flows that would reassert once again writing's privileged against a "vulgar" mass media complex.[39] Instead, a compensatory response to the ostensibly overpowering claims of mass culture ends up generating its own lines of flight, explorations of the utopian potentials housed within late modernity. The challenge the media laboratory poses is thinking these oppositional tendencies simultaneously. It requires us to put pressure on the very seductive reading according to which alternative interpretations are necessarily agentic—that agency and interactivity are ipso facto a kind of power—given the ease with which this discourse slips all too comfortably into neoliberal accounts of contemporary media usership.[40] But it also asks us to consider how these same flows are not monolithic, at least in the halfway house of fiction.

If the laboratory is not a refuge but an operational site, authorship must be reconsidered accordingly. As in Olivari's "Starstruck," one of the persistent features of the works I analyze here is the intentional blurring of narrator and commentator, invention and reportage, literary text and imaginary medium, and even author and protagonist. Narrators are frequently unnamed or share their author's name; quasi-autobiographical experiences are foregrounded; a redundant first-person appears over and over again, eschewing a vivid interiority or roundness of character for an interest in operations, tactics, and bodily responses. We witness the author grappling and experimenting with the boundaries of fiction and essay, with self and character, with literature and its constitutive outside.

In the media laboratory, the transformations authorship undergoes are registered in the body of the narrator-commentators. The body that writes, reads, views, feels, or listens as it submits itself to the sensorium of cinema, radio, and the typewriter is constantly foregrounded. Like Olivari's narrator in "Starstruck," many of the anonymous protagonists of the late modernist literature I explore here suffer from "hyperaesthesia" (165), an excessive, exquisite sensitivity, as bodies are easily pricked by pain, pleasure, quivering, or tickling. Through the spectator and user's vulnerable body, authorship becomes a porous membrane that registers changes in media reception and, beyond, technological modernity. As these texts explore, media are machines of sense-production; they intensify our sensory relationship to and knowledge of the world: "extension[s] of the sight" (in Epstein's definition of cinematic *photogénie*) but also of touch ("the skin of the film," in Laura Marks's pithy formulation), as well as sound.[41] In this sense, the media laboratory approximates the Benjaminian "room-for-play" (*Spiel-Raum*) that Miriam Hansen argues opens up with film, a space of the spectator's appropriation of technology through the senses.[42]

In recent years many modernist scholars have done compelling work to show how literature must contend with and manage threats from the media that emerged during the late nineteenth- and early twentieth centuries.[43] Writing works in tandem with other technologies, practices, and institutions of viewing, listening, and consuming, in a relay that requires each to rearticulate itself continually.[44] Among the most vocal proponents of literature's subsequent demotion vis-à-vis the new media of the late nineteenth and early twentieth centuries is Friedrich Kittler, whose focus on various inscription and storage media that compete with writing to usurp its privilege can be felt in many recent works on modernism and media in Latin America, the United States, and Europe.[45]

In employing the term "media laboratory," I mean to signal a divergence from such inspiring accounts, and more specifically from their emphasis on media ecologies. In general terms, the metaphor of media ecology describes a scenario in which media fight, survive, become residual or obsolete, at times without institutions, human actors, or living bodies making their presence known or felt. Media ecologies also rest on the premise of media qua media, a premise that many media theorists enjoy pushing toward tautology.[46] Anachronistic or otherwise disobedient forms of use have little place in a media ecology in which dominance or obsolescence is at stake, and in which technological (capitalist) development is the underlying narrative, albeit one often repressed. The concept of the media laboratory, on the other hand, foregrounds literature as the site of use and practice over invention, habituation over emergence, the "meanwhile" over rupture, and the residual or obsolescent over novelty.[47] It is less invested in the novum—the introduction of the new "species" that spurs a realignment among media and technologies—than in how media are refunctionalized by writer-users who may have quite different agendas than their inventors or developers.[48] It is interested in counterfactuals, residuals, belatedness, and misappropriation. It therefore inquires into the *where* and *how* of media reception from the perspective of writing as a late medium and the author as an actor in transformation.[49]

Ultimately, while useful for providing a thick description of a given scenario, the concept of media ecology conveniently brackets the problem of access. Many works of Latin American literature, scholarship, and film, in contrast, keep our focus there. What is central for critics like Jesús Martín-Barbero, the early Sarlo, and others is the utopian dimensions, however truncated, of early twentieth-century media, their democratizing potential. This interest recurs in twentieth- and twenty-first-century Latin American art: it is there in the scrap materials accumulated in the amateur's basement that prevent planetary colonial domination in the seminal Argentine graphic novel *El eternauta* (Héctor Osterheld and Francisco Solano López, 1957–59) and in the desire to use the discarded objects in slums or garbage dumps to make art in contemporary documentaries such as Federico León's *Estrellas* (Argentina, 2007) and Brazil's *Wasteland* (Lucy Walker, 2010). It is also there in the strange itinerary of the recently discovered version of Fritz Lang's monumental global modernist classic film, *Metropolis* (1924), whose preservation in a dusty basement in Buenos Aires is the stuff of a Borges story.

I am less interested, then, in the "thingness" of literature (Murphet; Kittler) than in shifting definitions of authorship and their relationship to the author's body, the page he or she reads or writes, and the world "out there" from which he/she has temporarily withdrawn. Broadly speaking, the fantasy of the "non-living agent" that David Trotter compellingly analyzes in Anglo-American modernism, also resonant with arguments by North and Murphet, is of much less interest to the modernist artists and writers I explore. In this way, South American late modernism can defamiliarize the posthumanist accounts that have themselves become consolidated (naturalized, taken for granted) as a sign of the contemporary, accounts that are increasingly extrapolated back onto modernism itself.[50]

A brief excursus helps illustrate how late modernist disenchantment led to a transformation of authorship in the media laboratory. The celebration of rupture that we find in the historical avant-gardes is nowhere so clearly manifested as in the manifesto, a performative genre that has become synonymous with these movements: a defiant assertion of rupture and metonym for modernity in its multiple forms, including its disavowal of the past's lingering influence.[51] Under late modernism, however, the manifesto is threatened with extinction. In its place, we find a genre that I call the "anti-manifesto": a rejection of the avant-garde manifesto that critiques it as an automatized genre, overly invested in a discourse of futurity that positioned authorship as its privileged mouthpiece.

With a few exceptions, beginning in the late 1920s the manifesto is demoted as a legitimizing discourse. In its wake, writers traced the sense of failure or collapse of these confident claims for inaugurating an origin. In 1930, for example, the Peruvian experimental poet César Vallejo publishes his "Autopsy of Surrealism" (Autopsia del superrealismo), declaring the movement defunct; he ends with the powerful image of a revolution of the masses threatening to grow out of surrealism's "open tomb."[52] Like Viktor Shklovksy's "Monument to a Scientific Error" (1930), with its chastened distancing from the recent Soviet avant-garde experimentation, Vallejo's text attempts to imagine a future for writing and the author in the post-avant-garde world. As Patrícia Galvão suggests in *Industrial Park*, a novel I analyze in the following chapter, the perceived bureaucratization of both the political and aesthetic avant-gardes of the 1920s had become a key source of anxiety in the 1930s. In one scene from the novel, a character arrives draped in "a new Futurist scarf," the gift of a rich lover; later, a rich patron of "the new arts" proclaims: "How can I not be a Communist, since I am modern?"[53] Given this historical juncture, Galvão's novel asks: How is revolutionary art possible? What happens when the manifesto itself is employed like a "futurist scarf" around the artist-intellectual's neck, or when an *ism* becomes a bureaucratized ornament rather than a catalyst for change?

In 1933, Galvão's partner Oswald de Andrade published his novel *Seraphim Grosse Point* (*Serafim Ponte Grande*), originally drafted between 1924 and 1928, the twilight of the first wave of modernism in Brazil. *Seraphim* is a highly experimental work, brimming over with ludic encounters and paratactic approaches to modernity in Brazil's most prominent example of a telegraphic novel. Oswald was the virtuoso of Brazilian manifestos: he wrote two of the most famous contributions to the genre, "Manifesto of Pau-Brazil Poetry" (1924) and the "Cannibalist Manifesto" (1928). In the latter, he put forth a vision of Brazilian aesthetic freedom that would represent the overcoming of the sterility of Europe: "The world undated. Unmarked. Without

Napoleon. Without Caesar." As he will in the pages of *Seraphim*, Oswald's language here intertwines the language of the "New World" (the Americas) with the language of aesthetic and technological novelty.[54] The preface cites this earlier moment—including its playfulness, emphasis on aesthetic experimentation, cinematic innovation, and obligatory pilgrimage to Europe—only to repudiate it.

After *Seraphim*'s publication, his family's coffee fortune mostly liquidated by the economic crash of 1929, Oswald began to draft two thesis novels that would attempt to translate the mass experience of the 1930s into prose: *A Escada Vermelha* (1934) and the two-volume *Marco Zero* (1943–46). *Seraphim* is thus a self-consciously periodizing text, marking the closing of one era and the beginning of the late modernist or *pós-modernismo* moment. In the year of its publication, Jorge Amado, a rising star who would soon become Brazil's most prominent writer of proletarian literature, declared of *Seraphim*: "With this book modernist literature—the literature of São Paulo, the coffee-baron bourgeoisie, and also a phase of Oswald de Andrade—comes to a close"; with *Escada Vermelha*, he writes, we witness "the passing of modernist literature" to social realism.[55] In a sense, Amado is merely reiterating what Oswald had declared, in a much more performative fashion, in his preface. *Seraphim*'s provocation is related less to its own prose than the very decision to publish it during a moment that so clearly seemed to belong to the recent past: "I'm publishing this novel in its integral text, finished in 1928. Necrology of the bourgeoisie. Epitaph of what I was."[56] The notorious preface authorizes a self-consciously belated act: authorship as a mea culpa and a machine that produces repentant self-citations. Now is the moment of what Fernando Rosenberg has described as the "repentant homecomings" of the erstwhile avant-gardists.[57] This last performance of the earlier modernists becomes, per Oswald, a "document," "a graphic" (5). As it will be so frequently in 1930s Brazil and Argentina, the avant-garde text is mobilized as residual, as a ruin. The authorial demiurgic performance—new world, new writing, new technology—is deflated in the process.

Jorge Luis Borges began to draft his own anti-manifestos during the 1930s and, in tandem, to fashion a different role for himself as author. Beginning with his adolescence in Europe, where he translated expressionist texts and wrote *ultraista* poetry before returning to his native Buenos Aires and contributing to the avant-garde journals *Prisma* (1921–22), *Proa* (1922), and *Martín Fierro* (1924–27), the early Borges was intensely engaged with the avant garde tenets of rupture and experimentation. In the 1921 "Ultraist Manifesto," for example, he had written that its new aesthetics "demands from each poet a fresh view of things, clear of any ancestral stigmas; a fragrant vision, as if the world were arising like dawn in front of our eyes"—language that resonates with the "undated" world that we saw in Oswald's cannibal manifesto. During the late 1920s and increasingly throughout the 1930s, however, he turns away from these bold claims. Like another Brazilian contemporary, Mário de Andrade, he begins to retrospectively clip the wings of his earlier avant-garde writings.[58] A literature of youth, Borges begins to deem it, disdainfully.

Like Oswald, the Borges of the late modernist period also begins to self-consciously cite himself, enlisting his earlier writing as a means of recasting his former projects. In the essay "Historia de la eternidad," published in an eponymous collection in 1936, he explicitly invokes self-citation, mobilizing an earlier text, "Sentirse en la muerte" (Feeling in Death, 1928), as a means of establishing historical distance with his recent avant-garde past. Again an abyss has opened up in a few short years; Borges's narrative voice places the two moments against each other to sketch their contours. He will cite the same fragment once again in an essay from the mid-1940s, "New Refutation of Time"; with each repetition and juxtaposition, he posits writing as a return to the past with minor variations.

While Borges's cool repudiation may seem far removed from Oswald's impassioned cry for the leftist struggle, both canonical modernist writers converge in their suggestion that the future tense required a different strategy during a decade in which the confidence in unadulterated rupture—with the manifesto as its medium—had now become a material trace of the recent past. The late modernist anti-manifesto cites and recycles the utopianism of modernist media and posits the author as spectator of his own past, tinkerer in the ruins of modernism. The role of the late modernist writer is emblematized in the anti-manifesto: not to inaugurate yet another rupture but to mine its traces, in particular its embrace of technological and aesthetic modernity.

LATE MODERNISM AND PERIODIZATION

Under late modernism, the very notions of origin and rupture, period and change, become objects of inquiry. As signaled by the prevalence of verbs like "vacillating," "tripping," "dispersing," "forking," and "halting" in the archive, late modernist writers grappled repeatedly with the difficulty of narrating the present.[59] If the tendency of Latin American literary history has in recent years been to elide the distinction between the 1920s and the 1930s, and the tendency of classical historical accounts has been to overdetermine the 1930s in terms of political/economic crises, this study seeks out a different way of reading transnational late modernism. It values the period in its own right as a unique inflection point in our understanding of modernity, both literary and technological, in and beyond South America. If there is a risk in positing an overdetermined period as a measure of analysis, then, there are risks as well in rejecting periodization as barren, stodgy, or "coffin-like" in juxtaposition to a vitalist conception of literature.[60]

Late modernism is a global phenomenon and can be found wherever the avant-gardes had a robust and self-conscious articulation; indeed, it requires this robustness to stipulate its own, at times sour, energy. Just as 1922 functions as a nodal point to periodize modernism across different contexts, 1930 provides a means of grasping late modernism's global reach.[61] This simultaneity of late modernism is important. The media I examine here, for example, were first experienced in parts of South America more or less at the same time as (and sometimes even prior to) they were in the United States and western Europe; in Argentina and Uruguay, radio arrived very early; as in Brazil, cinema arrived within months of its Parisian debut.[62] This simultaneity is uneven—just as all periodizations entail asymmetries. (There is no such a thing as an "even" modernity or "symmetrically developed" media ecology; even in the heart of the metropolis, technological modernity was as much a phantasm and fantasy as it was a set of concrete material practices and institutions. What is clear, however, is that "evenness" is more vexed in the South American context.)[63]

Anglo-American modernist studies has had difficulty addressing the fact that many non-Western modernisms were produced simultaneously with European ones, despite their differing experiences of modernity. Outside of Latin American studies, the region is often figured as belated, even in accounts that purport to critique belatedness itself. Within modernist studies, an influential origin for this interpretation is Perry Anderson's "Modernity and Revolution" (1984)—"For in the Third World generally, a kind of shadow configuration of what once prevailed in the First World does exist today"—but it has found renewed energy in the calls to globalize modernism.[64] These calls have often hinged on the tacit assumption that periodization is the problem, border-patrolling modernism and ostensibly keeping later modernisms out. Yet the premise of belatedness founders on any substantive engagement with the Latin American context and, I suspect, other Global South contexts as well, for the historical avant-gardes of the continent were nothing if not "up-to-date" with global modernist movements, texts, and artists.[65] At the same time, the way in which the term "global modernisms"—as an additive, supplemental, or anthological corrective to the dominance of its Anglo-American variant—is continually produced as an intervention suggests a difficulty in recognizing the lengthy critical traditions of non-Anglophone modernisms. The problem that theorists like Sarlo, Rama, Martín-Barbero, Néstor García Canclini, Roberto Schwarz, and Renato Ortiz have long noted, the difficulty of thinking "modernism without modernization" (or with various versions of modernization) makes Latin America a compelling case, yet one seldom taken up substantively by scholars calling for worlding modernism.[66] Ultimately, the expansive gesture is an unsatisfying response to the perceived stinginess of periodization. Exploding temporal boundaries—"giving world modernisms a voice"—is an act of generosity that, like all gifts, might favor the giver as much as or more than the ostensible recipient.

A goal of this book is to provincialize the persistent U.S./U.K.-centrism of modernist studies, its reliance on English as an unmarked term.[67] Modernism's complexity, we know, is compounded when one works across multiple languages, amplifying the term's already notorious bagginess.[68] Even within the relatively self-contained field of Brazilian literature modernism seems to exceed itself; in Silviano Santiago's visceral definition, *modernismo* is a devouring monster: "Everything done in its name and even against its names and its ideas is subsumed into its enormous belly."[69] The temptation to collapse into nominalism once we begin to travel with modernism is therefore strong; we founder for lack of a conceptual model when we do so: "A dialectic does not yet exist that is capable of coordinating the incommensurable conceptualities of the national-literary and the international."[70] This incommensurability is not a side effect but rather a motivating principle of this book.

At the same time, in comparing areas as geographically proximate as they are culturally different—Brazil and the River Plate region—I query both the national literature and area-studies models still quite powerful in various disciplines, including in Latin American literary studies. In a letter to his Argentine translator, the Brazilian novelist

Graciliano Ramos remarks upon the circuitous route by which a book written in São Paulo or Rio de Janeiro has a better chance of being read in his peripheral northeastern state if it is first crosshatched through the literary sphere of Buenos Aires.[71] Given the great regional disparities that marked a country like Brazil during this period—disparities that had a direct impact on its literary system from the question of prestige to access to literacy—thinking comparatively makes more sense than assuming an unremarked national coherence. As Graciliano suggests, the nation-state is itself fragmented, and literature travels in often surprising itineraries. In this way, the book joins a burgeoning conversation about the multiple but, until recently, overlooked axes of comparison between Brazil and its Spanish American neighbors.[72]

Beginning in 1930, in Uruguay, Brazil, and Argentina, the promises of what had been up to this point a most experimental and hopeful moment of progressive modernity—political, economic, technological, and aesthetic—seemed to be radically foreclosed. Liberal democracy, the sense of freedom the avant-gardes espoused, and a presumed link between technological and political modernization all seemed precarious, if not impossible. Dictatorial regimes that came to power in 1930 linked the experiences of Argentines, Uruguayans, and Brazilians, as well as many of their contemporaries across Latin America. These economic and political crises dovetailed with critiques of dependency during Latin America's neo-imperialist phase, leading to the first politics of import substitution and the beginnings of the eclipse of oligarchical elites. Indeed, one historian has argued that the nineteenth century in Latin America ended not in 1899 but in the 1920s. "The partying was over," Emir Rodriguez Monegal writes succinctly of Argentina on the eve of 1930.[73]

Prevalent in the archive but relatively absent from subsequent literary histories, the Brazilian term *pós-modernismo* illustrates the sense of an ending that characterizes the period. In literary and cultural journals beginning in the early 1930s, writers across the political and aesthetic spectra employed this term to define themselves negatively vis-à-vis the experimental projects of their avant-garde predecessors.[74] The latter were frequently caricaturized as bent on a gleeful destruction that *pós-modernismo* would then reconstruct. Such an argument is evidently rhetorically convenient: it allowed late modernist writers to position themselves as erecting a foundation over the remnants of their predecessors, essentially burying them in the process—a ritual of mourning at times that approached gloating, or at the very least schadenfreude.[75]

As Afonso Arinos de Mello Franco writes in his article "Poesia, 1936," these innumerable ruins are also an opportunity; or, as the conservative Tristão de Athayde puts it in his "Synthesis," "*pós-modernismo* breathes the somber air of . . . a crisis that does not end, of revolutions that continue, of heroic and cruel reactions."[76]

Studies of 1930s modernisms beyond Latin America also resonate with my own research. The articulation of the avant-gardes' failures that occurred in western Europe, Japan, Korea, the United States, and the Soviet Union in the late 1920s and early 1930s was equally, if not more, strident in Latin America. The dictatorships of the 1930s paralleled contemporaneous events unfolding in Italy, Germany, and the Soviet Union, where Stalinism truncated, albeit without disappearing, one of the world's most prolific sites of avant-garde experimentation. In their emphasis on intensified forms of incomplete modernization, German modernist media theory, especially the work of Walter Benjamin, with its simultaneously melancholic and hopeful approach to the relationship between mass culture and modernization, has been particularly important for Latin Americanists, and that is why its presence can be felt keenly throughout this book.

In each case, modernists confronted the shifting terrain in pronounced but different ways. In Brazil, for example, the unique intertwining of modernism and the state, wherein the modernist author was sutured into the latter's at times violent modernization project, contrasts sharply with the expulsion of modernist artists from the military dictatorship that came to power in Argentina in 1930.[77] Yet modernists in both contexts shared a language of failed potential, of the automatization of modernity's promises. Indeed, the 1930s seems to spawn metaphors of truncated possibilities around the globe. The moment draws, like a magnet, meta-reflections on literary history and literary modernity, as well as on teleological narratives of all kinds. Thus Hansen writes of the shutting down of modernity's utopian approaches in Germany in the 1930s; modernism is "cut off" in the Soviet Union during the period (only to be rerouted underground); in Korea, the "future disappears" during a moment known as the "dark period"; and Argentine scholars have coined several potent metaphors of truncation: "the decade of the suicides," "the sad thirties" (*los tristes treinta*) "the years of the great funerals," and, most famously, "the infamous decade."[78]

While differing significantly from the South American context, Anglo-American modernist studies offers us a robust theorization of modernism's late phase. It remains germane to this study despite its myopia—"the blindness of the center"—and despite the fact that the major models for literary modernism in Latin American were French.[79] Its difference helps sketch the contours of South America's specificity. (The inverse might prove to be equally true.) Drawing on Tyrus Miller's interpretation of late modernism in the Anglo-American context as a "failure to repress" the materials of history, and of late modernist works as "allegories of the end of modernism" (32, 23), we could say that South American late modernism allegorizes the end—or one possible end—of the fascination with rupture and modernity that has characterized its specific postcolonial experience. Miller describes how his late modernist writers approached high or "classic" modernists' texts as ruins (14), opposing their own "leaky forms" to their predecessors' investment in form to shore up a world in dissolution. As the anti-manifesto shows, however, in South America late modernists approached their avant-garde predecessors as a different sort of ruins: of the utopia of the new, of Latin America's endlessly deferred promise as a site of modernity, one that the author had been in a particularly privileged position to voice or enact.[80]

Thus, rather than hinging on the collapse of modernist formal mastery in the world war interregnum (Miller), anxieties surrounding the waning of an empire and a subsequent shoring up of the national (Jed Esty), or a reaction to the consumer-driven art market under a burgeoning late capitalism (Jameson), South American late modernism emerges in response to the phantasmatic desire for progress that posited the artist and intellectual as a special voice or seer, at the vanguard of change for a part of the world that had and has frequently been relegated to a space outside of history but for which the future always seemed just around the corner.[81] Here, in the "new world," which Hegel and later Ortega y Gasset would still read as devoid of history, was where the promises of modernity were held out and foreclosed in a very short period of time.[82] Here, where the author held a particularly privileged status, is where we can see most clearly how late modernism made possible an intensive and vexed critique of modernity's periodization and of the artist as the engine and telos of this same modernity. Because it takes shape in the wake of the most starkly innovative moment in South American literary and artistic production, late modernism is uniquely poised to critique the relentless pursuit of progress, its capacity to transform innovation into its proper machine without contents, the homogeneity that threatens modernity's incessant search for the latest thing.

Scholars periodically chasten the period as crude or historicist (terms often unfortunately equated). Yet the pervasiveness in late modernism of narratives tripped up, rerouted, thwarted, of dead ends or regressions or truncated ruptures, requires that we take them seriously. The overdetermination of periodization in these accounts of modernism, starkly different yet united in their simultaneity under the sign of state violence, left melancholy, and failed promises is perhaps nowhere as pronounced as in 1930. Yet, paradoxically, this overdetermined periodization is forged through an interrogation of the very possibility of rupture, modernity's privileged mode. If late modernism seems to stubbornly resist both media and literary histories, it is precisely because works from this period both invoke and trouble the very notion of periodization and breaks. If the avant-gardes produced crisis as an opportunity to stage their intervention, here the crisis is not staged to produce a "ground zero" (Krause) but is understood as a chronic condition. My choice of "late modernism" over *pós-modernismo* or "post-avant-garde" is meant to query this emphasis on rupture. "Post" implies a beyond, whereas "late" implies the lingering, the residual, the *longue durée*, the at times agonic and at other times anachronistic relationship to the avant-gardes that we find throughout this book. "Late" indexes the difficulty of conceptualizing rupture, the waning or residual forms of modernism once it has turned against itself.

Thus, while there are compelling reasons to query periodization, its suppression risks missing the strident critiques of the avant-gardes that mark 1930s production—critiques that are also opportunities for understanding what intellectual, aesthetic, and affective needs periodization indexes, both then and now.[83] In *A Singular Modernity*, Jameson builds on his suggestion, in *Postmodernism*, of the centrality of lateness as a mode of positing historical change.[84] Offering a distinct definition of late modernism (or "neo-modernism") in the postwar period, he also echoes Tyrus Miller's insight that late modernism allows us to interrogate our most sacred, and polemical, categories, to organize literature: rupture, periodization, telos. Similarly, Raul Antelo's description of *pós-modernismo*, in a discussion of the Brazilian modernist anthropologist Gilberto Freyre, suggests an understanding of the 1930s as threshold and critical appraisal of the idea of periodization and the modern itself.[85] In the Brazilian context, both the terms *pré-modernismo* and *pós-modernismo* were coined in the 1930s, suggesting that modernism itself as a self-consciously historicizable moment was born in a retrospective gesture that consecrates it vis-à-vis a present in crisis.[86] The late modernism defined here thus represents an attempt "to work on a period only if it originates from a *problematized periodization*."[87] Throughout the book, "1930" acts both as an opportunity for returning to the rich and at times overlooked polemics of the time and as a heuristic for tracing the shifts that modernism undergoes in the region, a bend in the road from which we see the inflection of a different way of charting literary history, as well as a different understanding of technological modernity and media history.

The late modernist conviction that authorship was transforming as a result of crisis would only increase in intensity throughout the century. Its emphasis on its own untimeliness would morph, throughout the twentieth century, into both a cliché and a tactic. In Virgilio Piñera's microfiction "Grafomanía" (1970), writers are gathered together and accused of the eponymous crime.[88] Writing is consigned to the margins, and even to excess or madness (*mania*), and yet it will continue. It is this "and yet" that moves me, inasmuch as it does not disappear but recurs throughout twentieth- and twenty-first-century literary theory and criticism. "Why does anyone decide to be a writer? Why does he or she decide to work alone as an artisan with words with the view of writing a book, a book that is becoming more and more obsolete in the era of mass culture?" the Brazilian novelist and critic Silviano Santiago asks in his essay "Literature and Mass Culture." Writing, like Piñera, in the 1970s, Santiago insists that literature is "functionally untimely in the era of cinema and arts of technical reproducibility."[89]

Late modernist literature dwells in what Santiago calls "the contemporary out of its era."[90] In the late modernist media laboratory, fiction becomes a medium to think with precisely because it is out of step with the contemporary. It can now be positioned as a residual medium vis-à-vis the increasingly prevalent technological media that surround and shape it.[91] The 1930s is a moment when South American authors were especially self-reflexive and pessimistic with respect to their privileged position as heralds or vanguards. As a result, authorship could become something other than the self-styled leader of a nation, people, or time. Rather than the origin of a new order, it could be transformed, in the previous century and our own, into a strategically residual practice. This practice did not need to compete with the worlds created by increasingly dominant media. It could instead stage partial interventions into daily life under the increasingly powerful and often homogenizing experience known as modernity.

CHAPTER 1

Conscripting Global Cinema

Men of the different Americas are not in contact with one another—a lack of communication which the cinema, with its direct presentation of destinies . . . will undoubtedly undermine.

—Jorge Luis Borges, "The Other Whitman"

No one is permitted to be disinterested anymore. It's a deadly fight between two irreconcilable classes.

—Patrícia Galvão, *Industrial Park*

In contrast to the first wave of the avant-gardes, the problem of the masses takes hold with surprising force under late modernism, especially through the collective, sensorial experiences of cinema. The earlier avant-gardes had implicitly posited themselves a temporal and spatial elite, in opposition to a broader collective.[1] When the Argentine writer Leopoldo Hurtado writes in 1931 that "today the historic accent, the decisive factor in historical occurrence, is the masses," he expresses a preoccupation absent from the avant-garde journal *Martín Fierro* (1924–27), where he had begun his literary career and where he first began to write about cinema. He now ends with a question repeated by artists and intellectuals throughout the decade: Who will answer the call of these masses? And how would writers' approach to cinema, arguably the central mass medium, change as a consequence?[2]

Emergent forms of populist politics and industrialization and the large-scale migration to cities like Buenos Aires, Rio de Janeiro, and São Paulo combined with mass media to alter the status of the masses during this period.[3] In the 1930s, radio, cinema, popular books, and magazines, ushered in by publishing houses dedicated to newer, cheaper publication formats, joined prominent mass spectacles of both religious and political persuasions. As the continent's first populist leader, Getúlio Vargas, rose to power in 1930, the late nineteenth-century naturalist crowd, inflected by Gustav Le Bon's pessimistic theories, gave way to a discourse of the multitude.[4] The problem of proletarian literature spawned intense debates in the little magazines of the period. A glance at prominent titles from the first half of the decade makes this preoccupation clear: Elías Castelnuovo's *Art and the Masses: Towards a New Theory of Aesthetic Activity* (Argentina, 1935); the journal *The Man of the People* (Brazil, 1931–32); and Ortega y Gasset's *The Rebellion of the Masses* (1930), very influential in contemporaneous Argentine circles. While radically opposed in their aesthetic and political valences, these phenomena found a new center of gravity in the mass body.

Focusing on popular periodicals and mass media, in particular the cinema, this chapter considers how this new imperative of the masses allowed authorship to refashion itself as spectatorship. Authors were to be allied with the masses by joining them as fellow viewers. They would no longer be ahead of the pack but immersed in it. If their avant-garde predecessors posited their own writing as homologous to the still-new medium of cinema through the privileged criterion of innovation, they would engage the masses directly, especially those gathered in and around the cinema—not the only available instantiation of the crowd, evidently, but a paradigmatic space in the media laboratories of the 1930s. In this sense, late modernist writers did not merely respond to a positivist category like "the historical emergence of the masses" but also helped shape it as they underwent their own transformations.[5] As in Olivari's "Starstruck," the withdrawing into the media laboratory that I define as a feature of late modernism happens in the specific spaces of the movie theater and screen, as well as the contiguous space of print media.

This chapter opens my study of the various shifts authorship undergoes in the late modernist period through an analysis of the literary and journalistic production of two very different contemporaries, both of whom employed spectatorship as an authorial strategy. Published in serial form in the colorful Saturday supplement of *Crítica*, South America's most widely circulated periodical of the time, Jorge Luis Borges's *A Universal History of Infamy* (*Historia universal de la infamia*, 1933–36) is the culmination of his multiple experiences as writer, editor, and burgeoning film critic.[6] Writing in the wake of experimental cinema's impact on the Argentine avant-garde, he encounters the Hollywood studio system, which he parodically engages. In contrast to Borges's penchant for Hollywood, his contemporary, Brazilian author and activist Patrícia Galvão, turns to the other principal language of global cinema during the late modernist period: Soviet montage, the elaboration of meaning through the stitching together of often oppositional shots and sequences.

Both writers sought an interface with a popular, globalizing cinema during its consolidation. Through their experiences as writers, editors, and spectators, they explored cinema's alternative practices in their first forays into fiction. Yet, as the epigraphs that open this chapter suggest, their models were quite different. Borges saw Hollywood cinema as a "connection machine"—a way of linking the world, albeit one Creolized (recast through local conditions) and made possible through the individual spectator's lateral gaze. For Galvão, on the other hand, cinema is an oppositional forum for staging the inequalities of global capitalism.

This chapter thus reflects the logic of montage itself: an inherently asymmetrical confrontation between Hollywood and Soviet cinema that exemplified the struggle over mass spectatorship taking place on global screens and pages. By the late modernist period, cinema would indeed connect the men of the Americas through its "direct presentation of destinies," as Borges writes in a special issue of the literary magazine *La vida literaria* at the close of the 1920s, in the epigraph that opens this chapter. Yet, as Galvão shows, this connection was also a disconnection, this network prone to short circuits, problematizing the ostensibly uniform processes of cultural importation and Americanization that were major sources of anxiety for Latin American intellectuals and artists during the period.

JORGE LUIS BORGES, VERNACULAR LATE MODERNISM

In 1935, Borges's first work of fiction, *A Universal History of Infamy*, was published by Tor, one of the numerous publishing houses founded in Buenos Aires during the interwar period. With its cheap editions and graphic, color-saturated covers, Tor was a natural choice for this motley collection of capsule biographies of tricksters, assassins, and thugs from different parts of the globe. Here, Mark Twain's *Life on the Mississippi* was juxtaposed with Sir Percy Skye's *A History of Persia*; Argentine and New York gangsters volleyed for attention within a few paratactic pages. A very different Borges surfaces in the 1930s, in no small part because of his experiences with this text. On one hand, *A Universal History of Infamy* stages what will become Borgesean signatures; the lack of hierarchy and sense of accumulation that organizes its stories anticipate his beloved encyclopedia. On the other hand, this minor work represents his most sustained engagement with mass media, popular journalism, and Hollywood films, a unique moment in his own relationship to writing, the market, and the materials of a burgeoning culture industry.[7] No longer linked to the avant-garde movements that shaped him as a young writer (the *ultraísmo* movement; the avant-garde little magazines, *Martín Fierro*, *Prisma*, and *Proa*) but not quite the celebrated author of fictions that will become his global signature, this is a "pulp" Borges, a refashioned fiction writer who finds his materials in the stories of others, especially those produced by Hollywood. A Borges who has proven, like late modernism more broadly, more difficult to pin down—and for precisely that reason, a welcome addition to this alternate periodization.

Prior to their collective publication, the majority of the stories in the *Universal History of Infamy* had been published in the *Multicolor Saturday Magazine* (*Revista Multicolor de los sábados*), a cultural supplement of *Crítica*, a newspaper that proudly proclaimed on its masthead "Largest South American circulation." A singular force in modern Argentine culture, *Crítica* was responsible for publishing many of the most notable writers of the 1910s through the 1930s, including many former avant-gardists like Borges himself. The periodical also incorporated into its elastic form a wide swath of genres, modalities, and geographic and historical referents.[8] Borges not only published frequently in the Saturday supplement from 1933 to 1934, he also co-directed it during those same years. This dual role as writer and editor shaped his understanding of authorship. Reception became the engine for a different author-figure, forged against the earlier avant-garde self.[9]

While Borges has occasionally been positioned as a proto-theorist of new media, the material practices that influenced his shifting understanding of literature as a technology have received less critical attention. Beginning in 1930, he began to submit literature and writing to encounters with its audiovisual others, mining and undermining its specificity in the process. *A Universal History of Infamy* has tended to be read in terms of transition—as a pit stop on the way to a fully realized Borges, the one whose global fame (the international prizes, the guest stints at Harvard, the homages by Foucault and Deleuze) would take shape on the basis of stories written in the 1940s.[10] Yet, rather than think of the text teleologically, as a stepping-stone to the more compelling stories and essays that he will write in subsequent decades, I argue here that analyzing this ostensibly minor text allows us to uncover a different Borges—neither the avant-garde poet of the 1920s nor the crafter of polished stories in *Garden of Forking Paths* (1944)—revealing the process by which authorship becomes recast as spectatorship, a process that works in tandem with a bureaucratizing and globalizing mass culture.

Mass Journalism and the Media Laboratory

Borges's 1930s writings represent the most heterogeneous moment in his lengthy career. This is a period in which he wrote for radically different publications and publics. At the beginning of the decade, he embarked on two definitive experiences: in 1931, he published his first film reviews in the pages of Victoria Ocampo's *Sur*, the little magazine that would soon introduce Latin American readers to Faulkner and Woolf; in 1933, he began to coedit *Crítica*'s Saturday supplement. Throughout the decade, he will also write for the women's magazine *El hogar* (where he published one of the first international reviews of Faulkner), as well as for a publication sponsored by the Buenos Aires subway system. In short, this is a moment in which Borges directly and frequently experienced the contingency and fragmentation integral to mass culture, more specifically modern print journalism and Hollywood cinema, media that mutually conditioned one another throughout the early twentieth century.

Just as cinema will, the sensorial dimensions of the comic strip and the juxtaposition constitutive of modern print journalism offer a provocation to the author. In his prologue to the first edition, Borges diagnoses the formal strategies of his *Universal History of Infamy*: "Certain techniques are abused: mismatched lists, abrupt transitions, the reduction of a person's entire life to two or three scenes" (3). This list not only describes specific elements of the stories but also gestures at the context of their initial publication. *Crítica*, their mass culture incubator, is characterized by just these elements: the composition of visual images saturated with colors; the "reductive" mode of its layout, privileging brevity over a sense of profundity; the "mismatched" juxtapositions of spaces and times that lack, as is characteristic of modern print journalism, connection to each other. Further cut up by subsections that bear the material trace of their presence in the Saturday supplement, the stories, like the publication where they first appeared, also borrowed from the emergent aesthetic of the cartoon, an effect further heightened by the color illustrations that initially framed them.[11] As though to acknowledge and exploit this position within the *Multicolor Saturday Magazine*, Borges draws extravagantly from both mass and popular culture, including his compatriot Eduardo Gutiérrez's gaucho tales, Herbert Asbury's *The Gangs of New York*, and the films of Josef von Sternberg.

Crítica's charismatic owner, Natalio Botana—"the William Randolph Hearst" of Argentina (although he originally hailed from Uruguay)—had founded a journal that would be passionately modern, connected to the latest technologies and rapidly expanding reading publics, but also interspersed with literature that would not immediately be considered popular.[12] Structured on the principle of the *fait divers* of modern journalism and its attendant shifts in writerly and readerly attention, the *Multicolor Saturday Magazine* mixed notices of local literary prizes with brief sketches reminiscent of *Ripley's Believe It or Not*, stories of garish crimes, erudite theatrical reviews, and reports of unrest among railroad workers.[13] *Crítica* was also one of the first Argentine mainstream periodicals to incorporate writings on film, over a decade before Borges joined the staff.

The first issue of the Saturday supplement debuted on September 12, 1933; over the next two years, Borges and his friend Ulyses Petit de Murat (also a film critic and burgeoning scriptwriter) would go on to collaborate intensively on its production as editors, soliciting and selecting what would appear in the supplement, as well as penning various sketches and articles, correcting others, and collaborating with the multiple workers involved in the various processes of typesetting, layout, and graphics that led to the journal's striking colors.[14] This practice, with its multiple planes, was also a way of underscoring feedback loops between words and their physical supports, of bringing literature into the visual realm and of creating visual-verbal formats that would be consumed by reader-viewers.[15] Involved in the process of selecting, editing, writing, and laying out the pieces that comprise this strange admixture of high and low, avant-garde and mass culture, Borges, through the *Multicolor Saturday Magazine*, entered the media laboratory and emerged with his own strain of post-avant-garde literature. Along with his new habit of filmgoing, his experience with the *Saturday Magazine* radically transformed his understanding of authorship—after it, "Borges" would not be the same.

These experiences inflected the self-conscious materiality of the *Universal History of Infamy*. In editing and retooling the works of others, a different relationship to writing was forged: "We never dreamed that we would move from the modest, almost familial edition of our books and the small circulation of our little magazines, to a circulation like that of *Crítica*," Petit de Murat writes in his memoir (144). On this reading, the Saturday supplement constitutes a point of inflexion, in which the earlier avant-gardes' sense of a private and intimate circle, abstracted from the world, is exposed to the logic of modern print capitalism. The intensity of the avant-garde self is recast as part of a larger, collaborative effort to produce and sustain the new reading publics and consumers. The transformation from writer to reader that Borges inaugurates in the first preface to the *Universal History of Infamy* as his personae of authorship—"I sometimes think good readers are poets as singular, and as awesome, as great authors themselves"[16]—mirrors, and is to a certain extent made possible by, this transformation from authorship as a nodal point of authority to the reader-spectator. A reader-spectator who perused the shifting surfaces of the mass periodical competing for his attention.[17]

Hollywood, History

The erosion of the figure of the expert and the exaltation of the figure of the viewer, mutually constitutive phenomena that Borges's contemporary Walter Benjamin put forth in his "Work of Art in the Age of Its Technological Reproducibility" (1936), is fulfilled in *A Universal History of Infamy*.[18] The book represents Borges's first engagement with a medium that was no longer new in Buenos Aires, although certainly novel to his oeuvre: cinema. In his role as *Sur*'s first film critic, he reviewed von Sternberg's *The Docks of New York* (1928) and *Morocco* (1930), along with other films.[19] By 1930, Argentina had long established its position as the filmgoing capital of Latin America; since the beginning of cinematic production and reception in the region, export wealth of coveted primary products led to its rapid modernization and market primacy. Coupled with the influence from European immigrants at the turn of the century, it became a synecdoche for modern, worldly cinema spectatorship.[20] In 1930, the British avant-garde film journal *Close Up* published "Cinema in the Argentine," H. P. Tew's paean to Buenos Aires's film culture. "Though the Argentine is, comparatively speaking, a non-producer," Tew writes, "it must be one of the world's greatest consumers." Invisibilizing Argentina's film production, Tew defines its reception in terms of what he deems the "impartial" receptivity of its "cosmopolitan mass."[21]

Arguably, this desire for the cosmopolitan was even more pronounced than in the United States or western Europe. Beginning in the late 1910s, South Americans received European film theory and avant-garde films in piecemeal fashion but with a short or at times infinitesimal time lag. The Brazilian avant-garde *Klaxon*, for example, was in dialogue with the Belgian film magazine *Lumière*; it would also incorporate articles and images from France, Japan, Belgium, the United States, and Spain, including works by Bergson, Epstein, Stravinsky, Picasso, Cocteau, Chaplin, Guillermo de Torre, and Apollinaire. Artists and intellectuals also began to circulate their own homegrown theories of *cinéma pur*, the medium in its irreducible specificity, uncontaminated by the novel or theater. With few exceptions, this cosmopolitan film culture was realized by writers, not filmmakers. (There is no precise South American equivalent to an Epstein or an Eisenstein, figures who doubled as both experimental filmmakers and proto-film theorists.)

In fact, through the work of Latin America's central modernists—broadening our geographical scope to include not only Borges and Mário de Andrade but also Alejo Carpentier in Cuba—readers experienced many foreign films first on the page, rather than the screen. There are, of course, exceptions: as I indicate below, the public had access to some Soviet films, and trade publications from the period enthusiastically promoted the arrival Fritz Lang's *Metropolis* (1927)—a film that was to fare better in posterity than when it first debuted. In Buenos Aires, the Asociación Amigos del Arte (1929–31), in which Borges participated along with other key figures in modernist writing and photography in Argentina, had one of the earliest film clubs in Latin America. Its screenings were heterogeneous and often projected in fragments that the organizers could obtain, accompanied by lectures on world cinema: Disney animation, Eisenstein, Epstein, René Clair, Man Ray, Dalí, Buñuel, Murnau; its first screening was of Carl Dreyer's *The Passion of Joan of Arc*. A breakout group of the Amigos del Arte, led by the photographer Horacio Coppola, would go on to found the short-lived *Clave de Sol*, one of the first Argentine journals to approach cinema as an art, rather than popular form, and an equivalent, of sorts, to Western European film periodicals like *Close Up* and *transition*. In Brazil, the Chaplin-Club of Rio de Janeiro (founded in 1928), with its journal, *O Fan* (1928–30), would fulfill a similar function. Both were sustained by very small circles of friends and acquaintances.

In contrast to these peers, however, Borges was unmoved by European avant-garde cinema. His participation was on the margins of this proto-cinephilia; his preference was for Hollywood, whose narrative efficacy he embraced over more experimental film production.[22] In his film reviews he is often intrigued by the industry's capacity to produce infinitely compelling variations from within a rather limited formal structure: "classic" Hollywood, he observes, shares this with the Greek tragedies.[23] Hollywood films have a dual potential: for radical innovation and utter predictability. In fact, the innovation depends on the formulaic and generic expectations and the pleasure they produce for readers, writers, and viewers.

In light of this doubled possibility, *The Universal History of Infamy* strategically adopts metonymies of Hollywood cinema. Rather than critique it as an ironclad structure, as many of his contemporaries were beginning to do, Borges adopts its fragments as one possible procedure among many. As in the striking images that undergirded his first poetic experience, as elaborated in his "Ultraist" manifesto (1921), the author privileges the potent image. But here he does not produce it; instead, he steals it from the films he watches and displays it for his fellow reader-viewers in the pages of his pastiche. The viewer appropriates in metonymic fashion, through the glance over the rapt gaze.

The author-spectator's focus on a potent image can rescue a film from utter failure. Borges's take on King Vidor's *Billy the Kid* (1930), for example, features an assassination whose indirection he finds powerful, even if the film itself fails. Borges would rewrite Billy the Kid in "The Disinterested Killer Bill Harrigan," part of the *Universal History of Infamy*. This intermedial text unites the print legend of the mythic figure to Vidor's film version to create the *Universal History*'s most citational episode. In his review of Vidor's film, Borges had criticized its pseudo-epic sweep, deeming it the "shameful chronicling of the twenty murders (not counting Mexicans) committed by the famous fighter of Arizona, a film made with no other distinction than the accumulation of panoramic takes and the methodical elimination of close-ups in order to suggest the desert."[24] In his view, Vidor's film works with various spatial clichés that cannot be rehabilitated. His critique of the director, however, does not preclude him from initially borrowing these same strategies.

Borges's "Bill Harrigan" also proceeds by takes: "History (which, like a certain motion picture director, moves through discontinuous images) now proposes a risky saloon."[25] Manifesting a paradox central to film, *défilement*, history operates through discontinuous images, through interruption rather than flow—or a flow that always depends on fragmentation. As a result, Borges suggests, history itself is altered under film's gaze.[26] His "Bill" opens in this way: "The image of the lands of Arizona, before any other image." A figure appears within this setting. "Within this landscape, another image—the image of Billy the Kid, the rider sitting firm upon his horse, the young man of loud shots that stun the desert, the shooter of invisible bullets that kill at a distance, like a magic spell" (37).

As these examples reveal, his author-viewer opts for the presentational strategy of film—that "direct presentation of destinies" that he identified as unique to the cinema in this chapter's epigraph—over the representational strategy associated with literature. Rather than offering us a detailed realist description, the stage is set with the utmost brevity and efficiency, as though merely showing us what we can already see. This indexical strategy, signaled by the omission of verbs, points to and displays the materials of mass culture, as a camera would, or as the *Multicolor Saturday Magazine* did with its text-image pairings. The shift away from both realism and psychological depth will become part of Borges's definition of late modernist literature (as I explore in greater detail in Chapter 5); here, it is made possible by cinema as a continual alteration of surfaces. Borges the author-spectator watches the frames of someone else's film unfold.

At the end of "Bill Harrigan," the wide-angle shots that signify "desert" in King Vidor's *Billy the Kid* are replaced with literary close-ups of the protagonist. As though to seal the sense of performativity and borrowing from popular culture that marked Billy's entire life—"he felt no scorn for theatrical fictions: he liked to go to the theater (perhaps with no presentiment that they were the symbols and letters of his own destiny)"—this hero ends up exhibited in a shop window, surrounded by spectators: "On the third day, they had to put makeup on him" (28, 41).[27] Again, Borges's narrator is presentational, rather than descriptive or explanatory. In this case, like the authorities in the short story, he displays the garish corpse of Billy the Kid. The grotesque and pulpy ending, a mise-en-scène of mass culture, also implicates the reader of these stories of infamy, connecting him in a mirror effect to the spectators described in the story, gawking at the outlaw's cadaver.

Yet, while offering his readers consumable stories, Borges nevertheless fails to fulfill his promise, nearly always ending with a grotesque, specular, or emphatically banal image—a garish corpse ("Bill Harrigan"); an unpoetic case of pneumonia ("The Cruel Redeemer Lazarus Morell"); a cat encircling the body of a gangster, assassinated anonymously ("Monk Eastman"); deaths evacuated of any meaning or narrative buildup ("The Improbable Impostor Tom Castro"). Together, the stories in the *Universal History of Infamy* reject narrative as explanation, as the "grasping together" we expect from stories and from history, as well as from "classical" Hollywood cinema that sought to manage the shock effect of death present in cinema's origins, as in the cinema of attractions.[28] Elements are not linked together through either coordination or subordination; rather, they are incomplete, somehow truncated, failing the promise of the *terminus ad quem*. Eschewing causality, they counter the explanatory thrust of narrative that traditional historiography exploits: the slippage between *this happens after this* and *this happens because of this*.[29]

These stories are inassimilable to a broader historical narrative; they are shop windows of curiosities. The collection appears devoid of a meaning that might become visible through the accrual of different stories. "The endeavor to explain and interpret [historical events] directly is accordingly like the endeavor to see in the forms of the clouds groups of men and animals," wrote Borges's beloved Schopenhauer. "What history narrates is in fact only the long, heavy, and confused dream of humanity."[30] In the prologue to the 1954 edition of the *Universal History*, Borges describes his own book in similar terms: "Gallows and pirates fill its pages, and that word *infamy* strikes awe in its title, but under all the storm and lightning, there is nothing" (5). This makes Borges's decision to publish and republish them over subsequent decades (in contrast to several of his other earlier works, which he actively suppressed) especially telling. Why continue to reissue a collection of citational *faits divers*?

Schopenhauer's early influence on Borges primed him to be suspicious of grandiose claims for universal history—claims that received serious attention in the circles he moved in during this period, courtesy of Ortega y Gasset and Keyserling's rehearsal of Hegel's *Lectures on the Philosophy of World History*.[31] Ortega's very late reassertion of Hegel's hyperbolically Eurocentric text positioned Latin America, once again, as a space devoid of history. In contrast, in the *Universal History of Infamy*, the miniature nature of the capsule biographies seems to cause the frame—that pompous title—to collapse. Disconnected stories rub up against other sketches in different issues of the supplement, yoked together only by the paradoxical and absurdist banner under which they are grouped, *A Universal History of Infamy*.[32] Patchy and incomplete, it flaunts its large gaps. In his critique of Hegel's persistence in contemporary historiography, Ranajit Guha writes that Hegel's was "a short story with epical pretensions."[33] In turn, we could call the *Universal History* the parodic inversion of the same: an epic of fragmented or truncated proportions. While we search in vain for the inside of this universal history, we find only a piling up of colorful stories.

Borges's universal history also differs from Hegel's and Ortega's—as well as from the skepticism of his admired Schopenhauer's—because it shapes history itself to Hollywood, and to U.S. mass and popular culture more broadly. Despite their invocation of a variety of spaces and times, the stories in the *Universal History* are disproportionately weighted toward the United States, as though to suggest the inevitable particularity that undergirds any claim to the universal. For Borges the author-spectator, Hollywood, and U.S. mass culture more broadly, speaks the language of the globe. A universal history for this period, he suggests, will necessarily be written with and through its materials.

What Gramsci called the "American phenomenon" had unique implications for Latin America in and beyond the literary sphere. By the post–World War I period, the United States had become the dominant producer of mass culture, above all cinema, consumed in Latin America; after the European markets, Argentina was Hollywood's largest importer.[34] In the Latin American context, it is impossible to speak of mass culture without speaking of the United States' increasingly prominent role, as well as the relationship between media (above all the cinema) and globalization, a transformation that marked generations of writers. Along with the telephone lines that connected Argentina and the United States in 1929, the spread of U.S. economic and cultural influence beyond Mexico and the Caribbean, and into countries far removed from it geographically and politically like Argentina and Brazil, cast a long shadow. Progress in modern technology was undergirded by a diffusionist account, whereby the U.S. center would bestow technological progress on a backward Latin America; in nearly every U.S. military and economic intervention in Latin America beginning in the late nineteenth century—from the United Fruit Company to Ford's rubber plantation in Brazil to the most recent dictatorships of the 1970s—a discourse of technological progress, including journalism, filmmaking, radio, advertisement, and even the exportation of typewriters, was central.[35]

The equation of Hollywood with Fordism also made inroads in Latin America during the period, as it had in Italy, Germany, and the Soviet Union.[36] By 1920, the Ford Motor Company had already began production in Buenos Aires and São Paulo and would spread beyond to other large Latin American cities; Ford's pedagogical films for workers also circulated in Latin America, in tandem with the company's increased investment there.[37] By the following decade, both Fordism and its products were well-known to most educated Latin Americans, a major source of both fascination and, more frequently, fear. Regardless of the different degrees of incorporation of the Taylorist model into an increasingly, if unevenly, industrialized South America, Ford as a metonymy for rationalized, administered modernity began to take root in the 1930s. In the words of *The Man of the People*, the Brazilian post-avant-garde journal I examine below, Latin America, along with the rest of the world, was now in the "machine age," under the sign of "the divine Mr. Ford": "We want the technical revolution and American efficiency."[38] An increased presence of modern U.S. brands (Quaker, Ford, Palmolive, etc.) decorated the mainstream publications of the period, alongside works by modernist writers. Even the rural, peripheral northeast of Brazil was "under the Ford flag," writes an author in 1935.[39] The practice of planned or "engineered" obsolescence also begins in the 1930s with General Motors' "yearly model change."[40]

For many Latin American intellectuals, Fordism/Americanism/Hollywood had become an entangled knot, an ill that had to be rooted out of both the cultural and economic realms. It offered a fresh arsenal for the reinscription of *arielismo*, the articulation of a "Latin" aesthetic, intellectual, and spiritual superiority over the "Yankee" materialistic, mechanistic positivism. Hollywood cinema, in particular, threatened the local because of its potential to transform all times and spaces into its pernicious play of surfaces. The overall effect was a bleeding of definitions between hard and soft power. For many writers, U.S. film is increasingly framed as a surreptitious, almost oxymoronic form of imperialism: "a peaceful invasion," in the words of one writer, threatening the local.[41] In the more strident words of an anonymous worker in Galvão's *Industrial Park*, cinema is the "imperialist opium" sent by the United States to curtail the Revolution (109). The Brazilian leftist journal *Momento*, published far from Galvão's cosmopolitan São Paulo, also predicted that Hollywood cinema was finally revealing, in spite of itself, the contradictions of capitalism: "The suffering cry of the proletariat of that great colossus is making its way to comrades in other parts of the world. 14 million unemployed. . . . The death rattle of the land of Rockefeller and Ford is beginning to be heard."[42]

The neo-*arielista* arguments that position Latinate culture against the barbaric U.S. play of surfaces, so frequent during the period, do little for Borges. Instead, he stakes out a position as a spectator from the margins. In the story "The Improbable Impostor Tom Castro," he invokes his reader in the opening sentence, which establishes the "return" of the title character to South America, "even if only as a ghost, or a Saturday pastime." In a footnote added after the stories were compiled as a book, the narrator states, "This metaphor allowed me to remind the reader that these infamous biographies appeared in the Saturday supplement of an evening newspaper" (31). The reference not only reminds us of the work's initial context of production in the *Multicolor Saturday Magazine* but also situates the itinerary of the trickster Tom Castro as part of a larger traffic between North and South. The reader is localized, momentarily, in his position as spectator before beginning to roam once again through this peculiar gallery of universal history.

In this sense, we can read the *Universal History of Infamy* as an example of what Miriam Hansen has defined, for the realm of cinema, as vernacular modernism, with its emphasis on local adaptation to global (or Hollywood) modes. Hansen's contribution to modernist studies was to reorient the term to include U.S. industrial film production and its itineraries, offering an early argument for transnational film history that she would subsequently expand upon.[43] Hollywood's extension, she argues, is due to its ability to manage (or "mediate") different approaches to modernity/modernization, in no small part because it had to forge consensus—or what she calls, through Kracauer and Alexander Kluge, an alternative public sphere—at home for an extremely heterogeneous population. A process not without its own violence, although Hansen tends to deemphasize it for the sake of her argument, this forging resonates with Borges's *Universal History* on the level of content, for the stories that comprise it are slanted toward popular U.S. narratives of slaveholders, cowboys, and gangers who themselves manage heterogeneity through violence. Borges's "Bill Harrigan," for example, is a totem of the transformation of popular culture into mass culture, from the legends of oral culture to the myths of the Hollywood screen. Other stories in the *Universal History* are also equally interested in this shift, the moment in which outsider figures are yoked into mass culture via new technologies of circulation, distribution, and reception, at the moment of their ostensible demise.[44] In the gangster tale "Monk Eastman, Purveyor of Iniquities," "the conventional gunman of the moving pictures is modeled after *him,* not the flabby and epicene Capone" (32–33). Hollywood's mythic gallery is also a cemetery, its novelty predicated on the reanimation of older figures into ostensibly new, Frankenstein-like amalgamations.

As a vernacular modernist, Borges adapts his fascination with Hollywood's ability to update these mythic figures, as well as its administration of difference through narrative and sensorial pleasure, for his Argentine public. In describing the backdrop of a treacherous slaveholder, for example, he describes it to his readers as such: "The Mississippi is a broad-chested river, a dark and infinite brother of the Paraná, the Uruguay, the Amazon, and the Orinoco" (8).[45] To employ terms germane to Latin American cultural studies, Borges Creolizes, indigenizes, or transculturates the scene that has arrived to him through U.S. culture. Billy the Kid, for example, becomes a *compadrito*—the local term for an Argentine thug. For Hansen, the "vernacular" that modifies cinematic modernism meant "working with genre formulas (both local and imported) and popular motifs, if not clichés . . . putting them into play, twisting, denaturalizing, or transforming them, thus making them available for an at once sensorial-affective and reflective mode of reception."[46] As this quote make clear, her work also highlights the non-narrative dimensions that equally interest Borges in *The Universal History.*

At first glance, Borges might initially appear to ally himself more readily with David Bordwell and Janet Staiger's model of classical Hollywood cinema, the target of Hansen's critique. After all, U.S. commercial cinema, as we have seen, was attractive to Borges precisely for its successful narrative order. Writing in response to Bordwell and Staiger's influential if polemical argument, Hansen emphasizes instead Hollywood's transculturated itineraries, rather than its internal coherence, calling for studies of embodied responses to cinema's circuitous routes, rather than maps of its narrative patterns. Similarly, Borges's emphasis on the author-spectator's constant oscillation between the global and the local through moments of material, corporeal experience allies him in compelling ways with Hansen's thesis. In her emphasis on finding "currents of modernist aesthetics *within* the field of commercial mainstream cinema," her work approximates Borges's attempts to inhabit

Hollywood's latent defamiliarizing tendencies, rather than rehearse, as many of his contemporaries were doing, the burgeoning opposition between avant-garde and popular cinema.

Refusing affirmative national culture in the face of an increasing Americanism, Borges opts for strategic metonymies of Hollywood that zero in on the reader thumbing through the Saturday supplement or exiting the movie theater on the busy Corrientes Street of Buenos Aires. He borrows Hollywood's mythic characters but robs them of poetic justice ("Lazarus"); he pans over the desert but shows the truncated nature of these pans ("Bill Harrigan"); he blatantly displays a preference for the poetic choreography of the Argentine thug over his North American equivalent. The story "Monk Eastman" begins with an unexpected paragraph, titled "Those from this America," which features a highly stylized knife fight between two Argentine gangsters (*compadritos/cuchilleros*): "This is the detailed and total story of our thugs." This story, of course, is anything but "total," but what follows next gives a cue to how Borges intends his readers to define Argentine identity vis-à-vis its counterpart: "The story of the fighting men of New York is much dizzier and clumsier." The following subsection submerges the reader further into this other underworld; it is titled "Those from the other [America]."[47] In order to enter into the world of New York thugs, a portal through Argentine popular culture is required. The subsections, bearing the trace of their popular press circulation, define with brevity and concision the differential element of all identities and position Borges's understanding of world-making as one of paratactic opposition.

Borges suggests here that tinkering with cinema's materials, translating and adapting them, offers another possibility, one that writing can take up in the vacuum created by a struggling local film production culture.[48] (Borges was notoriously hard on Argentine films.) This interest in permutations or combinations of preexisting materials, rather than origins, echoes his experience as a writer/editor for the *Multicolor Saturday Magazine*. Order and creativity, original and copy, rules and riffing, would now be mobilizing tensions in Borges's corpus. The *Universal History of Infamy* thus probes the limits of novelty, demonstrating a paradoxically productive resignation to this ceaseless recycling. When, in the second prologue to the 1954 edition of the *Universal History*, he links his strategies to the Baroque—"the final stage in all art, when art flaunts and squanders its resources" (4)—he invokes his work's sense that the new has become exhausted.[49] Shifting away from the novelty that had undergirded authorship in the avant-garde period, he posits the author as the locus of reception of mass culture; at the same time, this spectator is not a passive consumer but a sly, strategic retooler.

MONTAGE TO THE LEFT: PATRÍCIA GALVÃO'S ALTERNATIVE GLOBAL VERNACULAR

As Borges was writing and editing his pulpy, Hollywood-inspired supplement, a Brazilian contemporary had begun to explore a different cinematic idiom in her media laboratory. Like Borges, in the early 1930s, Patrícia Galvão experienced a confluence of material practices: she coedited her first periodical, which featured its own play between the verbal and the visual; began reflecting on the power of cinema for writing; and drafted her first work of fiction, the novel *Industrial Park* (1933).[50] And like Borges, Galvão also went to the movies, but she did so in order to experience a very different kind of spectatorship: while Borges posited a new role for the individual spectator of mass culture, she sought to sketch the terms for an elusive, collective gaze that would supersede the individual. Moreover, if Borges positioned himself as a spectator as a means of negotiating his disenchantment with avant-garde originality, Galvão did so in order to mingle with the heterogeneous bodies that converge together, haggle and talk in the alternative public sphere of the cinema.

An often-overlooked figure from her emergence on the avant-garde scene in the late 1920s until her death in 1962, Galvão's rich and fascinating life reads like a compendium of modernist interventions: avant-garde muse during the 1920s; beauty contestant in a Fox Film competition (she lost); interviewer of Freud on a boat to China (where she brought back the first soybeans to Brazil); protester incarcerated in France; narrowly missing the grasp of the Nazis in Germany during these same years; a trip to Hollywood; publications of pulp fiction under the pseudonym "King Shelter"; the introducer of Faulkner and Joyce into Portuguese; the first woman arrested in Brazil on ideological grounds, at a rally protesting the Sacco and Vanzetti trial.[51] At the beginning of the 1930s, a recent convert to communism, Galvão sought out a form that would reflect her newly engaged stance, and she found one in the slightly belated, fragmentary access to avant-garde Soviet film.[52] If, for Borges, Hollywood constituted the focal point for his media laboratory, for Galvão it is the "alternative vernacular modernism" of Soviet cinema that Hansen mentions in passing.[53]

In Galvão's proletarian novel *Industrial Park* and her ephemeral little magazine *The Man of the People* (1931–32), Soviet films provide the rhythms for the juxtaposed labors of writing, activism, and the machine labor that gives her novel its title. By this point, São Paulo had become the paradigmatic example of what José Luis Romero has analyzed as the "'irruption' of the masses in the cities," intimately bound up with the struggles of industrialized labor.[54] As the story goes, this Milan—or, per Oswald de Andrade, "Chicago"—of South America was the cradle for Brazil's most experimental strain of artistic movements in the 1920s.[55] Yet the economic and political crises of 1930 afforded a different vantage point from which to view the city's rapid-fire modernization. It would be up to those writing in the wake of Brazilian modernism to approach the underbelly of this futurity.

During the 1920s, São Paulo's most important modernist painter, Tarsila do Amaral, painted the mythical figure of the Abaporu, a visual icon for Brazil's most radical literary avant-gardes. Along with her earlier representations of Brazil's abundant flora and fauna, this singular, modern primitive captured a gesture of the era: the ostensibly innocent gesture of discovering Brazil. In the 1930s, however, this imagery abruptly came to a halt. In her painting *Operários* (Laborers, 1933), Amaral replaced her mythical Abaporu with rows of seemingly interchangeable proletarian faces, a line of smokestacks in the background. Like the Argentine Antonio Berni's canonical painting *Manifestación* (Protest, 1934), these workers stare back at the viewer and at the artist herself, interrogating her. Meeting the gaze of the elusive figure of the masses had become the imperative of early 1930s cultural production in Brazil, as in much of the world.

In the context of the regime of Getúlio Vargas (1930–45), Brazil's late modernist writers would also be forced to contend with a state invested in harnessing the masses, in part through cinema and the radio. In his elegiac essay "O Movimento Modernista" (another late modernist anti-manifesto), the Brazilian Mário de Andrade marvels at his own "drunk" audacity during the earlier period. By 1930, he writes, modernism had exhausted itself, having completed its mission: "In the streets, the people, rising up in mutiny, were shouting:—Getúlio! Getúlio!"[56] Mário's synthesis juxtaposes two historical moments: on one hand, the ecstatic pursuit of pleasure of the early years; on the other, the masses in the streets who call for the populist leader, Vargas.

In their ephemeral journal *The Man of the People*, Galvão and Oswald struggled to interrupt this fiction of a call-and-response from Vargas to the people, and to instead speak for and to these masses themselves, circumventing the consolidating discourse of populism and replacing it with the internationalist rhetoric of solidarity. This fascinating little magazine featured a large, tabloid form, emphasizing concision and brevity in its appeal to the working man. Totaling eight issues, it would be suppressed by the authorities after a series of violent polemics, contributing to its urgent, ephemeral status. The journal's leftist thrust, interest in mass culture, and experiments with typography anticipate *Industrial Park*. Traces of the periodical appear throughout the novel, suggesting that the former functioned as a site to essay strategies that would make their way into the latter, especially in the relationship it attempts to forge with the masses.[57] In the third issue, the masthead states that the journal has no director, headed up instead by "the man of the people himself."

Galvão's *Industrial Park*, Brazil's first, and long unrecognized, proletarian novel,[58] is also Brazilian modernism's most intensive effort to engage the problem of the masses through an intermedial encounter between cinema and print culture. Like Borges, Galvão posits that late modernist writing must engage mass culture through the figure of the spectator. As opposed to Borges, however, the monadic spectator gives way to the collective, finding her purpose in the encounters, clashes, and friction with others. And, in contrast to Borges's privileged *fait divers*, his metonymic cabinet of strategic appropriation, here we find an Eisensteinian dialectic. Throughout the novel, the narrator watches the screen but more often the audience, attentive in both cases to the potential for an embodied experience that may turn an inert series into a politicized group.[59]

The Praxis of Montage

While tracing an overarching narrative arc of the execution and repression of a strike, the multiplicity of its characters and narratives means that *Industrial Park* resists any straightforward synopsis. Galvão's novel draws from the city-portrait genre of books and films that appeared in and beyond Brazil in the 1910s and 1920s.[60] Like her contemporaries John Dos Passos (New York) and Alfred Döblin (Berlin), Galvão attempts to grapple with her city's heterogeneous spaces. Yet sex, race, and gender, as well as stark class inequality, are more pronounced in her novel than in the works of these predecessors and contemporaries. Set in São Paulo during the early 1930s, *Industrial Park* consists of short, pithy scenes that exposed the reader to jagged shards of daily life. It is immersed in mass experience, from the dense network of factories described in its title to seamstress shops to bars to salons to street protests to workers' tenements to the cinema: spaces as characters, and characters as unapologetic social types. Crosscutting between classes, races, and genders, the novel creates a portrait of a city in economic and political turmoil.

Industrial Park presses modernist form into the service of exploring intersecting classes and lives that comprise a city on the cusp of a global upheaval, beginning with its epigraph, which locates us squarely in an "economic depression that afflicts the whole world and whose repercussion we began to feel in the month of October 1929." References to this recent global economic crisis recur throughout the novel, establishing an explicit parity between the context of the novel's production, its audience, and its content. As a result, the uneven texture of Brazilian life during the 1930s becomes the grounds for a critique of global capitalism. In contrast to the primitivism of earlier modernism in which decontextualization meant freedom,[61] *Industrial Park* historicizes the present as a clash of forces. Throughout, Galvão posits that there is no gesture, moment, or image that is not contextual, not linked to another in the web of class struggle.

The year of *Industrial Park*'s publication was critical for debates surrounding the proletarian novel in Brazil and globally. As in Soviet avant-garde cinema, albeit with different formal strategies, proletarian novels envisioned a collectivity that would supersede the plots of individuals and families, challenging the realist novel's emphasis on roundness and interiority.[62] Galvão's novel is an example of what Michael Denning has called "subaltern modernism," a moment in which 1930s writers globally "abando[n] established family plots and the individual Bildungsroman to create experimental collective novels based on documentary and reportage (terms both coined in this period)."[63] In South America, the boom of novels in the 1930s focused on primary products for the export market—with titles like *Cacao* (Jorge Amado, 1933) and *Tungsten* (César Vallejo, 1931)—represented the rural counterpart to Galvão city-novel. In contrast to most Brazilian proletarian novels of the period, however, *Industrial Park* engages fully with cinema, its fragmentary principles, and its mass sensorium. At stake is what undergirded Eisenstein's failed plan to film Marx's *Capital*: how to render perceptible and visceral the invisibilized forces of global political and economic injustice.[64]

In the context of a global economic crisis that threw into relief capitalism's inequalities, the form of the novel itself experiences a crisis, or transformation of sorts. In its first and scarce edition, Galvão employs short sections, graphic marks, and large print, foregrounding the book as a visual medium and entering into competition with the graphic power of cinema and advertising, mutually constitutive spheres. We find the same desire present in the tabloid form, art-deco letters, photographs, and graphics, including some of her own hand-drawn cartoons, of *The Man of the People*. These strategies recall the experimental graphic design and fascination with the cinema found in *Klaxon*, Brazil's first avant-garde little magazine, albeit with an emphasis on the masses that her avant-garde predecessors ignored.[65]

They also recall the *Multicolor Saturday Magazine*, and in particular the overlapping realms of mass print culture and cinema that Borges was simultaneously mining in the *Universal History of Infamy*. As for Borges, for Galvão cinema spectatorship has a dual potential for innovation or regression, and her fiction operates as a testing ground for this duality. Her understandings of the innovative and regressive, however, are much more explicitly politicized, seeking out a clash on a geopolitical scale: Soviet cinema's innovation versus Hollywood's regressive energies. While several critics have noted the cinematic effect of Galvão's prose, including the influence of Soviet montage, in their descriptive catalogs of the novel, these observations are often mentioned in passing, begging further questions. Was this a relationship exclusively formal?[66] What is the relationship between montage and mass perception? What are the limitations in translating Soviet cinema to the Brazilian novel?

Soviet films were screened sporadically from the late 1920s through the 1940s in Latin America.[67] As in many parts of Europe, they were frequently banned or cut or found their circulation limited. Argentina was the first to screen Soviet films and would do so more frequently than many of its neighbors in the late 1920s and early 1930s; the Soviet Union opened a distribution center in Buenos Aires, URSS Films. In contrast, censorship circumscribed the showing of films like the celebrated *Potemkin* in Brazil as well as in other countries like Cuba, leaving writers to imagine the film with the aid of foreign periodicals or to travel to other countries to report back to their readers, as in the case of Galvão, who might have glimpsed her first Soviet films on a trip to Buenos Aires in 1930.

Yet even in countries where the screening of Soviet films was scarce or nonexistent, print culture allowed for a dialogue on Soviet cinema. Through marginalia, film reviews, journalistic sketches, and novels, as well as books and periodicals from Europe and the United States, writers interpreted cinema for readers who had limited access to the films themselves, exposing them to central debates surrounding Soviet cinema that circulated globally during the 1920s–1930s: the use of non-actors; the problem of synchronized sound; and concepts such as intellectual montage, the Kino-Eye, and simultaneity. (In the case of Brazil, this reception was most prominent not in Galvão's São Paulo but in Rio de Janeiro, through the work of the Chaplin-Club.) As he was globally, Eisenstein was the metonymic figure of this reception.

Galvão picked up the fragments of this circulating discourse as a promise for forging another relationship to the masses. It would take place through a confrontation between opposing forces on superimposed scales, from quotidian street slang to the global economy. In one scene from the novel, for example, working-class women are invited to "girls' night" at the movies; at school, young women gossip:

—Did you see today's *Cinearte*? It talks about Russian cinema . . .
—Listen! Do you know what communism is?
—I don't know and I don't want to know. (28)

In this abrupt archive of adolescent girls' speech, bourgeois norms supersede their alternative, Soviet cinema. The battle lines have been drawn; cinema has become a site of struggle, and different, competing publics come into view. On one side, we find *Cinearte* (1926–42), the most widely read film periodical in Brazil, featuring both beauty tips and articles on Hollywood as well as national cinema. On the other hand, a truncated potential: that of Soviet cinema, evoked only to be ridiculed and then occluded (just as it was on the pages of *Cinearte*, notoriously Hollywood-centric). Similarly, in the first and last issues of *The Man of the People*, Galvão and Oswald underscored this contrast, citing statistics on ticket sales for U.S. films that week, in contrast to "o cinema das massas [. . .] o cinema russo"; the first issue calls for an anticapitalist Brazilian cinema.[68]

Another iteration of this confrontation occurs in the later description of a cinema house, a poster of Greta Garbo on its façade:

> Opaque and illuminated, indifferent to empty stomachs, receives Braz's aristocratic petty bourgeoisie that still have money for

> the cinema. At the door, the pale enigma of Greta Garbo, in the poorly drawn colors of a poster. Disarrayed hair. Bitter smile. A prostitute feeding the imperialist pimp of America to distract the masses. (78)

Garbo's face, juxtaposed with proletarian print culture, is a cipher of the violence of global capitalism. The narrator immediately follows this image with its antithesis: "Crimson placards incite to revolt. Clumsy but ardent tones blend in speeches" (79). Crosscutting between the "pale prostitute" Garbo and the workers organizing in the streets, she redefines the star's image vis-à-vis the hot colors, inefficient and for this reason more authentic, of the rumblings of the revolution. This shot of Garbo attempts an x-ray of the violent processes that sustain globalization, while the subsequent image of the Communist placards reframes the image through contrast.[69] In *Industrial Park* the privileging of smeared, imperfect visuals—those crimson placards, the "smudged ink of the printed bills demanding more bread" (100)—provides an antidote to the slippery smoothness of Hollywood. The impassive, mask-like face of Garbo—as Roland Barthes would famously describe her—is here activated by the impoverished poster leaflets, delineating a struggle almost entirely absent from the world outside the novel.[70] Here, and throughout the novel, wherever a medium or site of inscription appears, its antagonist immediately follows.

As in Borges's *Universal History of Infamy*, *Industrial Park* adopts the presentational strategy of cinema. The narrator omits verbs to index images for her reader-viewers: "Blood mixed with milk." Yet the effect could not be more different than in Borges's text. Her novel's employment of juxtaposition and antagonism finds its inspiration in certain practices and beliefs that were often grouped under the broad rubric of "Soviet montage."[71] Linear, sequential narrative gave way to parataxis, and also to dramatic, "choppy" cuts with saturated images. Galvão appears especially interested in Eisenstein's assertion that montage works through collision, conflict, and opposition, which he opposed to Pudovkin's conception of montage as linkage. His theory and practice of montage entailed a dialectical conception of history, in which the confrontation of two oppositional shots produces something new.[72] Similarly, at key moments in *Industrial Park*, the narrator both links and separates similar cinematic images set apart from one another. An early image describes a worker's foot bleeding after it is cut on a broken milk bottle as he returns to the factory: the aforementioned "blood mixed with milk" (9). In the second, in the crescendo of a protest: "This gasoline is our blood!" (78). The shift from the simple, quotidian scene of milk to the powder keg of gasoline pivots on the repeated image of blood, depicted here as an escalation of violence, a coming to consciousness.

The spatialization of the class struggle also recalls Eisenstein's later concepts of associative and intellectual montage, in which two contrasting shots of the same kind of object throw class difference into relief. As the class struggle builds to a crescendo in the novel's second half, the revolution is preceded by a sense of the collective achieved through clashes and fluids, in a visual spectacle: "Shots, rusty swords, poison gases, horses' hoofs. The throng sees the light, in the stampede and the blood" (81); "The police advance, fire. A small woman lies on the ground, crying out with her leg shattered. Her blond Lithuanian hair flows smoothly over her sweaty forehead" (100). The potent image recalls the "We Won't Forget!" after the massacre on the Odessa steps in *Potemkin*; in Galvão's novel, it anticipates the martyrdom of the suppressed rebellion, a motif of proletarian literature that projects into the future the redemption of past repression.[73]

The strike scene in *Industrial Park* comprises the novel's most explicit parity with Eisenstein's praxis, but elsewhere Galvão also employs montage on different scales, including on the level of the chapter, section, paragraph, and even sentence. Chapter titles frame contrasting spaces of this broad social strata: at times revealing what custom has kept hidden ("Racial Opiate"); at other times cataloging labor and laboring bodies ("Looms," "Needle Workers," "Street Walker") and social spaces ("Birthing Houses," "Public Housing"); at times explicitly employing Marxist terminology as a means of situating a scene into a broader vision of the world ("In a Sector of the Class Struggle"; "Where Surplus Value Is Expended"; "Proletarianization"); elsewhere as a description of character types ("A Bourgeois Vacillates"; "Where They Talk about Rosa Luxemburg"). Suggesting an immediate affinity with both photographic captions and silent film intertitles—Eisenstein's *Potemkin* is separated into chapters such as "Killed for a Plate of Soup," "Of Man and Maggots," "A Dead Man Calls for Justice"—these chapter headings also participate in the operation of montage, connecting different sectors of São Paulo together through jarring contrast.

What is at stake is not just the adoption of formal strategies but also their political implications beyond the screen or page at a moment in which different forces are jockeying for the power to speak both to and for the masses. Soviet cinema, and Eisenstein's in particular, afforded a potent model because it suggested a way of producing a collective amid the seemingly individualized experience of film spectatorship. Eisenstein, Vertov, and others created films in an attempt to overcome what they saw as the legacy of the bourgeois novel with its patterns of one-to-one identification between spectator and protagonist. They focused instead on making the crowd a protagonist—for example, in the crane shots of the industrial park that opens *Strike!* or in the increased presence of long shots and crowd scenes as the sailors come together in *Battleship Potemkin*—hoping that film might inaugurate a subject (the masses) not reducible to a series of individuals. "Discarding the individualist conception of the bourgeois hero, our films . . . made an abrupt deviation, insisting on an understanding of the mass as hero," Eisenstein wrote. "No screen had ever before reflected an image of collective action. Now the conception of 'collectivity' was to be pictured." Given both its collective setting and formal strategies (the multiple angles, cuts, and viewpoints it embodies), film also produced a mass gaze, offering an alternative to individual subjectivity.[74]

This collective aspiration helps us understand *Industrial Park*'s refusal to privilege and resolve the narratives of its multiple and seemingly incommensurable lives. Like the Soviet filmmakers whose work she admires, Galvão seeks out the construction of a collective experience or body that cannot be discretely tethered to any individual, a figure that would constitute a new mode of perception, united by experiences at once grounded and embodied in specific sites and mobile and transnational in its scope. In this way, the mass on screen or page would reverberate with its addressee, the mass in the audience or the group of readers. Perhaps, the novel suggests, by being connected in their rather solitary experiences of reading, they might realize, too, their collective potential. While during these same years Humberto Mauro had declared Soviet cinema "inadaptable" to the Brazilian context, pushing toward a definition of national cinema, Galvão seems to be attempting just such an adaptation from Soviet screen to Brazilian page.[75] At a moment in which Soviet films themselves were banned in Brazil, she vernacularizes this elusive, internationalist potential and grounds it in the give-and-take of bodies watching film.

One scene in *Industrial Park* zeroes in on the embodied experience of filmgoing, displaying its potentials and its limitations. In the chapter "Proletarianization," the worker Otávia realizes her attraction to

Alfredo, the wealthy scion who has recently committed class treason and joined the Communist Party. The scene describes their first date, where they go together to see a Soviet film, a process depicted as at once intimate and political, naturalized and pedagogical. This is one of the few moments in the novel where we see sexual desire from a woman's perspective, as well as constituting a relatively rare late modernist depiction of female spectatorship. Significantly, it takes place in the cinema, a space that Galvão attempts to reinhabit as the doubled allure of this awakening. Immediately before this scene, Alfredo works and releases a "laborious and happy sweat," a temporary baptism of sorts into the working-class movement. Prior to the lights dimming, Otávia is drawn to the newly proletarianized Alfredo. Then her desire seems to spread to the collective that inhabits the theater: "In the dark, Otávia wants to wrench [*arrancar*] from each still spectator's head, from each silent arm, an allegiance to the emotional spasms that envelop her. She squeezes Alfredo's hand" (100). The description recalls Pudovkin's behaviorist assertion (also echoed in some of Eisenstein's writings) that "film is the greatest teacher because it teaches not only through the brain but through the whole body."[76] The pleasurable but also violent, even coercive process—*arrancar*: to wrench or root out—describes bodies reacting inadvertently to the stimulus of screen and collective spectatorship, a process that echoes varied modernist theories of spectacle, from Eisenstein's montage of attraction to Brecht's alienation and Benjamin's innervation.

And yet this collective political awakening, with its hint of a kind of political Carnival, is curtailed by some viewers' lack of interest in the Soviet film they are watching: "A lot of people don't wait for the end of the showing. A group of young women go out lamenting loudly the ten cents wasted on a film without love" (100). Waiting for the millionaire who will never appear from far away: this quote implicates the sublimation of libidinal political energies into romance that marks the enormous popularity of commercial U.S. cinema during the period. In the cinema scene the group of young women exits the theater in disappointment after the Soviet film, but not without a concluding, antagonistic commentary: "In the front row, two young male workers are enthusiastic, absorbed in the proletarian drama being shown. One of them talked so loudly that Otávia could hear every word: 'No one here understands this bombshell!'" (100).

As in the brief exchange on the cinema between working-class girls or the juxtaposition of Hollywood movie posters with smudged proletarian handbills, the cinema here becomes a site that makes possible revelatory clashes. Such encounters reflect not only Galvão's desire to employ the medium for revolutionary purposes but also her simultaneous ambivalence about the collective potential of cinema itself. On one hand, cinema would appear to offer a space for these identifications to flourish on an affective, corporeal plane. Although moviegoing in Brazil was originally a purview of the upper classes, by the time Galvão writes *Industrial Park* it was a more widespread form of entertainment, albeit not as extended as in Borges's Buenos Aires. In addition, given the challenges afforded by Brazil's vastly unequal education system—estimated national literacy rates for this period hovered below one-third of the population—cinema's potential was greater than for its neighbors Argentina and Uruguay, a fact intellectuals in the Vargas regime were beginning to notice. In this scene from the novel, Otávia's attention is continually diverted away from the film to the spectacle of the audience itself: what unfolds is not moving images on the screen but the words and gestures of spectators. The "talking back" to the screen and to one another that fascinates her in this scene indexes a potential flight line, of words and paralinguistic expressions that lead to divergent interpretations. While advocating for a pedagogy that would direct these bodies seemingly on the cusp of coming to consciousness, *Industrial Park* also allows us to glimpse alternative ways of conceiving community at the movies as, precisely, dissensus.[77]

On the other hand, while identifying Soviet avant-garde cinema as a possible model for imagining this urgent, if elusive, collectivity, *Industrial Park* hesitates when it comes to conceptualizing the masses through cinema spectatorship. The acknowledgment by the few remaining workers in attendance at the Soviet film, "no one understands this bombshell," hovers between an optimistic reading and a pessimistic one, between a revolutionary and reactionary spectatorship. "No one understands" is thus both a criticism and a lament. Cinema's potential risk for leftist politics is that it can subsume and supplant class-based identifications. In fact, its vast appeal lay in its apparent ability to transcend, and therefore erase, class (as well as race and gender) divisions and identifications. In this sense, we might see cinema as a parallel space to the workers' neighborhoods (*vilas operárias*) that pop up frequently in *Industrial Park*, where diverse groups cohabitated in housing constructed by São Paulo factory owners. This motley crew jostled together and shared experiences at the movies. Galvão's own work as an usher in a cinema house as she was drafting the novel, in fulfillment of the proletarianization imperative of the Brazilian Communist Party, may have taught her to observe spectators rather than spectacle, as well as given her access to the latest films.[78]

Yet this same collective of workers and spectators coexists uneasily in the novel, suggesting that political organization is, at best, an ephemeral potential. The mass at the cinema, after all, does not easily line up with the proletariat but emerges as part of a collective body even more mixed and difficult to define. In his classic study of Latin American cities, Romero argues that the masses is neither a right-wing nor a left-wing category. It is what exceeds political classification, its surplus. His own language suggests this unaccountable or uncontainable force: "a thousand-headed hydra"; at once "abstract and collective."[79] Galvão does not entirely escape this fear of cinema's seduction of the masses—that classless, amorphous collective that becomes an unlikely protagonist during the 1930s. In light of her conflicted understanding of the medium's potential for a revolutionary leftist politics of the masses, this scene of cinema spectatorship functions as a mise en abyme of the novel itself. For it, too, struggles with mass culture in the hopes of transforming it into a revolutionary energy. While it adopts Soviet cinema as an imperfect praxis, it is left with a sense of unease about the ability to create a cultural product directed toward the masses, forever betraying their heterogeneity in terms of interests, desires, and experiences.

If we look for where the stress falls in this overflowing account of proletarian life, we find that Galvão is ultimately more invested in moments of release through collective struggle, in the messy, cacophonous registering of an undisciplined mass, the anarchist happening of the protest, the interruption of the series in the protest, the sublimation of art into politics: "Braz awakens. The revolt is joyful. The strike a party!" (79). Here, São Paulo's recent history of anarchist worker culture—and its topos of the "strike as the emergence of a party, of fantasy, as carnivalization of the everyday," in the words of Brazilian historian Francisco Foot Hardman—seems to momentarily materialize and eclipse the directives of the Communist Party, which serves as an important interlocutor for Galvão as she was writing the novel.[80] This strike/protest/carnival may also be the historical substitution for the avant-garde happening where she first cut her teeth as an adolescent muse to Oswald, Tarsila do Amaral, and others. (It also overlaps with Eisenstein's own interest in excess.)[81]

It is not surprising, then, that the Brazilian Communist Party, knee-deep in its most strident proletarianization phase, ordered Galvão to publish *Industrial Park* under a pseudonym; the novel implicitly invokes a collective spontaneity that is difficult to reconcile with its directives. (In the years immediately following the novel's publication, she would be forced to break with the party, only to be imprisoned and tortured soon after for her involvement with it.)[82] The cinema spectators agitate in front of the screen, but the crowd writhes joyously in the streets, underscoring the desire for immediacy that constitutes her work's productive limitations. The space of the cinema—screen and seat—is ultimately insufficient for the intervention she desires. For, in contrast to Borges's view of the spectator as a nascent bricoleur, employing the metonymies of Hollywood to deflate their globalizing thrust, she finds politics where a clash between opposites brings forth something new: a group of bodies whose tense interactions extend beyond the silent, darkened space of the movie palace.

In one of his first film reviews, even Borges begrudgingly recognized Soviet cinema's importance. After describing certain images in what he deems the best Soviet films—Eisenstein's *Ivan the Terrible*, *Battleship Potemkin*, "and perhaps *October*"—he observes that Soviet cinema was able to have great impact through efficient, inexpensive devices (such as the oblique angles of certain objects). It revitalized the saturated worlds of Hollywood films, crammed with objects and extras: "The Russians discovered that the oblique (and deformed) photography of a jug, column, or nape of a bull's neck was superior in its expressive value to the 1,001 *extras* [in English] of Hollywood, hurriedly disguised as Assyrians and later shuffled into utter meaninglessness by Cecil B. de Mille."[83] Yet Borges goes on to read these Soviet innovations as valuable only temporarily, as a palate cleanser of Hollywood excess, rather than enduring works of art in and of themselves: "The greatest virtue of the Russian film was its interruption of a continual California regime." Once acknowledged by "the world," Soviet films no longer have value. In fact, Hollywood improved the aesthetic quality of its shots and continued its imperial march, having at its fingertips an infinitely vaster repertoire. For Borges, as for Miriam Hansen, Hollywood triumphs by subsuming difference through uniquely effective formulas for managing modernity's heterogeneity (for example, immigration). Hollywood has no adversary worthy of its capacious incorporation.

The only strategy, his work implies, is a pointedly minor resistance: to reassert the spectator's prerogative to poach on its strategies.

For Galvão, in contrast, the solution is quite different. The glaring juxtaposition of Soviet montage informs a dialectical conception of history that requires a collective—a mass as much desired as present—to posit a counterweight to Hollywood, among the most potent figures of capitalism and imperialism during the 1930s. To employ an anachronism, Borges's approach is de Certeauian, emphasizing tactics and reappropriations, while Galvão's is Adornian, more deeply pessimistic, even as it casts its lot with formal experimentation. Moreover, in their very juxtaposition, we see the blind spots of each: the limited and monadic nature of Borges's Hollywood cinephilia; Galvão's own indecision with regard to the Soviet model. Read together, then: if Borges Creolizes Hollywood, Galvão provincializes Borges's "modest" cosmopolitanism. The author as spectator cannot be a solitary bricoleur but must be thought with and through the alternative practices of cinema spectatorship that also surface during the late modernist period. Together, they establish the spectator—a discursive, cryptic, and irreducibly heterogeneous nodal point that makes cinema possible[84]—as an alternate figure for the late modernist author. In the chapter that follows, the visuality of their filmgoing experiences cedes to a more elusive sensory realm, the audible.

CHAPTER 2

Tuning In

The Late Modernist Acousmêtre

At first they reached him in what seemed like watery murmurs, as if he were wearing a diver's helmet. Then he woke up and realized some of the sounds were trying to tell him something, as if he were being singled out from among a number of persons snoring in the room. But when he tried to concentrate on the sounds, they scattered like frightened mice.[1]

—FELISBERTO HERNÁNDEZ, "The Daisy Dolls"

LATE MODERNIST VOICES

In this passage from Felisberto Hernández's "The Daisy Dolls," the protagonist attempts to tune into indistinguishable voices. Sound moves from the illegible to the communicative and back to the incomprehensible. It eludes his capture, "scatter[ing] like frightened mice," even when directed toward him, a receiver apparently uniquely poised ("as if singled out") to capture it. It is as though he were unsuccessfully seeking out a radio frequency for noises positioned at once outside of and within him. Hernández's furtive description provides a shorthand for a late modernist approach to sound. Sounds of unknown or muddled origins run stealthily through many of the texts I analyze in this book, from the disembodied "clumsy and ardent tones" of the amorphous masses in Patrícia Galvão's *Industrial Park* (Chapter 1), to the clock radio ticking off the hours in Clarice Lispector's *Hour of the Star* (Chapter 3), to the phonograph record uncannily droning "Tea for Two" in Adolfo Bioy Casares's *The Invention of Morel* (Chapter 5). Sounds often exceed receptors' aural grasp, despite efforts to home in on and locate them.

Beginning in the 1930s, three concomitant phenomena galvanized sound and in particular the voice and their political and economic deployment in South America. The status of the radio shifted from that of a new, nearly magical technology into a broadcasting medium linked to the market and in certain cases to the state; synchronized sound was introduced and rapidly consolidated in the cinema, flooding silent film with human voices; and populist regimes emerged that would, in the decades that follow, privilege the spoken contract between a charismatic leader and "the People" (*el pueblo/o povo*). The simultaneity and at times interpenetration of these phenomena are crucial to understanding the period's soundscape. In all three cases, the voice's massification threatened to privilege materiality over signification. The voice's materiality was now capable of being shared by individuals far removed from one another; in turn, it shored up a new understanding of these same individuals, reconstituting them (and not always willingly) as participants in a virtual collective.

In contrast to the visual emphasis of the previous chapter, here I show how authors and their narrators engage with the aural dimension of literary and media interfaces. The voice, of course, has a lengthy pedigree in literature and literary studies, in particular the layered or hybrid voice of Bakhtinian polyphony and heteroglossia.[2] While informed by this legacy, with the voice I refer to something less metaphorical: the audible sound emanating from entities (mostly, although not exclusively, human) with the objective of communicating with others.[3] My emphasis is on how literature in this context grapples with the voice's materiality: the textures and "grains" of the voice that produce tangible effects in the world, effects that often exceed language's representative function.[4]

A prose sketch that navigates the boundary-crossing voice of Greta Garbo; a microfiction that uneasily incorporates the radio's insidious interiority; a short story that interrogates the freakish ventriloquism of populism; a novel's suturing of the proletarian voice-body weld; and multiple film chronicles that reflect on the "old novelty" or "domesticated monstrosity" of synchronized sound: these are some of the stations on which I land. Without seeking to erase the specificity of loudspeakers, radio, or synchronized sound, I want to convey a sense of the different voices jostling for the attention of the late modernist ear. Departing from the single or dual author readings of the book's other chapters, I shuttle among literary texts; I also move among different media, privileging the experience of the writers' often-frustrated desires to decipher the period's competing voices.[5] This chapter is thus shaped by the dialectic of distraction and attention that preoccupied late modernist writer-listeners.

The historical avant-gardes had their own sound obsessions—the triumphant drumbeat of futurist war and its technologies; Dada's celebration of "senseless" (often racialized) sound; the declamations of São Paulo's Modern Art Week, celebrating the acoustics of jazz and the typewriter; the *klaxon* that inaugurates Brazilian modernism, the most euphoric wing of the Latin American avant-gardes; the experimental radio poetry of the Mexican Estridentista movement; Marinetti's self-fashioning as a radio, which led to radio appearances in Brazil and Argentina.[6]

The late modernist voices I analyze here differ from these earlier celebrations of technological noise as a metonymy of modernity. Late modernist texts continue their predecessors' exploration of the tensions produced in the soundscape of modernity: between signal and noise, culture and nature, voice and speech, between trying to say something and the multiple, non-signifying sounds made audible in and through media.[7] Yet they reject the earlier, implicitly celebratory analogy between writing and the sounds transmitted by radio and cinema. With the consolidation of technologies that inscribe and transmit the voice with a seeming faithfulness of which literature could only dream, and with the rise of leaders who claim a special privilege to speak to and for the masses, authorship finds itself demoted. It must reconsider its prerogative to inscribe or herald the voice of the people.

Alternatives appeared in this at times dysphoric landscape. Late modernist authors found them in the missed encounters of the *acousmêtre*, the voice whose source is invisible. They explore how voices acquire power by hiding their origin or, inversely, by attempting to suture themselves to representative bodies. Instead of seamlessly welding bodies to voices, writers can struggle with the disjuncture between one and the other. They traverse the scars of conflicting voices and bodies, rendering sound's rough edges; expose the seams of the voice-body weld as technological industries work to stitch them back together; or reveal the emptiness behind the disembodied, and ostensibly omnipotent, populist voice. Authorship, they suggest, is especially apt to trace the politics of the voice's materiality and its embodiment, including its failures.

Late modernist authors and their narrators became receptors or antennae of conflicting voices: capitalist and populist, new and automatized, national and global. In its debut issue of 1931, the Argentine journal *Nervio* (Nerve) published an editorial titled "Antenna" that emblematizes this role: "Short and long waves. Messages from all zones, agonies from all latitudes." The editors promise, like the antenna, to capture the frequencies of the contemporary global crisis.[8] Authorship has become a tuning in, corresponding to a period in which the voice itself was transformed into a crucial medium in cultural politics. It shifts from celebratory proclamations of the sounds of modernity to an acute, and at times paranoid, mode of listening in, even *eavesdropping*, into the intimacies of an increasingly massified experience of sound.

BROADCAST RADIO: INNER EXTERIORITY

In the *acousmêtre*, the voice's power derives from the invisibility of the body from which it emerges. According to Michel Chion, its most impassioned theorist, the etymology of the *acousmêtre* is a Pythagorean sect whose disciples, in *Wizard of Oz*–like fashion, listened to their leader from behind a curtain in order to absorb fully the power of his words. The power of the *acousmêtre* lies in this invisibility, which produces the sensation that he (the figure is almost always masculine) is ubiquitous, omniscient, omnipresent, and panoptical. Conversely, revealing the source of the origin—what Chion deems *de-acousmatization*—functions as a kind of de-auratization, collapsing the distance between speaker and listener by exposing the former's vulnerable body. While often situated in terms of a universal primal origin (the voice of the God or of the mother, whom Chion deems the ultimate *acousmêtre*), the term became reanimated through the increasing presence of technological media, beginning with the phonograph and including radio and the telephone. Authorship finds itself in competition with these forms of "secondary orality," because before them script had been the only way to fix the voice.[9]

The radio is always acousmatic, concealing the body that produces the voice (except for when viewers would watch the filming of radio shows). Before radio, the term "broadcasting" referred to oratory contexts, in which the human voice underwent a transformation into "a nonhuman, invisible source of nature."[10] This uncanny power constructed a virtual collective, as it would continue to do as radio emerged as a mass medium. Yet its very collectivity usually depended on a privatized speaking to: the voice issuing from the domestic apparatus, in the privacy of the listener's home. This experience does not so much blur the boundaries between inner and outer as occupy them both, simultaneously.[11] The broadcaster's voice "mystifies" despite being human, Sartre writes, because it mimics the reciprocity of discourse we experience in daily conversation but prevents this reciprocity from actually taking place. Sartre uses radio as one of his principal examples of seriality, and radio listeners as a collection of people that cannot recognize themselves as a group. Listening to radio, he writes, I can turn the dial or turn the apparatus off, but this doesn't change the fact that the voice is still being heard by millions of listeners who form a series: "I will not have negated the voice; I will have negated myself as an individual member of the gathering."[12]

For Sartre, broadcast radio had long achieved the status of a consolidated medium, a process that begins in the 1930s and was theorized by German artists and intellectuals with particular force, as well as taken up by their counterparts throughout the United States and Latin America. In his "The Radio as a Communications Apparatus" (a manuscript from 1932 that he intended to read aloud), Brecht, as Sartre would later, expressed a deep distrust of radio's one-sidedness: "It is only a distribution apparatus, it merely dispenses."[13] To make radio a medium that does not pacify, to "refunctionaliz[e]" it, requires artists to imagine its transformation into "vast system of channels": "to let the listener speak as well as hear"; "to bring him into a network instead of isolating him" (42). Brecht does not have in mind a radio public that is already constituted as consumer-citizens. He wants to intervene before the medium's relationship to either the state or the market is consolidated; his public participates by talking back, through a dual process in which it both instructs and is instructed (43). In his "Reflections on Radio" (also written around 1931, unpublished during his lifetime), Benjamin, similarly concerned about the dividing line between performer and audience, wants to convert the latter into an expert—a shift he also argued takes place in cinema in "The Work of Art in the Age of Its Technological Reproducibility"—as opposed to its current state, "the relentless fomenting of a consumer mentality."[14]

These reflections signal a historical shift in how radio began to be understood during the late modernist period. For Beatriz Sarlo, when radio first appears in Argentina, the listener could be at once a spectator and a producer, a listener and an emitter. Early approaches to radio underscored it as a technological marvel, with spectral or even fantastic immateriality. The radio in the user's hands; the radio as a magical medium—both of these approaches seemed occluded by the 1930s and 1940s. During this period, radio appeared to become "opaque" to its users; amateur tinkerers became captive audiences, and the radio's utopic ephemerality was increasingly linked to expansionist projects under the rubric of both nationalism and capitalism.[15] The transformation of radio from a new medium to a consolidated one inspired two opposing responses on the part of authors: on the one hand, an eagerness to participate as handmaidens in the construction of an etherized national voice, regardless of the inevitable difficulties this imposed; on the other, sheer terror of the medium as a vehicle for what they saw as a stealthy and rapid erosion of interiority.

In 1931, Mário embarked upon his first forays into radio through a series of polemical articles in the *Diário Nacional* of São Paulo. By this point, the "pope" of Brazilian modernism had already embarked upon his life's project to explore the contours of a national language and music, mining the longstanding gulfs between written and spoken language, live and notated music—gulfs, in his view, that secured the *letrado*'s privilege at the expense of Brazil's rich and hybrid popular culture. In light of Brazil's overwhelming heterogeneity, including a majority population without access to literacy, his radio texts thus form part of a broader project to redefine the national. In his early sketches on radio, Mário protests the "primordially foolish" nationalism that had sprung up during the post-1930 revolutionary fervor, producing an admixture of schmaltzy music and "ads for curing the indiscreet annoyances of *senhoras*."[16]

To underscore his disgust, he imagines a hypothetical Argentine listener tuning in and judging the Brazilian people accordingly. These first writings on radio take place during a pivotal moment in the history of Brazilian cultural history, one that sees what we might call the first import substitution of a specifically mass national culture that defines itself negatively vis-à-vis its neighbors and influencers: peninsular Portuguese, the United States, and Spanish America. If Benjamin describes the voice in broadcast radio as a "visitor" in the listener's home (391), Mário imagines that this guest is joined by another, explicitly foreign one. The radio is beginning to be depicted as the voice of a nation, but one that paradoxically depends upon outsiders eavesdropping on this imagined community.

Nearly a decade later, Mário elaborates his interest in the radio as the medium of a national voice in a lengthy *crônica* titled "Radiophonic Language" (A Língua Radiofônica).[17] The critical historical distance required to reflect on the technology's status as a national consensus medium had been established, and he finds that the broadcast medium has formed its own language. Here, the radio is grounded neither in technophobia nor in technophilia but rather a meditation on the voice itself as a medium of national identity, forged through a confrontation among unequal voices, including those at the nation's exterior edges. The acousmatic (disembodied) nature of the radio makes possible an alternative language that can merge this heterogeneity.

Mário begins by describing a survey on the language diffused by radio: Does it "contaminate" the national tongue? Should there be censorship of words on the radio? How to approach regionalisms, slang, and variations in pronunciation? Tellingly, Brazil's neighbor once again appears on the horizon of his understanding of radio as a national medium, for the survey that prompts his reflection is from Argentina. It is as though the medium itself prompted a transnational and comparative angle. In fact, while his privileging of the radio as fostering a specifically Brazilian language suggests Jesús Martín-Barbero's later view of the medium,[18] for Mário the search for a national voice always exceeds the national, evoking its constitutive outside—just as his earlier modernist works would seek out the specificity of Brazilian language amid a polyglot confluence of voices, notably in his experimental opus, *Macunaíma* (1928). As his reference to the Argentine survey suggests, both Brazil and Argentina were experiencing a period of intense regulation of the radio, part of a struggle to posit a national voice in unified terms of gender, ethnicity, race, and class.[19] In response, Mário argues for a second-wave imagined community, forged within a nascent national culture industry that has its eye on its own borders.

In "Radiophonic Language," Mário rejects the opposition present in the Argentine survey: the idea that the mass medium contaminates either elite or popular speech. Language, he insists, is an abstraction (as in Saussure's *langue*; what Mário calls *Língua* as opposed to the plural and lowercase *línguas*). In reality, there is a multiplicity of languages, each generated by a specific constellation of laws, customs, geographical separation, and technical specialization. Each is generated according to its own context, not just to the subject enunciating it: the "petit bourgeois" coos to his lover in one language, curses in a fit of rage in another, and uses yet another "at his little daughter's birthday party." In this heady stew, elite or lettered speech is just one subset.

Radio, too, is developing its own language, one as specific as those of "engineers, thieves, or mothers with their infants who cannot yet speak." This short list is telling, combining the heterogeneous discourses of the technocratic, the marginalized (as in the figure of the *malandro*, or hustler), and the intimate prelinguistic. Radio, Mário argues, yokes together. It is more than the sum of its parts. The imperative of accessibility gives birth to a "mixed, complex language; one with its own unique flavor," in Mário's words, "a particular, complex, multifarious, mixed-up [*mixordiosa*] and anti-elite language" (178–79). Forged within the plural Spanishes and Portugueses of the world, this new radiophonic language has its own defined territory, one located in the strength of frequencies of the capital cities and realized through their specific accents, which subsume all of these *línguas* under its hybrid banner.

His primary example of radiophone language is the use of the *você*—today the most common form of the informal second person in Brazilian Portuguese, especially on television and in the major cities. He describes the at-first nearly offensive over-familiarity with which the radio voice addresses his unknown listeners through the *você*, cultivating the "demands of sympathy" (178). In this first example of Brazilian mass media, the radiophonic voice shrinks and manages class and regional difference (as television will in a formidable way beginning in the 1960s in Brazil). On the other hand, the *você* preserves a distance that the *tu*, at this moment spoken in more intimate contexts, does not possess. It is, as he says, a mixed or paradoxical mode of address: a familiarity with brackets, a mass intimacy.

An interest in orality had structured Brazil's postcolonial literature during the first wave of modernism; here, this same interest encounters a technological medium capable of, and with pretentions to, transmitting the national voice during the more centralized, anti-experimental period that followed the avant-gardes. Ultimately, Mário sees the intertwined relationship between popular forms of expression and the popular medium of the radio as mutually constitutive. Singers and musicians are creating a "super Brazilian" (*brasileiríssima*) language on the radio, replete with its own terminology, one that is superior to the elite lexicon. The "new" radiophonic language is not, then, precisely new but rather an admixture of the nation's ever-present, constitutive heterogeneity. Mário mines the Brazilian modernist trope of *discovering what had been there all along*, a paradoxical novelty. This elusive aural territory has yet to be mined by intellectuals. This extant Brazil was to be discovered at the moment of transmission of its national voice.

The author here is a giant ear: one of the many listeners tuning in to the national voice and its exteriorities, albeit one who is especially acute, prone to elaborating his listening experiences and remediating them through print. In this sense, radiophonic language sutures over certain differences (of class, race, region) and speaks the language of a privileged difference, national identity, with the author as "aural witness" (or ear witness). The receptivity of the author-as-listener may seem passive; ultimately, however, it negotiates a contract between literary texts, such as Mário's own essays, and the broadcast medium. In his view, and in tune with his own burgeoning work on ethnomusicology, print culture and radio will complement, rather than compete with, one another, as a caption fleshes out the photograph's muteness. This complementarity is secure only inasmuch as the author gives up his elite (*letrado*) perspective. Authorship finds its place not in speaking for but in listening to the national voice.

For other late modernist authors, however, radiophonic language interpellated in nightmarish fashion not a national listening community but a series of isolated listener-consumers. While it was blurring the edges of interior and exterior, broadcast radio was also busily installing other divisions that favored the interweaving of mass media and capitalism. As Brecht and Benjamin feared, it would continue to divorce users or listeners from producers and position them unilaterally as consumers. In his *crónica* "Why I Stopped Speaking on the Radio" (1932), the Argentine writer Roberto Arlt quotes a friend who declares, "The radio receiver has become a piece of decorative furniture; covered with a cloth, it serves to hold a flower pot, and nothing more."[20] The radio's immaterial magic was grounded, its noises part of a ubiquitous background. The stress now falls on the insidiousness and domesticated tenor of these ostensibly exterior sounds and voices, their low-grade, chronic, and disembodied aspects. Like other consolidated media, it subsumes what was once seen as a harbinger of futurity into capitalism's repetitive rhythms.

In a process that echoed cinema's own consolidation, but much more rapidly, in Brazil, Argentina, and Uruguay, radio had become structured by the logic of the market. The state's presence increased, but it was not to be the definitive influence on the medium (at least not until Perón in Argentina, in the mid-1940s). Sponsors reoriented programming away from the programs of aficionados and bricoleurs and toward publicity and vertical consolidation, restructuring it through product placement—in which merchandise is sewn into the narrative itself—and the episodic rhythms that lent themselves to commercial breaks, most notably the powerful genre of the *radionovela*, first imported from Cuba and funded by multinational corporations.

The "Radioteatro Palmolive del Aire" (sponsored by the U.S. detergent company) ran in both Argentina and Brazil during the 1940s, for example.

While for Mário the radio provided a way of making audible a composite national voice, Felisberto Hernández was preoccupied by the radio's protagonism in suturing consumers into a consumption network, whether they liked it or not. In his short story "Lovebird Furniture" (Muebles "El Canario," 1947), an unnamed first-person narrator traveling on a streetcar unexpectedly receives, along with his fellow passengers, an injection from a smiling salesman.[21] At home, he finds he has been infected with a different kind of radiophonic language. Before falling asleep, the birdsong of the story's title begins to play inside of him, an assault of the radio's alternating noises. This micro–science fiction underscores a common fear that the radio's omnipotence was molding listeners' capacity for attention and reflection through its serialized, segmented structure. And while for Mário this listening had its own timely power, one that authors, self-fashioned as listeners, were uniquely poised to trace, Hernández's narrator is a captive listener.

"Lovebird Furniture" belongs to the genre of fantastic, a privileged one in Latin American literature, but here it is dysphoric, disenchanted. One of the features of fantastic literature is its tendency to literalize the metaphoric:[22] here it is the injection that literalizes radio's "occupation" of private space and the simultaneous breakdown of the monadic interior. The syringe depicts commercial broadcast radio as part of a disciplinary regime of daily life. It injects radio programming into listeners both willing (like the narrator's fellow passengers on the streetcar) and unwilling (the narrator himself). In Jameson's concept of modernist homeopathy, the alienation of mass culture was tamed by selectively incorporating its fragments.[23] Here, however, Hernández's narrator cannot tame the medium through selective incorporation—homeopathy has morphed into a viral injection. Any possibility for agency has been evacuated. Nor is the "sabotage" that Benjamin saw as the radio listener's only option available to the narrator, for he cannot simply switch the apparatus off.

While all voices trouble the division between inner and outer, the radio as a broadcast medium appeared to writers and theorists to amplify this blurring, to underscore and expand its scope. The acousmatic inner speech the syringe induces in "Lovebird Furniture" is of a very specific nature: it produces the episodic fantasies of consumer acquisition. The narrator pulls the bedclothes up over his head to stamp out the radio's noises, only to find them growing stronger. The human body becomes a medium of transmission of a message ostensibly exterior to it. No apparatus is necessary and, in this respect, the radio's ubiquity foreshadows contemporary technologies that track and trace our every move, especially our consumption.[24] The radio voice's lack of a material support is transformed from a privileged vehicle for the artist's unconscious—as it was for Breton and the other surrealists whom Hernández formed an uneasy dialogue (Chapter 4)—into ideological contagion.

"Lovebird Furniture" suggests that authors became unwitting antennae for this new role for the radio, if only because writing appears to afford no way to shut out these disembodied voices. Significantly, the title of Hernández's short story comes courtesy of a sonnet for a furniture company the narrator is forced to absorb. The reference to the commercialized sonnet immediately evokes an earlier anxiety about the role of the artist vis-à-vis the market. In Rubén Darío's famous parable, "The Bourgeois King" (El rey burgués, 1888), the poetic voice is also sutured into the economy of commercial goods in the shop window/mansion of the nouveau riche.[25] Yet Darío's poet is a neglected seer, crying out in the literal wilderness against commodification. He dies outdoors, frozen, with an ironic smile on his lips. In contrast to Darío's heroic Messiah, Hernández's narrator is not a poet, nor does poetry afford heroic resistance. The narrator is instead forced to listen to the commodification of the sonnet form, and even incarnate it in his very receptivity. In this sense, the sonnet written for a furniture company does not index so much a new economy of goods (new products coming from abroad, a noted obsession of *modernismo*) but rather a shifting role for authorship, signaling its demotion from production to (compulsory) reception. At the same time, the transformation of poetic expression into advertising jingles is reinforced in "Lovebird Furniture" by the incorporation of music—a form of artistic production especially important for Hernández—into the jittery forms of an episodic commercial.

This dysphoric aurality undoubtedly reflects Hernández's experiences working at a radio station in 1948, in which he was responsible for organizing time slots for advertising and other programming, the poor man's equivalent to Adorno's contemporaneous Princeton Radio Research Project. His job required a certain corporeal experience with broadcast radio's episodic timetable, its short attention span. (This is a very different role than that of modernist writers who wrote *for* the radio—among them, Eliot, Woolf, Pound, Beckett, and Benjamin, as well as Mário and the Argentines Olivari, Arlt, and Raúl González Tuñón.) Radio has gotten under his narrator's skin and into his brain, its episodic forms a symptom of administered life. The act of "tuning in" has become his daily bread, one that requires him to monitor radio's truncated, episodic structure. What frightens Hernández is the seemingly involuntary nature of listening to broadcast radio, the way it transforms interiority into an endless alteration of the voices of others.

Evidently, Hernández's is a much more sinister construction of the inner-outer blurring—or, better, reverberation—that we saw in Mário's "Radiophonic Language." If Mário's radio *acousmêtre* is the nation's inner speech rendered palpable and shared, Hernández's is a chronic invasion, one that derives its power precisely from disappearing its origins. What connects the two writers, however, is their articulation of a shifting role for writing with respect to the no-longer-new medium of the radio. Tracing its own supposed obsolescence—or sublation into broadcast radio in that sad little sonnet for the furniture company—it tunes in to the site at which inner speech becomes part of the public domain, a shift that reorients authorship away from production and toward the specific reception of listening.

SYNCHRONIZED SOUND CINEMA: OLD NOVELTIES, TALKING DOLLS

As radio was finding its own language, film was finding a voice box.[26] While the transition of radio from a bricoleur to a broadcasting medium inspired unease in Latin American writers, the arrival of synchronized sound in cinema was often depicted as an outright crisis. During the transitional period 1928–33, along with innumerable filmmakers and journalists, major Latin American writers—including Mário, Borges, Horacio Quiroga, and Alejo Carpentier—reflected on the shift from silent film to synchronized sound with a sense of urgency that more closely paralleled their European, rather than U.S., counterparts. For many, sound emerged to "dilute, fog up, and falsify the precise, clear eloquence of a gaze, a gesture, an intention barely visible in the tips of the fingers," in the words of Quiroga. At the very moment in which the specificity of cinema as a medium appeared to be consecrated, having acquired "una personalidad marcadísima," synchronized sound threatened to render such distinctions precarious.[27]

In this sense, the arrival of sound coincided with, and helped to foment, intellectuals' desire to shore up a definition of cinema's uniqueness. South American writings on cinema repeatedly critique synchronized sound for preventing a thoroughly "cinematic" experience. For the most part, they presented it not as a celebrated technological innovation but as a superfluous trick—or at the very least, a fall into a more generalized noise of modern life: "all those sounds and noises that wound our ears," Brazil's most prominent filmmaker wrote in 1932, as he worked on his own silent-to-sound transition film.[28] Sound film's de-acousmatization was a doubled threat: to the medium specificity argument that implicitly valorized a role for literature and to the cosmopolitanism of a global film culture that did not speak the increasingly monolithic tongue of English.

The arrival of synchronized sound inaugurated a shift in cinema, reorienting its formal and industrial properties in multiple ways.[29] Of central importance for our purposes here, the human voice became the primary auditory code. (Per Rudolf Arnheim in his well-known essay on sound film, "A New Laocoön," it drowns out all other sounds, gestures, and objects.)[30] In this sense, synchronized sound was another, powerful step in a longer journey of privileging the technologically mediated human voice, a process that had begun with the phonograph. The sense of disjuncture that sound film inspired was of particular concern to Latin American artists and intellectuals because they had only recently begun to articulate an understanding of (silent) film as a specific medium, one in which they could potentially participate. If silent film appeared to offer an "Esperanto," sound film underscored differences between national and linguistic contexts in all their messy and uneven specificities.[31]

The dominance of the voice over other sounds had implications not only for formal properties of film but also for literature. Writers' adoption of arguments about cinema's medium specificity—drawn from artists as diverse as Jean Epstein, Louis Delluc, Chaplin, and Eisenstein, all of whom appear in South American journals from the mid-1920s through the early 1930s—was not only a way of participating in a cosmopolitan culture of film spectatorship. It was also a call, I would argue, for a division of labor, in which literature should not cede its increasingly tendentious authority to another realm. The repeated assertions of cinema's uniqueness were premised on a negative definition: cinema was not a novel, it was not theater. True cinema did not need to borrow from other media. These kinds of assertions were also, implicitly, a last-ditch attempt to underscore what literature *was*, in a corollary to *cinéma pur*. In other words, inasmuch as writers insist upon how verbal language "burdens" cinema, they implicitly claim speech for their own jurisdiction. Literature under silent film could be depicted as a companion medium, flooding its muteness, extradiegetically, with its metaphorical voices, in the form of intertitles, commentaries, or fantastic fiction about the cinematic apparatus. There, it finds its purpose. Inversely, if cinema and radio could now register the rich specificity of local and national voices—Buenos Aires *lunfardo*; the particular cadences of the *carioca* (Rio de Janeiro) or *nordestino* (northeastern) accents in Brazil—what could writers offer with their own inscription technology? If the cosmopolitan Esperanto of silent film was disappearing, where did that leave literature, the mouthpiece for the local since the Romantic period?

Without the material resources or technical know-how to answer this question through sound film itself, authors employed a powerful element of their repertoire, the metaphor. Two appear with frequency across the early *crónicas*: that of synchronized sound as a technological "toy" and the more grotesque image of the talking doll. The former was especially prominent in the first years of the debate on synchronized sound, with artists and intellectuals underscoring the awkwardness of the novelty over its technological prowess. A "child's toy" (*juguete infantil*), in the words of one *cronista*; "just a curious toy, without transcendence," for another.[32] If these images appear to echo the importance of childhood for avant-gardists like the surrealists (and Walter Benjamin), it is important to note that here they lack any utopian dimension. The toy implies instead regression, of technological novelty as working against progress, or as a farcical simulacrum of that same progress. Synchronized sound cinema was a hybrid amalgamation, rather than a new form, and, often, part of a repurposed bag of tricks designed to seduce viewers and consumers, an interloper in the territory of literature. The latest thing, a passing fad, it adds nothing to a global project of artistic development. In this sense, sound film inaugurates the oxymoron of a "novedade velha"[33]—the old novelty—a key contradiction for late modernism, when the engine of modern media seems to sputter without the narrative arc of progress to guide it. Sound film is a prime example of the bureaucratization of technological novelty: the rehearsed promise that can never truly deliver because it generates a chronic desire for more. The sense of innovation as itself growing old that I have identified as constitutive of late modernism, its strangely melancholic energy, is inflected here in sound film.

If the child's toy sought to manage the perceived threat of sound film, the metaphor of the talking doll makes explicit this underlying anxiety through its far more sinister, grotesque register. The doll is also a toy, and speaks similarly to a stilted progress or infantile regression, but its effects are far more sinister, even grotesque. The image is overdetermined, manifesting interlocking anxieties: the automaton-like quality of the Fordist assembly line; the freakishness of unfettered technological progress embodied in the mismatch or *desencuentro* between voice and body, the human reduced to discrete parts and operations; the severing of intimacy through media that ostensibly seek to connect people. Underscoring the very rift it attempts to suture, synchronized sound seemed to breed its own "unnatural" family, "the anti-artistic monstrosity just around the corner."[34] It inaugurates "an automatized figure that moves under the brays of an idiotic command, acting without the least bit of spontaneity." It grates on the ears: "The human voice, amplified, loses its naturalness entirely. A canary whistles like a locomotive. . . . The first time I heard my own voice in the cinema I could not believe that grunting was truly my own!"[35] For another writer, "the character has no voice" of its own in sound cinema "but a family of voices" that seem to crop up from all directions. Its initial estrangement does not produce wonder but alienation. In this sense, it merely adds to the indistinguishable noises of modernity. "The feeling of uneasiness" that Arnheim attributed to sound film in "A New Laocoön" inspired in South American writers a corporeal repulsion.[36] In addition, the new practice of dubbing had its own bestiary. In one of Borges's few excursions into the technical dimensions of the cinema, he describes dubbing as a "mythological freak" or "ventriloquist's trick."[37] This assemblage—dubbed, divergent versions of Spanish, awkward sound reproductions—also brought the status of localized, global, and/or disembodied voices to the fore.

There is, of course, a material explanation for this "freakishness": the failures and gaps in synchronization that produced ineffective sutures or illegible words and whose infelicities writers were especially eager to note. As in Europe and the United States, but to a far greater extent, the transition to sound in South America was not instantaneous—the abracadabra miracle of innovation—but was, rather, a discontinuous, "stuttering" one.[38] Sound arrived in fits and starts, impeded by various material constraints, especially the cost of adapting movie theaters to the new technologies (including the shift from Vitaphone to optical discs) and anxiety about the discontinued labor of live performers, especially musicians, who worked in the "silent" film realm. At the level of production, moreover, Argentine and Brazilian cinemas were able to regroup fairly quickly after this initial period, but other national cinemas in Latin America were quite devastated by the arrival of sound. (Uruguay's national film industry was much smaller, in contrast, throughout the 1930s, with its first national talkie debuting in 1936.)

While all of these constraints are important for an understanding of sound film's perceived threat, I would argue that writers' repeated insistence on the gaps in the voice-body weld ultimately had a different goal than the denunciation of uneven material conditions in the medium's development. Such articulations, frequent throughout the archive, sought instead to territorialize the voice in the realm of prose, where it would then be refunctionalized by the writer's typewriter or pen. In a *crónica* on sound film, Quiroga writes that the technological frenzy for innovation requires "the hand of the writer" to "guide it firmly" back into its proper place.[39] In contrast to his earlier texts with their enthusiasm for cinema's novelty, a gap has now opened up between the medium of cinema and the medium of writing. The former's consolidation requires the latter to assert its specificity as sound film encroaches upon its territory.

GOAT-GLANDING AND THE TERRITORIES OF SOUND

The reassertion of literature's medium specificity vis-à-vis the cinema was one frequent response. Other writers, however, probed the rifts in the voice-body weld that sound film produced in spite of itself. These rifts or gaps were also potential sites in which authorship could dwell. At the very moment in which film began to be dominated by words, authors stepped in to chart the slippages between words and the bodies that produced them. This approach shares with the defensive one sketched above an anxious search for literature's role within the massification of the voice through communication media. However, in contrast to the discourse of children's toys and talking dolls, which implicitly coated literature with the patina of history and legitimacy, this approach posits a "weak" power for literature: that of charting the slippages or failures between dominant voices and their origins.

The stakes of synchronized sound in South America are underscored in the discourse surrounding the sensationalist phenomenon of "goat-glanding." A term for the adding of synchronized sound to silent films by dubbing one actor's voice over another's body, goat-glanding referenced a surgical procedure made famous in the late 1920s: the suturing of goat testicles onto the male body as a cure for impotence. As such, goat-glanding was also a metaphor for the "unnatural" addition of silent sound. In Timothy Armstrong's analysis of the Anglo-American context, goat-glanding glossed the arrival of sound in its doubling effect of separation and suture, as sound film constantly rehearses—in spite of itself—gaps in the voice-body nexus.[40]

If, per Armstrong, the metaphor of goat-glanding indexes a "crisis in writerly authority" (235), the South American context adds a new dimension, for the problem of cultural importation and the geopolitics of influence had their own fraught histories across the continent. While sound film held out the possibility of being able to provide listeners with something like a national voice—just as the radio had for Mário's author-listener—it also seemed just or even more likely to impose American English on their receptive ears. In a frequent complaint, these ears were exhausted from the constant struggle to understand foreign speech. In Brazil, the minor status of Portuguese (even with respect to Spanish) compounds this experience. "We are so tired of hearing foreigners and not understanding" is a frequent lament, one often followed by a call for the expansion of national film production.[41]

The creation of multiple-language version films (MLVs) during the early sound film period (1929–31) only exacerbated the sense of a rift between sound film's voices and its viewers. These predominantly Hollywood productions were an attempt to supersede the need for subtitles and to corner the global film market by folding multiple languages into its studios, inspiring their own problems in the form of the wide varieties of Spanish found across Latin America and Spain. ("Grunting in Spanish" was how a Mexican writer described them).[42] Films shown throughout the three national contexts were thus frequently underscored with the possessive pronoun *ours*. These kinds of responses mark a clear key difference with the arrival of sound film in English-language milieus: while sound might have been a threat to the avant-garde artistic community internationally, it evidently posed unique problems for more marginalized languages.[43] It is a difference that will persist into our present, with the status of dubbing and subtitling in the global market for cinema affecting the majority of the world's viewing public with what Nataša Durovicová describes as "a thin but distinct coating of difference, supplemented by an additional layer of graphic or acoustic matter."[44]

During the late modernist period, how does the authorial ear locate this potential cacophony of asymmetrical voices? In Nicolás Olivari's sketch "The Voice of Greta Garbo" (Voz de Greta Garbo, 1932), the cataclysmic effect of hearing the international film star in her first talking picture indexes the predominance of the U.S. English voice, which the author attempts to simultaneously materialize (through inscription) and deterritorialize (through listening).[45] As in Galvão's *Industrial Park* (Chapter 1), Garbo is once again a figure for the geopolitical clashes of mass culture in late modernism, but here she is an aural cipher, a voice-type, rather than a visual icon.

The projection of Garbo's voice for the first time in cinema was often recounted as a fall. In *Annie Christie* (Clarence Brown, 1932), her voice unhinged viewers—throaty and accented, it appeared at odds with her fine features. As for the writers who attempted to manage sound film through recourse to metaphors of talking dolls, her recorded voice was depicted as a narrowing or limiting of an expansive imaginative potential. Chion describes the first audition of this voice in this way: "Garbo in the silent era had as many voices as all of her admirers individually conferred on her. The talkie limited her to one, her own."[46] In Olivari's text, however, this ostensible fall is also an opportunity. Unlike the voices of other silent film muses, who "bray painfully" (67) Garbo's synchronized voice is depicted as constitutively ambiguous, border-crossing, located on different, ostensibly mutually exclusive territories. Writing traverses these missed encounters, even as sound film attempts to suture them together.

Garbo appears in the opening sentence of Olivari's text standing on a threshold (*umbral*), in the position of an "anticipation" or "promise." The closing image echoes this, with her poised "on the hill of our memories, situated between two docks"—the docks of the film where *Anna Christie* takes place but also the liminal space between worlds that her voice occupies. It traverses the border between sound and silent film by bringing the star of the latter into the realm of the former, but it also crosses other borders culled up in this initial transgression: between masculine and feminine, dirty realism and the auratic star system, the unattainable idol and the proletariat, the local and the global. It is as though for Olivari's author-listener the transition to synchronized sound functioned as a magnet for all sorts of strange overlappings. His role is to tune in and chart the disjunctures that take shape in the wake of the revelation of this strange "new" voice.

Garbo's voice does not issue forth seamlessly into the author's ear but is instead produced through specific materialities that, in turn, produce their own material effects in the form of her voice. Olivari's listener underscores the contrast between the voice's ephemeral, ether-like quality and the stubborn, if mute, materiality that brings her voice to him: "Her words went away in the celluloid that the operator stuck into a can of guava paste"; her voice "eternally buried in the can of guava paste, which holds the roll of celluloid." This is not the first time Olivari has expressed interest in the materiality of the film canister; in "Starstruck," the short story that opens this study, the narrator also compares it to a tin of guava paste, carried into the cinemas of Buenos Aires by "four men dressed in 'over-all' [*sic*]."[47] As we saw in the preface, Olivari's narrator will go on to describe how he follows these canisters in their class-based itineraries through the city, vernacularizing the Hollywood import, demonstrating the circuits by which it arrives to the spectator. The attention to the materiality of the foreign object allows Olivari to sketch the circuitous routes by which it becomes part of the South American context. In "Starstruck," Olivari's gaze makes possible a fragmented, privatized version of the Hollywood film; here, it is his ear that repositions authorship.

"The Voice of Greta Garbo" depicts the revelation of Garbo's voice as a kind of reverse de-acousmatization. Rather than revealing the source of the voice—the revelation of the body from which the voice emerges, which Chion describes as a "deflowering" or "striptease" of the godlike and "virginal" *acousmêtre*—the source finds a tongue; rather than embodying a defamiliarizing voice, a familiar face becomes "voiced." In this sense, it is metaphorically goat-glanded. In one of the sketch's more bizarre images, "Her ineffable voice extracted [*arranca*], like a musical chord, from her hermaphrodite clitoris." The description recalls Kaja Silverman's analysis of the "extraction" of the female voice in Hollywood cinema of the 1930s–1940s.[48] As Armstrong shows in his study, the transition to sound film was also often depicted in terms of a supposedly unnatural transformation in gender roles. The conversations around cinematic goat-glanding were often gender-bending; silent film was strategically feminized, especially by women modernists, with the new sound film positioned as a violent masculinization.[49] But in Olivari's text the poetic ear is fascinated, rather than repelled, by this transvestism. This reverse de-acousmatization shoves the goddess

Garbo not, as Chion would have it, into the world of human beings but into the space of an earthier, more primitive goddess. His Garbo is all "small hard breasts" and "thick Amazonian legs," feminine brocades and thick masculine overcoats. She is totemic, primordial, rather than an illustration of misplaced technological novelty (65).

On one hand, the narrator laments both the Vitaphone's apparently impoverished technology and the overpowering English voice, which function as obstacles to a desired pure transmission of the star's voice: "Her marvelous voice amplified by the Vitaphone, shameless and crude, robbing us of her best inflections. Her voice the ineffable music of a song we never understand." It is clear that the anxiety over synchronized sound dovetails with a new fear of the dominance of English. Yet, the narrator underscores, this English has an accent: "Her Swedish English, taught and relentless in its '*us*' and its '*vs*,' requires the agnostic key of an interpretation of dreams." Garbo's accent makes possible a transvestite English. It is *gargarizante*—gargling, an onomatopoeia. Indeed, the narrator repeatedly underscores the difference between voice and speech—the rich materiality of the former, which lends itself to be subsumed by or confused with the latter, for which it serves as vehicle. Accents underscore language's overlooked, sensuous dimensions, evoking the voice's materiality; culled up in synesthetic descriptions such as that of Garbo's "hoarse smile that comes from deep in her whiskey-burnt throat" (66). In this sense, Olivari's is a self-consciously failed attempt to translate this voice through metaphors and similes that become increasingly distanced from one another ("a field of poppies girded tightly by the wind"; "harsh, beaten down by sarcasm and the great fatigue of living" [66]). His ear attempts to isolate and inscribe this voice as it rolls over film spectators. Yet the excess of his description, the piling up of these oppositions, also points to a certain futility in the endeavor, as signaled in the repetition of the adjective "ineffable"—etymologically, *unspeakable*, *unutterable*. Later, Olivari's own work on the *radioteatro* will allow him to work hands-on with acousmatic voices, but here his narrator audibly wrestles with the *acousmêtre*. Garbo's voice is precisely the seam where poetic language finds its limits and displays them.

The last sentence of "The Voice of Greta Garbo" does not resolve but exacerbates these different sites of tension. It positions the narrator-listener at the feet of Garbo, depicted as a totemic earth idol:

> And if the whistles of the tugboats should vibrate, we would crawl towards her thick legs, more robust than her erudite waist,

> and we would strike her statue so it would vibrate too and the echo would return to us her ineffable voice on the Vitaphone of an unprecedented twilight, under whose awning we might slice off our calluses. (67)

This bizarre passage combines the grotesquely banal and the operatically auratic, the last in a series of oscillations—between the voice's ephemerality and the monumental quality of the star, its neumatic qualities and the brute reality of the film canister, the speaking English voice and the Hispanophone listener, between the noise of machines and the heat of the star's sexuality, between her masculine and feminine drives. Olivari provides us with a different understanding of authorship as listening, one that does not depend on an assertion of its specificity but precisely on its ability to tune in to the contradictions between Garbo's new voice and her now-classic body and face.

MISSED ENCOUNTERS OF THE POPULIST VOICE

While "The Voice of Greta Garbo" situates the author as the receptor of a jagged global English, many late modernist writers sought to reinscribe an unmediated national-popular voice: unmediated that is, except by their own pens or typewriters. As their response to the arrival of synchronized sound reveals, and as Mário's "Radiophonic Language" also suggested, they were especially concerned with registering voices—including dialect, regionalisms, and the working-class speech of the emergent proletarian novel—even as these seemed to come under the purview of mass media. In an aural equivalent to the visual montage that structures her novel, the narrator in Patrícia Galvão's *Industrial Park* juxtaposes the proletarian voice, depicted as an ephemeral monumentality, with technologically mediated voices. In one scene, for example, a radio "vomits foxtrots from the wall" (70). "Foxtrot," a synonym for U.S. popular jazz, appears in the novel in explicit contrast to the live voice of the Brazilian worker. Unlike Mário in "Radiophonic Language," Galvão posits the unmediated voice—unmediated, again, only if we disavow her own writing—as a naturalized force that interpellates working-class listeners to produce collective identities. This voice is first offered up as an antidote to the manipulative monochords of U.S. capitalism.

From its very first words, *Industrial Park* positions itself as registering the conflicting voices that encounter one another forcefully and violently in 1930s São Paulo. Its epigraph greets the reader with statistics of human suffering, whose language, we are told, is "spoken by this book." The proletarian novel here becomes a heightened recording device of marginalized speech; the turn of phrase recalls Dos Passos when he refers to his *U.S.A.* trilogy capturing the chords of humanity (1937); or the "attempt to catch the rhythm of our common city speech, its brassy sound, its trick of repetition, etc.," that Sophie Treadwell instructs in her stage directions for *Maquinal* (1928).[50] Like Dos Passos, Galvão's is a labor on the colloquial, an "attempt to invent a modern vernacular" for a large, heterogeneous space (here a major city riven by global capital). But if Dos Passos showcases in his 1930s trilogy the labor of "word-workers"—those who mediate the language of the people through jingles, slogans, or songs or by selling books, writing speeches, and so forth[51]—Galvão's is a more explicitly proletarian polyphony, and her prose is even more slangy and jagged, quite raw, even scandalous. It constitutes a deeper immersion into these working-class worlds than the newsreels and snippets of speech that characterize either her North American counterpart or Oswald's *Seraphim Grosse Point*. Her novel wears its populism—a direct challenge to its modernist predecessors—on its sleeve. It longs for immediacy with the laboring body.

The first chapter of *Industrial Park* fulfills the epigraph's promise by featuring slices of conversation with no bodies attached to them, as though recording the city's working-class tones in pure sonority. Yet the novel is not content to allow these voices to circulate on their own. It will later struggle to attach them, in an attempt to transform their ephemerality into monumentality. In this late modernist iteration of the lengthy Western tradition of privileging presence, the unmediated voice is positioned over and against the archiving and transmitting functions of technological media. In *Industrial Park*, certain "live" proletarian voices are speech acts, for they inaugurate a collective subject. When they issue forth from an identifiable proletarian body, the crowd of listeners becomes "galvanized" (87), conscious of itself.

This process occurs by attaching the voice to two metonymical bodies: Rosinha, the immigrant activist modeled after Rosa Luxemburg, with her diminutive revolutionary cry; and Alexandre, the Afro-Brazilian worker who promises to anchor the voice's ephemerality in a legacy of struggle that extends from chattel slavery to wage slavery: "The mighty voice dominates, spreads, registers an act of social revolution. . . . Alexandre doesn't know how to read or write. But social reality, coming from his mouth, excites the crowd: 'It's the words of one worker to other workers!'" (93). In the novel's climax, Alexandre's martyrdom makes possible the transmutation from vocal ephemerality to monumentality as he pronounces his last words: "His immense voice breaks in: 'They kill the workers, but the proletariat doesn't die!'" (96). While initially crafting itself as a giant ear tuned in to the city's multiple voices, the novel ultimately cannot but suture these voices back onto representative bodies.

While Galvão was drafting both *Industrial Park* and her journal *The Man of the People*, the Vargas regime was equally concerned with suturing speech to its own representative bodies—in this case, Vargas's own, as "The Father of the Poor." This consolidation will be central to the nascent practice of populism, most notably in the Argentine case, by Juan and Evita Perón—originally a radio actress, whose voice became a powerful medium.[52] While not an especially charismatic speaker, Vargas would be the first Latin American leader to begin to employ the mass media as an increasingly powerful means to speak *for* the people, as Perón and Evita would with more success in the subsequent decade; he would also adopt the radio to create the effect of an unmediated speaking *to* them. Vargas's declaration after the military coup of 1930 defined the new Brazil as one in which the difficulties of class, ethnic, and racial difference, including labor strife, would be subsumed under his unifying speech. In this heightened context, Galvão offers up the proletarian voice as an antidote not only to the "vomiting foxtrots" of U.S. mass culture but also, implicitly, to the populist construction of politics as mass spectacle. Her novel asks us to consider who speaks for the masses but also who listens to them.

As in *Industrial Park*, acousmatic fictions of the populist voice appeared with greater urgency during the 1930s and 1940s. Throughout the period, the voice would be increasingly employed by a variety of regimes as a means to domesticate class struggle and racial and gender inequality by positing a uniform national culture. Yet if Galvão's novel focused on creating a polyglot chorus of the masses through representative proletarian bodies, others honed in on the dystopic dimensions of the populist leader and his voice. Borges's "Hakim, the Masked Dyer of Merv," one of the citational tales of *A Universal History of Infamy* (Chapter 1), explores the power of the *acousmêtre* in the twinned realms of politics and religion. "Hakim" tells the story of a veiled prophet whose power derives from the fact that his followers can hear his voice but not see his face. Like many of the tricksters in *A Universal History of Infamy*, he leaves his homeland and makes himself anew. In his first public appearance, he emerges shrouded in a giant bull's mask, accompanied by two servants who have been blinded after looking upon his face.

Hakim's first iteration of a masked identity occurs with his birth into a family of dyers, whose trade entailed altering the original appearance of objects. These veiled origins are incorporated into his awe-inspiring speech once he begins to amass power.[53] It is notable that Borges cites (with his own customary variations) at length from this speech, in one of the *Universal History of Infamy*'s longest citations of spoken language. Hakim possesses a "singularly sweet voice, or at least it appeared that way in contrast to the brutality of his mask."[54] With it, he constructs a narrative in which his head was severed by an angel; after ascending to heaven, he was granted by the Lord "words so ancient that their repetition burnt the mouth and endowed a glorious illumination that mortal eyes could not bear" (87). His face will only be revealed when all are converted to the true faith. At the center of his cosmogony lies a similarly veiled figure: a "spectral God," who lacks origin, name, and face (90). The blankness of his physiognomy resonates with the talking dolls of early sound film, in as much as it operates on a disjuncture between physiognomy and voice. However, in contrast to those authorial attempts to domesticate sound film by linking it to the infantile, Borges suggests here that this same disjuncture consolidates Hakim's political power.

Hakim's downfall occurs when his true face is revealed, destroyed by "the peculiar whiteness of leprosy." The narrator lingers on this de-acousmatization: "It had no eyebrows; the lower lid of the right eye hung on the senile cheek; a heavy cluster of protuberances ate away at the lips; the flattened and inhuman nose was like a lion's" (92). This particularly grotesque revelation renders the powerful voice impotent. The voice itself has not changed; it is the mouth and face attached to it that alter its capabilities. Now able to return his gaze, his followers strip him of his power, consigning the all-powerful voice to babble. As he tries to intone his narrative, he is shot through with arrows.

Lest we think this is simply an example of Orientalist curios, recall that during the years of the story's execution, Borges had witnessed in Argentina, much to his dismay, a military coup replace a democratically elected president and inaugurate a right-wing regime that abounded in censorship and mass rituals under the name of a nationalistic Catholicism. Like the U.S. stories in the same collection, Borges "dyes" Hakim's life in a Creole bath through terms like *caudillo* (a provincial strongman, an echo of the military generals who ruled Argentina during this moment); he makes their very exoticism resonate with contemporary Argentine life. "Hakim, the Masked Dyer" depicts the voice as a mystifying, stupefying force that emanates from a power contaminated at the very site of its manifestation. Invoking a time and space so far from interwar Argentina that it employs a different calendar, Borges nevertheless draws the foreign epoch into his own. The *acousmêtre* makes possible a charismatic, obfuscating power, one that would be increasingly present in 1930s–1940s Argentina.[55] The narrator listens to Hakim's words and lingers on the moment of deacousmatization to locate political power's mystifying source, a mouth corroded by sickness.

Written in Borges's native Argentina the following decade, and likely inspired by Perón, the Cuban writer Virgilio Piñera's short story "The Dummy" (El muñeco) also posits an intrinsic emptiness at the heart of attempts to speak monolithically for the people. Written in 1946 during Piñera's lengthy stay in Buenos Aires—where he met many major Argentine modernist figures, including Borges, Bioy Casares, Silvina and Victoria Ocampo, Macedonio Fernández, and Oliverio Girondo—"The Dummy" traverses Argentine and Cuban literary histories of the late modernist period, having been published more or less simultaneously in both Havana and Buenos Aires.[56] Piñera's story draws together and trumps the different approaches to the voice I have explored thus far, culminating in this chapter's most sustained approach to vocal and auditory politics in late modernism: it incorporates the problems of the national masses, populist leader, and broadcast media under the sign of a talking doll, at once monstrous and absurd, threatening and ridiculous.

Told through the perspective of a listener-turned-bricoleur, the story posits an unnamed country where a populist leader (known as the President) asserts his presence through a variety of media, from handbills to newsreels to public broadcasting to street posters depicting him as "the first worker of the nation."[57] The story shuttles among absurdist episodes to describe the quest of the first-person narrator, one Jonatán Fernández, to save the President from being transformed into a dummy through the continual transmission of clichéd words and gestures.

The title figure is a jerrybuilt invention, a rubber doll that will replace the President in public and recorded events. It draws from acousmatic technologies, above all the phonograph, to stitch together a voice and a face that will construct a populist spectacle. Built from a mold of the leader's naked body, it features an opening for air to enter and exit, and "a record player at mouth-level where the appropriate record will be inserted and operated by remote control." To achieve the desired effect, "the mouth—perfectly synchronized to the speech the record player is delivering—will move its lips accordingly" (104). This aural technology also includes pauses for the obligatory applause of the masses in the populist pact of recognition.

In constructing the dummy, Jonatán inadvertently performs his own de-acousmatization, revealing the bizarre and far-from-charismatic assemblage of voice and body that undergirds the populist performance. Piñera, like Chaplin in *The Great Dictator* (1940), suggests the etymology of dictator as "one who dictates," the voice of absolute authority that will, in a later moment, be recorded by technologies like writing or the radio. There is something sinister but also absurd about Jonatán's contraption, designed to save the President from the expenditure of his voice's aura through mechanical reproduction. Where the national-popular voice appears in the story, it brims over with pompous foreign words and phrases (French, English, Latin). It features periodic eruptions of nonsense words ("plats, snnubg, mjuyye, lkashddd") and onomatopoeia ("miau miau" or "meow meow"). These two opposing tendencies—the power of the leader's voice and his vocal absurdity—are mirrored in Jonatán's reactions. In a textbook example of disavowal, he both creates the awkward contraption and simultaneously desires its seamless functioning, to forget how it operates. Jonatán is a listener who exposes the very gap he seeks to suture over in the name of a patchy, incomplete entity known as the national voice.

From the story's opening sequence, Jonatán is attentive to the minutiae of sounds, from the screams of crowds to whispers in the presidential palace, from audible language to the uncanny sound of heels clacking against marble floors. As in Hernández's "Lovebird Furniture," the sense of a constant alteration of sounds positions the narrator as an antenna of sorts. However, this time it is not capitalism's insidious encroachment onto the interior but populism's use of communication technologies that defines the frequencies. The story opens in a cinema where Jonatán and his fellow spectators watch national newsreel footage. The voice-over "was speaking about the fatherland"; this voice is almost immediately "covered up by background music."[58] The President's voice then alternates with this music and repetitive, serialized images. In these rapid alterations of sound and image, we experience Jonatán's disjointed reception, his sense that things are already coming apart at the seams that stitch the voice of the populist leader to a body that will subsequently speak for the people.

An episode leading up to his first encounter with power is structured around a rift between sound's intent and its effect. Jonatán encounters various obstacles as he waits patiently for the President to receive him. The scene provides us with the story's most intense eruption of absurdist language. A single word—"whisper" (*cuchichear*)—is repeated so that its meaning is evacuated, leaving only its scratchy texture:

> Convinced all is in order, [the President's aide] leaves the pink waiting room; we hear him whispering in the corridor, we sense that others are whispering to him, a little further down other whispers can be perceived, we end up whispering. He enters, not speaking, he whispers to us, we leave whispering, we cross the corridors amid whispers. I count fifty steps, we turn to the right, we emerge in a different corridor of whisperers, I count thirty steps now, a door appears. The official whispers for the last time, pushes the door sweetly, sticks his head in, pulls it out and, without whispering at all, introduces us to the presence of the President.[59]

As in the passage from Felisberto Hernández that opened this chapter, there is a disconnect between the whispers and their addressee. Piñera's irony evacuates the whisper of its supposed intimacy and locates it in the realm of audio stereotype, cliché, and tic. At the same time, the actual words pronounced on this endless variation of the root "to whisper" are never rendered audible. The effect produced is one of auditory texture: the very act of whispering, rather than any message transmitted; power's indecipherable secrecy, rather than its precise content. The threshold is this barely legible speech, as though access to power required a verbal incantation in which the voice's materiality becomes ritual, rather than signification. *Cuchichear* (whispering) is also an onomatopocia—the "ch," like the "s" sound in "whisper" suggesting the hiss that speaks volumes without saying anything, collapsing the distinction between noise and sense. For Piñera, "the law makes funny noises . . . the validity of the law can be pinned down to a senseless voice."[60] If for Olivari onomatopoeia provided an opportunity for a fine-grained form of listening, the emphasis here is on identifying the nonsense that subtends the incommensurable populist voice.

"The Dummy" is populated with other means of throwing and projecting voices. Along with the title figure, the radio, cinema newsreels, and loudspeakers together produce a satire of the short circuits of populism, a discourse that raises its leaders to auratic heights at the very moment that these pronounce their close proximity to the slippery category of the masses. Cinema spectators, for example, watch newsreel footage of the President donating blood: a public display of his inner life (80). Jonatán longs to call the President by his first name (81), to speak with him face-to-face, "in the most absolute intimacy" (88), despite—or perhaps because of—the technologies that surround and frame him. Indeed, at the very moment in which the voice was naturalized through populism, it was simultaneously separated from the body through radio and early synchronized film. If the fabricated smile represents the commodification of interiority, here as well as in other late modernist dystopias, the voice represents the truncated transmission between the masses and a populist regime that paradoxically speaks at once to, for, and of them.

Suturing the populist voice to its representative body requires another actor: the masses themselves. In the climax of "The Dummy," the invention is unveiled to them, the ultimate addressee of the populist voice. After staring at it mutely,

> Suddenly, those thousands of eyes broke free and the throats of the populace opened like chasms [*abismos*]. A deafening outcry followed that deathly silence . . . the shouts were increasing in strength, and the only thing that could be clearly distinguished was the word "dummy" issuing again and again from thousands of breasts. (110)

Like the whispering on the threshold of power, the unintelligible repetition of all but the word "dummy" circumscribes the voice, and the political pact it enacts, as one grounded in the sensory, rather than signifying, dimensions. Recall that for Romero, writing in the context of Peronism's complexity, the masses of the early to mid-twentieth century exceed a schema or classification: "a new force growing like a torrent and whose voices resounded like a clamor," a description that reverberates with the language of "The Dummy," with its mass throat opening up like an abyss. The mass body produces a noise without a signal; it demands, in turn, a nonhermeneutical approach to grapple with it. As with Hardt and Negri's more romanticized multitude, the mass, unlike the People, cannot be subsumed into traditional state or party-based politics. (Indeed, the very definition of the mass is that which cannot be subsumed.)[61] In "The Dummy," the masses are "the hot and pulsating substance of nations" (120)—an image, like the abyss-like throats, that suggests the primordial *informe.*

The unconstrained force of the masses must subsequently be brought back under control. In *Industrial Park*, as we have seen, this process required suturing the mass voice back into representative proletarian bodies, but Piñera's "cold" tale has a much less optimistic ending and one that registers, in a way that more closely resembles Borges's "Hakim," a burgeoning fear of populist politics on the part of artists and intellectuals. At the end of the story, "A very old record of the President repeating 'law and order' at least twenty times was inserted [into the dummy] and the difficulty was overcome" (111). The populist voice at once seeks authority over the masses and functions as an appeal/plea to that same figure; it is a surplus of both authority and exposure.[62] "The Dummy" thus depicts a strange symmetry that exists between the voices of the leader and the masses: both depend upon powerful, non-representational materialities. The mass voice and the populist voice mirror each other in their non-signifying power. The repetitive tautology (the whispers, the word "dummy") foregrounds the materialities of sound over signification. For if the repeated phrase "law and order" seems meaningful, Piñera has already suggested that just about any word would do. All that is required is a body to be attached to the voice.

And a writer-listener to point out the suture. "The Dummy" opens with a caveat from Jonatán:

> I am nothing more than an inventor of mechanical devices [*artefactos*]. If I consent now to write, it is precisely because I have been unable to design the device that might express the horrible events I am about to recount. If literature succeeds in communicating them, I will see it as yet another device. (79)

This declaration both invokes and challenges the primacy of literature. The word *artefacto* is more polysemic than the English translation "devices," which does not contain the original's layers of art and distortion. *Artefacto* draws attention to writing itself as a machine or device for falsifying reproductions.[63] For Jonatán, writing is a secondary, almost humiliating medium: neither his first choice nor the most efficient means of capturing, in contrast to certain fantasies of communication technologies, the immediacy of the grotesque story that will unfold. Yet if authorship's privileged relationship to the voice is eroded through the modern media with their paradoxically visceral immediacy, it fashions for itself a different function: that of tuning in to competing voices and all of their static. In this way, while it may make voices audible, it does so only insomuch as it calls attention to rifts in the voice-body weld. In late modernist fictions of the voice, authors and their protagonists pointedly and at times painfully traverse the gaps opened up in voices and bodies, approaching them as narrow openings within a broader disenchantment with the politics of dominant media. The next chapter moves from the author-listener to the author-user, from the authorial ear to the hand and body of late modernist authorship.

CHAPTER 3

Pounding Away at the Typewriter

Authorship and Proprioception

Since 1880, literature no longer has been able to write for girls, simply because girls themselves write. They are no longer taken by imagining sights and sounds between poetic lines, for at night they are at the movies and during the day they sit at their typewriters.

—KITTLER, *Gramophone, Film, Typewriter*

Rocking with the monotone tip, tip, tipirip tip tip of their machines . . .

—ALFONSINA STORNI, "La perfecta dactilógrafa"

In 1920, author and feminist Alfonsina Storni published a journalistic sketch titled "The Perfect Typist" in Argentina's most prominent newspaper, *La Nación*, under the pseudonym Tao Lao. Storni begins by describing a typical scene encountered when boarding the streetcar between seven and eight in the morning in the city of Buenos Aires: a sea of working-class women on their way to work, reading. The columnist then proceeds with a taxonomy of these women vis-à-vis their reading material: "If she carries a crime rag, she is a factory worker or seamstress; if she clutches to her chest an illustrated magazine of a clearly popular nature, she is a typist or employee of a store" (908). "The Perfect Typist" plays on different definitions of the word "type"—the term refers simultaneously to a system of classification (a mediation between the general and the particular) and to modes of mechanical reproduction (the "stereotype" and "cliché"). The working women who interest Storni seem to spring up in tandem with the typewriter, fascinating in their utter typicality.

The typist and typewriter make their first appearance in Latin American literature and cinema during the 1910s and 1920s. Advertisements for the technology began to appear in periodicals; shortly thereafter, writers staged their first experiments with typography. The typist was a handmaiden; the typewriter, a metonymy of technological modernity. For the avant-gardes, the typist represented not the fear of a "feminized" mass culture often associated with canonical Anglo-American modernism but a *melindrosa*, Brazil's version of the modern woman.[1] She was enshrined during the Modern Art Week of São Paulo (1922) when, in his speech introducing the public to "Modern Art," Menotti del Picchia euphorically drew the battle lines: the new modernists place their wager not on "the princesses of ballads in stony castles" but "the type-writer girl," "dancing the tango and typing up a ledger book."[2] In 1925, a writer in the modernist little magazine *Estética* similarly proclaimed the typist the most interesting material for the contemporary novelist.[3] In Humberto Mauro's late silent film *Lábios sem beijos* (Lips without Kisses, 1930), typing is sutured to the modern woman through a shot-counter-shot sequence that links her stockinged legs to the continuous clacking of the keys. As in Storni's "The Perfect Typist," the movements of her body and labor beat out the rhythm of the modern city like a metronome: the swinging of her legs, or the sound of her heels on the city streets mimetizes the machine's *click-click-click*, or *tip-tip-tip* (910). During this same period, Mário de Andrade was to write his famous "Typewriter" poem, dedicated to Manuela, the woman's name he bestowed upon his beloved machine—giving Brazilian modernism its most audacious experiment with typewriter literature.

Several accounts of modernist media locate the typewriter at the beginning of a posthumanist moment that whittles away at the authority of the author and his or her handwritten signature. For Kittler, the arrival of the typewriter had the salutatory effect of demoting writing's privileged position as the principal medium of expression. The typewriter's clacking keys sounded a death knoll: the death of writerly subjectivity and all its Romantic baggage. It reduced writing to discrete signs, rather than bundles of meaning; it trafficked in permutations and combinations. The natural "flow" from human hand to human ideas became a finite notation of signs.[4] Rubén Gallo extends this argument in his study of Mexican modernism (a chapter that is anchored by a detailed reading of Mário's "Typewriter" poem).[5] Earlier, Flora Süssekind argued that the undertheorized period 1890–1920 in Brazil witnesses writers' first rapprochement with new technologies, including the typewriter: while initially feared by the modernists' predecessors, by the mid-1920s, the medium "seemed to act as a de facto interlocutor in the process of literary creation" in the early modernist experimental writing that closes her study.[6]

While these emphases on the typewriter as rupture are valuable, my interest in this chapter lies elsewhere, for the relationship between literary production and the typewriter requires a different approach in the late modernist moment. The late modernist typist is neither Kittler's technophilic posthumanist Nietzsche nor his technophobic Heidegger. These poles of attraction/repulsion, themselves typical responses to emergent technologies, give way to a different relationship. With its extended use and portability, the typewriter begins to appear beyond the big city, indexing the ways in which modern technologies nestle into the most ostensibly backward parts of the region, such as the Brazilian northeast. It does so not as a rupture but precisely as an index of modernity's structural repetition, the new as a continual production of the same. In this sense, the typewriter parallels the domestication of the radio and the cinema, media that also spoke to anxieties over standardization and the shifting, increasingly decentered role of the writer.

With the figure of the typewriter and the typist, this study moves from the author-spectator to the author-user. From the very beginning, the typewriter existed as a much more privatized technology than either cinema or the radio, and one much more intimately connected to writing itself. Through this intimacy, authorship confronts a body that interacts in a more "hands-on" fashion than the cinema spectator or radio listener of the previous two chapters. On a scale of agency, the user is more active than the spectator; however, he or she is also more impacted and vulnerable. The spectator watches, the user intervenes; as a result he or she is "intervened" in turn. In this chapter, I trace the late modernist typist and her iteration of the author-user in two works, the Brazilian novelist Graciliano Ramos's *Anguish* (1936) and its mutation in Clarice Lispector's late novella, *The Hour of the Star* (1977). Strikingly different in many respects, they exhibit intriguing parallels in their invention of a typist who provokes their protagonists, both of whom are writers. The typist indexes not only the bureaucratized relationship to formerly new media that I am tracing throughout this book but also the proletarianized and serialized dimensions of authorship under late modernism.

The typist, I argue, provides a body for late modernist authorship to refashion itself as a kind of usership. She allows authors to recast earlier modernist experimentation through an emphasis on labor, in particular its bodily effects and sensations. This emphasis is at times erased in studies of the modernist typewriter, in which the focus on the medium's materiality is often accompanied by the explicit erasure of the body that operates it. In contrast, for Graciliano and Lispector, the typist is depicted above all through a heightened exploration of proprioception, "the cumulative memory of skill, habit, posture" that locates our bodies in space through our muscles and joints.[7] If, during the first iteration of Brazilian modernism, both the typist and her machine index an impassioned relationship to modernity—albeit one that already hinted at its habituation—here she indexes the proletarian contemporary, the automatized present tense that takes place through the body's repeated interface with a domesticated machine.

ANGUISH (1936): GRACILIANO RAMOS'S PROLETARIAN MODERNISM

A lower-middle-class functionary named Luís da Silva travels on a streetcar in the Brazilian northeast. His romantic and economic life in tatters, he is gripped in an existential crisis that spans from his familial past to his present alienation. In this context, a woman appears periodically in the crowd. She represents the only possibility for interrupting his chronic malaise:

> A typist appeared to me everywhere, a quite pleasing one. Pretty, with green eyes and a face like a saint. I would be turning a corner and I would bump into her; I would be on the trolley and she would be my fellow traveler. After so many random coincidences, we began to greet one another, even though neither of us knew the path the other would take. Sometimes I was distracted, my mind wandering over random things. When I least expected it, the typist's cat eyes would emerge. Other times the feeling I was going to meet her came to me all of a sudden. And then it would happen.[8]

For Luís da Silva, the anonymous typist offers the potential for a shared experience of writing as bureaucratized labor. Although he never speaks to her, she offers a counterintuitive alternative to his administered provincial life. While both labor in confined spaces, they also circulate in the city and this circulation facilitates their chance encounter. The grammar of the possible appears almost exclusively in relation to her—the conditional tense appears whenever she glimmers in his peripheral vision, as he makes his way through the city.[9] Only she is capable of punctuating the daily grind of this listless flâneur, emerging both literally in his field of vision and in his mind's eye, often when he least expects it. As the novel progresses, she takes on different roles in his fantasies: lover, writing collaborator, comrade ("hidden away in a dark room, the cat-eyed typist typed out a subversive pamphlet on the typewriter" [173]).

Why the typist? She is no radical other, promising unadulterated escape from the alienation of labor or a bucolic life divorced from the city. As he imagines her in different guises, she, like him, is bruised and damaged from the repetitive movements of her labor. Thus, while she embodies a flight line, the typist also represents the inverse: Luís's own subaltern status as a writer and copy editor. She is a proletarian who remains serialized, and who resists the linking together of the group.[10] (The typing pool, in this sense, is not the assembly line.) It is precisely her solitude, however, that spawns Luís's fantasies of solidarity.

Graciliano is among the most canonical Brazilian writers of the twentieth century, and certainly the most lauded of the so-called regionalist writers of the 1930s. In this context, *Anguish* stands out as his most experimental and least accessible work, a novel that traffics in the perverse and abject and, through its gnarled structure, defies the reader to take pleasure in the unfolding of plot or character development. While initially published to critical acclaim, its stock plummeted thereafter, as the two novels that sandwich its publication—*São Bernardo* (1934), the taut realist narrative of a violent parvenu, and *Barren Lives* (*Vidas Secas*, 1938), the minimalist story-cycle of itinerant farm laborers—became his most well-known texts, central to both the Brazilian and larger Latin American canon.[11] Yet *Anguish* shares important features with Graciliano's corpus, including his novels, *crônicas*, and the posthumous two-volume account of the year he was jailed by the Vargas regime in 1936, *Prison Memoirs* (*Memórias do Cárcere*). Throughout these varied works, with their motley casts of frustrated writers and ruthless strongmen, impoverished cowhands and subaltern copy editors, the reader's attention is constantly drawn to the material dimensions of writing: inscription surfaces, bodies in pain as they write, and the economic and political forces that simultaneously constrain and produce literature. His oeuvre exemplifies the mutually constitutive identities of labor and literary practice (of literature as labor and of labor as a source of literature) of the 1930s.

As its title signals, *Anguish* also shares with many other late modernist texts a focus on forms of malaise or unease, on chronic frustration that thwarts narrative development.[12] The novel is structured around images and sensations of clotting and repetition: fog, viscous shadows, a gelatinous consistency to the air; the reader is plunged into a sea of associative images that disappear and resurface with repetitive insistence. In this dense mesh, something resembling a story can be discerned. Luís, a lower-middle-class typesetter/functionary, becomes infatuated with his next-door neighbor, Marina. The two become engaged. Luís almost immediately witnesses Marina's seduction and corruption by the wealthy Julião Tavares, who deflowers, impregnates, and then abandons her. After stalking Marina when she travels to an illegal abortion clinic, Luís proceeds to pursue and kill his rival. In circular fashion, the novel begins and ends with a delirium and convalescence that follow this murder. The reader gradually realizes that past and present and even future are inseparable because of Luís's subsequent nervous breakdown. Ultimately, the book we hold in our hands is revealed to be a product of the protagonist's delirium, one that produces a state of constant eruptions and knotted superimpositions of historical and temporal regimes. In an eruption of automatic writing, a single nine-page paragraph closes the book.

Throughout, *Anguish* registers a very pessimistic portrait of the author. Luís returns obsessively to the same gestures with his habituated, proprioceptive body. This body writes not to produce new meaning but, tautologically, to write: to show one is writing, to make scratches on papers, a clacking noise with the keyboard. The multiple verbs Luís employs to describe his relation to words are pointedly distanced from creation and originality: *arrumar*, *arranjar* (arranging, ordering), *alinhar* (lining/aligning), *corregir*, *modificar* (correcting, altering), *redigir* (redacting), *sapecar* (throwing something together in a hurry), *bater* (pounding, to refer to typing). Variations are pointless: "I would write one more column which I'd written hundreds of times and which I always reproduce, substituting one word for another" (122). As a ghostwriter, his job is to reproduce opinions that he does not share, penning diatribes against local regional bosses. To make a living, he also reviews kitschy, poorly translated novels and offers haphazard consultation on literary works to young men who consider him a specialist. This alienation from writing had already begun early in life, when he began to sign over poems he had written to others for a small profit. He describes ripping the pages out of his notebook, sonnet by sonnet—"it wasn't even necessary to recopy them"—until he is left with a few yellowing pages, later gnawed at by the rats that occupy his apartment. These early attempts at romantic expression were published in marginal journals and can still be found in "backwoods weeklies," under different names.

The denigration of writing from production to reproduction, from the authorial signature to the effacement of his own labor, spawns compensatory fantasies. An incomplete novel—it will be extraordinary, translated into many languages—pursues him and erupts suddenly into his consciousness only to disappear once again into the thick fog of malaise. What dominates is a form of writing devoid of content, an automatism where language itself becomes neutral in its signifiers and requires only the reproduction of the voices, thoughts, and words of others. This dull time of repetition and fidgeting with texts and hand-operated machines is something of a topos of late modernist fiction and cinema,[13] as in this description of Luís melancholically rearranging the letters of advertisements:

> We move like pieces in an exhausted clock. Our old gears, their pieces worn down, interact awkwardly with the parts of other gears. The only things of value to us here inside are sluggish, drowsy. If the machine were to halt, we would not be affected: we would continue with our pen over the bruised and broken sheet, an extinguished cigarette between our yellowing fingers. We would stop blinking, but we would be unaware of the ceasing of even these slight movements. . . . The clack-clack of the typewriters takes me far away from the earth. That which outside is good, useful, true, or beautiful has no significance in here. We breathe in air swilling with particles of ink and paper, and we work in semi-darkness. (165)

The description defines authorship as melancholic usership. In the space of the office, withdrawn from the outside world ("far away from the earth," "semi-darkness"), Luís's bureaucratic labor allegorizes writing as the production of a habituated body that makes use of materials without recourse to technique. These habits shape and produce the writerly body: "Habits are socially or culturally contracted. But they reside in the matter of the body, in the muscles, nerves, and skin, where they operate autonomously."[14]

The use of the first-person plural, moreover, is striking in this passage, for so much of the novel takes place through the misanthropic singular. A series of laborers enact their own minute gestures, the senseless repetition of all the Luís da Silvas who do not recognize their shared experience of labor. This first-person plural also hints at a potential solidarity, one that shapes his fantasies of the nameless typist. She shares this experience of the administered labor of words, and perhaps is implicitly part of the "we" of this passage. She provides a figure for an authorship that no longer sees itself as creating but rather working on the almost invisible variations that stem from reproducing the language of others, when the value of authorial originality, like that of the typewriter itself, had lost its earlier purchase:

> Where might the typist be? . . . Poor little thing. Typing at the keyboard with her numbed fingers all day long, and for a salary next to nothing. Maybe she had younger siblings. A tenderness crept over me; I wanted to join my life with the plainly dressed girl, always in a hurry, her briefcase under her arm. We would be happy together. She would work less. On arriving home tired, she would amuse herself exchanging words with the parrot; she would run her aching hands through the cat's fur. I would write a book of short stories, which she would type in her spare time. (101)

While the typist represents an alternative to this automatized life, she also mirrors his own alienated labor. For Luís, she is simultaneously flight line and alter ego, a proletarian of letters and the very possibility of fictional creation. For not only will she help him give birth to a successful book, but her ephemeral presence, the curiosity she inspires, points to the desire and empathy required to begin to imagine another life ("Maybe she had younger siblings").

As these passages suggest, the typist provides late modernist authors with an extension of their own laboring body, one that senses itself as it works. Thus, while Kittler argues that the feminized typist is not a proletarian, it is more accurate to say that the typist became a proletarian to the extent to which she was feminized; what invisibilizes this proletarianization is precisely her gendered body.[15] The word for typing in Portuguese is *datilografia*: writing with the finger or the digits. For Heidegger, typewriting represented an artificial separation between the author and his production. The hand is separated from the body and rerouted through a machine, as the eye with the camera. But unlike the camera, here the ostensibly direct and organic link to writing itself is severed. The "flow" from human hand to human ideas morphs into a notion of discrete signs.[16] Yet in *Anguish*, the typist-author pairing is nothing if not embodied. She is characterized by the repetitive movements of her hands on the keyboard and by the position of her body as she writes. While tactility, the subject of the following chapter, refers to an encounter between self and object, produced on the surface of the skin, proprioception implies the body sensing itself, within itself, through the muscles: "the synthesizing viscera that produce orientation, balance, sensory location in space and time."[17] Massumi notes that proprioception draws the subject-object distinction into the body, in effect eradicating it, whereas tactility is a self-other encounter. In the passage above from *Anguish*, for example, "typing at the keyboard with numbed fingers, all day long" indexes proprioception, while Luís imagining the typist running her hand along the cat's fur corresponds to the tactile.

In describing the proprioceptive movements of the typist, Graciliano subsumes the self-other relationship between intellectual and manual labor into one another. The typist extends the author's body, rather than merely encountering or mirroring it. She embodies the writer's "cumulative memory of skill, habit, posture." Habit, which is forged through repetition, is "an acquired automatic self-regulation. It resides in the flesh."[18] Graciliano's interest in proprioception to depict Luís and "his" typist is his contribution to an analogy prominent in 1930s discourse, particularly on the left, that between intellectual and manual labor. In essence, the former often sought its own legitimation in its potential affinities with the latter. Journalists, for example, became "proletarians of the pen," in the words of a columnist in the Brazilian periodical *The Man of the People* (Chapter 1).[19] An Argentine contemporary epitomizes this analogical mode in an article in the post-avant-garde journal *Contra*: "Writing for me is manual labor. If what I write can't be projected into the lives of other men, as in the work of the bricklayer or carpenter, I wouldn't write. Some who write fashion jewels or make alcohol. I aspire to make bread from ink and pen."[20] Like his peers, Graciliano was fond of these kinds of analogies, although he exhibits a self-reflexivity about the limitations of the manual/intellectual labor analogy—a self-reflexivity that will reach its apex, in the second part of this chapter, in the work of Clarice Lispector.

Yet the relationship between writer and proletarian is not merely legitimating; it is inscribed in the experiences of many writers of the 1930s. Graciliano is a prime example. While he would eventually become one of Brazil's most lauded writers, he came to national literary attention not through his innovative fiction but through his *relatórios*, official reports from his position as the mayor of a small northeastern town. (In this sense, we find a parallel between his labor with words and that of Kafka's work in insurance claims; unlike well-known *cronistas* like Lispector or Roberto Arlt, these occupations demand invisibilized work.)[21] As the story goes, his dry, telegraphic style had repercussions in the then-cultural and political capital of Rio de Janeiro, and he was solicited by the era's most important publishing house, José Olympio, to write a book. Relatively elderly for one beginning his writing career, Graciliano never forgot the traffic between economic survival and language; in fact, far from diminishing, it was exacerbated during the economic crises of the 1930s and in the increasing politicization of the Brazilian aesthetic sphere. Throughout his adult life, he worked in local governmental agencies and performed various duties as a functionary, including fulfilling responsibilities that he found political and ethically repugnant. Yet the literary market was hardly more inviting. In his correspondence with his Argentine translator, Benjamin de Garay, his economic desperation and his simultaneous frustration with the changes required to make his stories more consumable are palpable; he painfully portions his novels out in pieces, like someone selling off parts of his home or his own body.[22]

Like his creator and many artists and intellectuals during the 1930s and 1940s, Graciliano's protagonist in *Anguish* works for a "government paper" and as such is responsible for quite literally reproducing official discourse, as a mouthpiece for the regime's local manifestations. In addition, the context of *Anguish* has the dubious distinction of being explicitly linked to the Vargas regime, for immediately after Graciliano handed in the manuscript to the typesetter, he was arrested and imprisoned without trial in the federal penitentiary of Ilha Grande.[23] (Ironically, his year in prison would be the only time he could devote himself fully to his own work.) In a prescient musing, Luís imagines himself writing a great work while in prison, "translated and read in many countries. I would write it in pencil, with butcher paper, in the margins of old newspapers" (219). Here, the prestige of international acclaim is almost immediately qualified by the roughness of the paper that serves as fiction's material base. While we could read this as a romantic depiction of the suffering artist—or a fetishistic one of the "concrete" labor of the working classes—it is important to underscore these kinds of descriptions as circumscribing the limits of the fantasy of writing as compensation. Dreams are always cut down to size by the bare materiality of writing's tools and the laboring body.

In this sense, Graciliano epitomizes the scrappy, semiprofessional writers from the peripheral northeast who came to the fore in the

Brazilian literary sphere of the 1930s. Per Sérgio Miceli, recent developments such as the acquisition of rotary presses, the professionalization and verticalization of the editorial market, new marketing strategies, and the founding of a number of influential presses occurred in tandem with the temporary decline of the southern elites whose sons and daughters had been the protagonists of the earlier *modernista* movement. Together, these changes marked a shift in symbolic capital toward the social regional novel and proletarian fiction.[24] *Anguish* belongs, albeit rather uncomfortably, to this boom of the northeastern novel of the 1930s. This genre obsessively charts a decadent family line, of which the protagonist—often an impotent, despairing writer—is the last representative. Within the symbolic economy of the genre, he attempts to ameliorate the loss of familial wealth and prestige once the region has lost out to mechanized processes of sugar extraction in the post-abolition period. In *Anguish*, Luís's obsessive, paranoid, and compulsive ruminations on his family's past on the plantation erupt repeatedly into the novel's urban present, charting a demise from his brutish, powerful plantation-owner grandfather, to his cruel, effete novel-reading father, and down to Luís, the laborer of letters.[25] In contrast to his predecessors with their lengthy, pompous names, Luís da Silva's name suggests an everyman, without rank or lineage; its "John Doe" quality links him to the larger cast of late modernist narrators in this study, who often appear without a name.

Luís also corresponds perfectly to what Mário de Andrade famously labeled the *fracassado* (failure) of literature of the period. Mário reads the *fracassado* as a symptom of authorial crisis in the 1930s: "a being with absolutely no force, stripped of his fibers, unable to live, unable to offer up a single personal element, a single trace of character, a muscle nor a single idea, in opposition to his environment."[26] This observation synthesizes a trope of Brazilian literary discourse of the 1930s, traversing different aesthetic and political orientations: the prevalence of characters who seemed to be dragged around by social forces under the period's neo-naturalist turn, a symptom of the "consciousness of underdevelopment" that António Cândido pinpointed precisely in the 1930s (introduction). The *fracassado* in Graciliano, as in his novelistic contemporaries, is above all a body incapable of shoring itself up against the crises of his environment. Wracked by indecision and pulled by the forces of contemporary life, Luís sees himself as a marionette, a boneless puppet, his vertebrae loose, hung up by a string (122). He lives a "barnacle's life" (9), clinging to his office desk like a mollusk, the position of a body conditioned by habit. He constantly describes himself as bent over, his body molded to typewriter, writing desk, and piece of paper.

In his frequent mental daytrips into the plantation culture of his past, Luís also recalls the humiliating position of Quitéira, his grandfather's favorite slave and concubine. Erupting back into the present, he discovers that, like her, he lacks control over his production, as when he refers to himself in the third person:

> What misery! Writing constantly, my spine wracked with pain, nostrils above the paper—all my strength and will gone. What did all that wordiness get me? "Write like this, Mr. Luís." Mr. Luís would obey. "Write like that, Mr. Luís." Mr. Luís arranged on the paper other people's ideas, other people's interests. (147)

Luís establishes a troubling analogy between Quitéria's labor and his own. Yet, in contrast to many of his contemporaries in the northeastern novel, the slaveholding past is not a site of nostalgia but of economic exploitation and bodily suffering on the most intimate scale; it produces schizophrenic narrators and writers who exist as battered and scarred bodies, long after the plantation had begun its decadence. Already on the novel's first page, Luís had gendered writing by explicitly linking it to prostitution; he periodically notes the lines on his palms and stiff fingers that come from writing by hand and with a typewriter. As with Quitéria, what he feels should be voluntarily given—love, companionship, the production of words—is no longer his own. The exploitive dimensions of the immaterial labors of art (in his case) and affect (in hers) come to the fore. The "frail" typist, "typing away at her machine," is similarly strained and constrained by her labor.

Emphasizing these constraints, and the parallels between intellectual and manual labor more broadly, is a means of breaking with the immediate avant-garde predecessors, for whom writing was rarely depicted as labor but instead as "play." Graciliano frequently rejected *modernismo* along these lines. When asked his opinion of modernism in an interview, for example, his response was acidic: "While others were attempting to examine something—to see, to feel—they were importing Marinetti."[27] His is thus a reluctant modernism, a "modernism of ill will."[28] Nor was he alone in his at times facile rejection of his predecessors—it is something of a late modernist tic, as I noted in the introduction—but here I want to emphasize how much of his criticism stems from what he saw as profoundly different conceptions of authorship. *Anguish* is Graciliano's most modernist, that is to say, experimental, work, but it treats modernist experimentation warily, even hostilely. Its fragmentation, surrealist imagery, interior monologue, and non-linear forms have none of the inspired energy of the avant-gardes from which they clearly borrow. The novel instead mobilizes avant-garde techniques to question the radical autonomy that characterized the experimental writers of the 1910s and 1920s. In their place, the writer is repositioned as a proletarian-user, whose body interfaces with the typewriting machine.

Author and protagonist mirror each other in this respect. Luís's own experiments with language differ strikingly in their effects from their predecessors'. In the opening pages of the novel, he breaks down Marina's name into letters that he constructs as anagrams, multiplying the individual characters/letters through the combination of fragments (8). Recalling Jameson's observation that "in modernist literature words are treated *like* objects" of mechanical reproduction, Luís also "plays" with announcements and writing pasted and superimposed on mirrors, movie posters, newspaper and book titles, in what he describes as an unfruitful pursuit of numbness (170).[29] He exhibits a constant need to mix letters, count on his fingers, and rearrange combinations of ciphers in his mind, tracing them with his hand (to employ an anachronism, he has an obsessive compulsive disorder):

> I would read the advertisements scrawled on the mirror, joining together letters of the longest words and forming new names. This exercise crystallized a habit from which I cannot free myself. I count on my fingers the combinations that are emerging, in series of twenty, corresponding to my two open and closed hands. When there are many vowels I manage to arrange sixty, eighty, sometimes a hundred words or more. . . . This idiotic hobby gives me a sort of *anesthesia*: I forget about the debts and humiliations, I stop thinking. (159; my emphasis)

The pursuit of language games has the goal of deadening (anesthesia), which will shore up against the repeated crises Luís has experienced.[30] The play with language functions as an inoculation that has become a habit, learned in the body without its needing to be aware of it. Homeopathically, it attempts to combat the alienation of modern seriality by gaining mastery over it, incorporating it into the work.[31] Such language games function in fact as a specular form of the novel, itself a kind of listless experimentation. They also suggest, more broadly, late modernism's melancholic relationship to rupture, and to the shift from authorial originality to writing as proprioception.

The late modernist accent comes across most clearly in Luís's obsession with errors and their traces, superimposed corrections that threaten to reproduce ad infinitum as his mind circles back upon itself frantically. These images knit together in a tangled knot as he writes:

> Impossible to work. They've given me a task, a report to type up at the office. I'm fine for the first ten lines. From then on Julião Tavares's bloated face emerges on top of the original, and my fingers encounter on the keyboard the soft resistance of fat flesh. And then the error appears. I try to overcome my obsession; I attempt, capriciously, to avoid the eraser. I finish the job, but much paper has been used up in the process. (7)

At the end of this section, he will end up scribbling on the page, "some stretched-out blotches and very dark borders" (9). Luís starts out "fine," meaning that his body works automatically as it types, a well-ordered, if anaesthetized, machine. But then the outside world intervenes. The error is the interruption that punctures even the rote job of copying. Material traces of it remain on the document in the form of those blotches and borders. Here, the avant-garde legacy of experimentation with language and its materiality does not disappear but is transformed into a modest and materialist incarnation of their typographic experiments through the error. The typing error introduces a variation in his rote reproduction. As with the typist herself, appearing and disappearing in the crowd, that slender possibility for an interruption of the daily grind, the error encapsulates a very skeptical but not entirely pessimistic relationship to rupture, with and through the proprioceptive body of the writer-user.

THE HOUR OF THE STAR (1977): CLARICE LISPECTOR'S LATE LATE MODERNISM

Four decades after Luís da Silva conjured up a cat-eyed typist on a tram in the northeast, a cat-eyed novelist began the story of a writer obsessed with a northeastern typist of his own. Clarice Lispector's novella *The Hour of the Star*, her last work published while she was still alive, resonates in unusual ways with *Anguish*.[32] *The Hour of the Star* and Lispector's contemporaneous journalistic production, the subject of the second half of this chapter, require a leap forward in the book's chronology, a leap that also reflects the return to the modernist period that occurred in Brazil and South America more broadly during the mid-1960s through 1970s, when the afterlives of late modernism become visible in the work of writers and visual artists.[33] Querying Lispector's late work and its affinities with that of Graciliano, her unlikely precursor, allows us to delve into a potent demonstration of the typewriter's *longue durée*. It will also allow for an exploration of gendered dimensions of typing that remained opaque to Graciliano.

Despite dramatic historical shifts from the 1930s to the 1960s, compelling points of connection link the moment of *The Hour of the Star* to that of *Anguish*. Both Lispector and Graciliano were writing in the midst of dictatorial regimes with pretensions of subsuming the popular, just as oppositional groups, such as the Brazilian Communist Party, struggled to do the same. During the 1930s, the author often positioned herself as a camera, phonograph, or x-ray that would denounce the crises of the era; this trope reemerged, with a difference, in the 1970s with the genre that Süssekind calls the *romance-reportagem*, or novel-exposé.[34] Lispector takes up this imperative self-reflexively through the form of the novella itself. The premises of the *romance-reportagem*, for example, are inscribed in *The Hour of the Star*'s title page, with its use of trigger words such as *registrar* (to record or archive facts), *grito* (the scream, as in a mass protest), and *obrigação* (the intellectual's responsibility or "obligation" to the subaltern classes). The "state of emergency and public calamity" that Lispector refers to in the novella's dedication (xiv) is thus at once utterly urgent—a realist description of the dark state of the present, with its political repression—and recursive, alluding to the persistent problem of Brazilian intellectuals' encounters with the subaltern. Ítalo Moriconi makes Lispector's response to the earlier *modernistas* explicit: "Macabéa is an allegorical representation of the relation between the Modernist intellectual and the poor, deprived sectors of the population."[35]

This allegory was central to both the proletarian and regionalist genres in the 1930s, but it did not disappear in this moment: it would resurface at various points throughout the twentieth century, whenever modernism's subsequent iterations became especially self-conscious of their own limitations to combat political and economic inequality. Throughout *The Hour of the Star*, Lispector underscores the changes the popular has undergone since its apex in the 1930s novels, as well as its stubborn persistence. On the novella's title page, for example, she also invokes *literatura de cordel*, the folk poetry sold in the northeast and in northeastern migrant communities throughout Brazil. *Literatura de cordel* recounts older and updated stories of battles and assassinations, girls lost in the city and bandits from days of old in simple prose, printed on the cheapest of paper. (The genre literally means "stories on a string" to refer to the way that are hung up, like laundry, for sale.)[36] At the same time, however, the author tells us, this is a "story in technicolor" (xiv), as Macabéa would want it, for she adores "horror films and musicals" (49); it frequently invokes the mass culture that its protagonist can access in fragmentary fashion on the streets of Rio de Janeiro: "You know what I want more than anything else in the world? To be a movie star. I only go to the movies on payday. I prefer a little theater [*cinema poeira*], it's cheaper. I love movie stories. Did you know that Marylin was all pink?"[37]

The Hour of the Star underscores the erosion of a division that had long been central to artists' and intellectuals' conception of culture in Brazil: the line between *cultura de massa* and *cultura popular*. The distinction between a popular (folk/"authentic") and mass (industrialized, often imported from the United States) culture was always a precarious one at best. Yet the difficulty of separating the two becomes much more pronounced in the postwar period. Beginning in the 1950s and reaching its apex in the 1960s–1970s, mass culture extends to broader sectors of the population; investment in advertising and consumption as economic engines increases; and, more broadly, a state-based model of cultural integration is displaced by one more closely aligned with market interests, including a national industry.[38] This period also witnessed the first generation of authors known as the "Coca-Cola boys"—indelibly shaped, since childhood, by the global mass culture experience, and with *The Hour of the Star* Lispector provides a portrait of a "Coca-Cola girl."[39]

While *The Hour of the Star* shares with *Anguish* an investment in the typist as an avatar of authorship, Lispector also suggests how the ground has shifted. The typist charts the recurrent apparition of the problem of the writer and the proletariat but also the further consolidation of media like cinema and the radio throughout the long twentieth century, along with domesticated technologies like the television, consolidated in the 1970s. From the 1930s until the advent of the personal computer, the typewriter's domesticated status will leave its mark on authorship without being cast as a new medium. Consider one of Lispector's *crônicas* from 1968:

> I use the rather light portable Olympia typewriter for my strange habit: writing with the machine on my lap. She runs well, she runs softly. She transmits me, prevents me from getting tangled up in the knot of my own handwriting. In a word, she elicits my thoughts and feelings. And she helps me as a person would. I don't feel mechanized because I use this typewriter. . . . The noise under her keyboard accompanies the solitude of whoever is writing. I would like to give my typewriter a present. But what could be given to a thing which modestly remains a thing, with no pretensions of becoming human?[40]

In this intimate portrait between writer and machine, the typewriter curls up on her lap like a cat, nearly purring. "She" (given the machine's gender in Portuguese) provides the opportunity for intimacy despite, not because of her distance from the author. It is a distant intimacy (for the typewriter remains in all its "thingness") that shapes the author as she writes.

This portrait resonates with the principal relationship of *The Hour of the Star,* the one between the narrator and "his" typist. The pendulum between distance and intimacy that we saw in Luís da Silva's relationship to the typist is also a constitutive dimension of Lispector's novella. Yet, in contrast to Graciliano's typist, Lispector's does not remain a flickering possibility but becomes instead an anthropophagic protagonist, one who threatens to devour the author who fashions her. As she emerges on the page, Macabéa struggles with her creator to gain something like autonomy, through a metafictional frame that draws our attention to her relationship to the author.

The narrator of *The Hour of the Star,* a writer by the name of Rodrigo S. M., discovers Macabéa, a young woman from Brazil's impoverished northeastern region adrift in the big city of Rio de Janeiro. The novella unfolds to show us the process of a misanthropic intellectual creating the book we hold in our hands, springing forth from his imagining of a fraught communion with the typist. Rodrigo states that he "glanced" at her in a crowd, catching her eye in that moment, before willing her into being: the same anonymous scenario that also conjured up Luís da Silva's typist. As in *Anguish,* Lispector's typist emerges from a crowd or mass to impose her presence on the narrator, paradoxically imprinting him with her very typicality. In the novella's opening pages, he underscores the anonymity and seriality of her life: "There are thousands of girls scattered throughout the tenement slums, vacancies in beds in a room, behind the shop counters working to the point of exhaustion. They don't even realize how easily substitutable they are" (6). Like Luís's typist, Macabéa embodies Sartre's understanding of seriality as a "plurality of isolations," made possible by capitalist modernity and exacerbated or thrown into relief by mass media.[41] It is the typist's typicality, her "easily substitutable" quality, which allows her to be immediately classified. That she is an impoverished migrant from the northeast compounds her role as a stereotype of the popular classes in Brazil.

Lispector's Macabéa also has something of Alfonsina Storni's messy, undisciplined typist, part of the masses accused of "contributing to the general level of joy on the streets of Buenos Aires," with "light stains of powder on her blouse" and clandestine carmine lipstick in her purse, with her "uninhibited laugh," "flashing glances," and the pattering of her high heels on the sidewalk.[42] Per Storni (as Tao Lao), the typist can be identified through the components of a recipe that the *cronista* offers us of an ideal type, "the perfect typist," or "typist-symbol": take a young woman between eighteen and twenty years old, have her live in an apartment building in a peripheral neighborhood, dye her hair blonde, paint her nails, "suck in her stomach, render stiff and calloused her index and middle fingers, sprinkle her generously with bad spelling," make her pay for a typing "academy," then "hire her on the cheap" (909–11). Lispector's Macabéa exhibits many of these characteristics—a young woman who lives in a tenement; an atrocious speller with an infelicitous relationship to cosmetics. In contrast to the middle-class housewives who protagonize Lispector's earlier novels, she possesses only three years of schooling, and she is malnourished from her early childhood, a lack she attempts to ameliorate through copious amounts of hot dogs and Coca-Cola.

Yet Macabéa is also a migrant from the peripheral Alagoas region, where Graciliano lived and worked and where Lispector spent her first, difficult years in Brazil as the child of Jewish immigrants fleeing a Ukrainian pogrom. She represents at once a radical alterity and alter ego for Lispector. A late work, *The Hour of the Star* was written after Lispector had already experienced life in the public gaze and was considered one of Brazil's most internationally acclaimed writers, albeit one constantly depicted as "exotic," out of place in Brazil and out of touch with urgent sociopolitical realities, in the persistent epithet/insult, "hermetic." (A caricaturist had consigned her to a grave of insufficiently engaged writers in 1972.)[43] As it was for both Borges and

Graciliano (and his Luís da Silva) in the 1930s, Lispector's own career had traversed multiple guises: a highly respected writer and a struggling paper- or print-smith, Brazil's most prestigious modernist of the mid- to late twentieth century, and writer-for-hire. In a challenge to the binary between the accessible and the hermetic that has long shaped scholarly and popular conceptions on her work, this duality becomes explicit during her late period, in both her journalism and last works of fiction.

Lispector's journalistic career paralleled the successive modernization of Brazilian print periodicals, including the publication of *Última Hora* and *Manchete* (Brazil's take on the *Paris Review*) beginning in the 1950s.[44] It was far easier for women to work as typists than as journalists, but journalism also partially enabled Lispector's novelistic production by exposing her to influential literary figures and allowing her a space to hone her craft.[45] In the period prior to the publication of *The Hour of the Star*, she published a regular column in the *Jornal do Brasil* (1967–73), a Rio de Janeiro newspaper, continuing a career launched in the early 1940s, when she began writing inoffensive *crônicas* for *Vamos Ler!* (Let's Read!), a supplement of the mass paper *A Noite*. If her earlier journalistic writing included obligatory apologists for the Vargas regime, her later contributions to periodicals included ghostwriting for a Rio starlet, as well as recipes for killing cockroaches and fabricating cold cream, the latter under the name of Helen Palmer, paid for by the Pond's cosmetics company, one of the many U.S. subsidiaries that came to prominence in mass print culture in the postwar period and fomented feminine consumption markets. In the column "For Women Only," she dispatched fashion and beauty advice to her feminine readers that ranged from very intimate exchanges to tips that would become part of the aspirational idiom of young women like Macabéa: "A good appearance is important for the working woman. So your bag should always have one of those powder compacts to retouch your makeup."[46] Late in life, Lispector began to dedicate herself to journalistic production more intensely out of economic necessity; for a divorced woman without family money (in contrast to many of Brazil's most lauded writers of the twentieth century), these columns paid. Ghostwriter, laborer of letters, modernist paragon: like Graciliano, Lispector found herself occupying these multiple roles, and often simultaneously. She was not given to assume them transparently, however. Many of the sketches she published in popular periodicals are surprisingly opaque and/or metafictional.

Lispector's sketches also made possible frequent traffic with her feminine readers. Recalling Borges's references to the "Saturday pastime" in *The Universal History of Infamy*, she writes in one, "So with great pleasure I sell you a certain part of my soul—the part of Saturday conversation."[47] In "Words from the Typewriter" (Máquina escrevendo): "If I could, I would leave my space on this page blank: filled with the greatest silence. And readers, on seeing this blank space, would fill it with their own desires."[48] As for Borges, these sketches were a laboratory for exploring writing's interfaces with bureaucratized technologies—in this case, the typewriter and its interface, the blank page. In a column titled "Fernando Pessoa Helping Me," she defines this mutually constitutive relationship: "In the literature of books I remain anonymous and discreet. In this column I am in some way letting myself be known. Am I losing my secret intimacy? But what to do? It's just that I'm writing at the typewriter's pace [*ao correr da máquina*] and, when I look up, I've revealed a certain part of myself."[49] Counterintuitively, it is not in the realm of the literary but in the anonymous clacking of the typewriter keys, and the body habituated to operating them, that she reveals herself.

Lispector returns repeatedly to these kinds of self-reflexive bodily interruptions into the supposedly insular and disembodied act of writing. Typing often cues them. In the sketch "Racing against the Typewriter" or "At the Typewriter's Pace" (*Ao correr da máquina*, 1969), "the typewriter races faster than my fingers. The typewriter writes inside me." These lines would appear to lend themselves to a posthumanist reading: the author as subject takes off and the machine takes over. However, this jag of automatic writing is interrupted by a quite different fragment, one that introduces the mechanistic repetitions of domestic labor: "And she, the maid, who lives on the outskirts of town and wakes up at four in the morning to work all day in the city before returning late at night in order to sleep in order to wake up at four in the morning and begin her work in the city."[50] This eruption of the working poor is part of the automatic writing that structures the sketch. It is one element in the racing brain that competes with the machine. It introduces a difference: the fingers on the keyboard cull up the automatized labor of the impoverished servant.

As for Luís da Silva, the relationship between narrator and typist in *The Hour of the Star* is thus both allegorical (the artist/intellectual and the working-class/*popular)* and autobiographical (given Lispector's own experience with writing). In the novella, Rodrigo the narrator underscores his own writing as a labor of the hand, seeking out moments of connection between his labor and that of "his" typist, Macabéa. He refers to himself as "the person sitting here typing" (11). The original is more emphatic about the simultaneity of the typing experience: "whom at this very instant is pounding on the machine" (20, my translation). (In Portuguese, "typing" is frequently depicted through the verb *bater*, to beat or pound.) At various points, he likens his writing to manual labor—etymologically and literally, a laborer of the hands—depicting himself as a carpenter or quarry worker, "all to put myself on the northeastern girl's level." "I am not an intellectual," he proclaims. "I write with my body" (8). "This story has no technique, nor style," he intones, "it lives from hand to mouth" (28). These descriptions of writing as labor and as a rather laborious (given his misanthropy) solidarity echo Luís da Silva's wrestling with language and his tentative approximation to his own typist.

On the other hand, *The Hour of the Star* underscores in a much more explicit fashion than Graciliano and his contemporaries the limits of such attempts to conflate different kinds of labor. Lispector employs the materials of writing, materials that narrator and typist share, to signal the very abyss that separates the two. We find out that when Macabéa's stomach rumbled as a child, she would chew up and swallow paper to trick her body's hunger. Meanwhile, Rodrigo's cook—one of the many figures of domestic labor who hover along the edges and sometimes migrate to the center of Lispector's fiction and journalistic sketches—mistakes her employer's latest writing for trash and tosses this paper out. Paper had once given Macabéa momentary sustenance. For Rodrigo's cook, it is waste. Both women approach paper in its pulpy materiality: in the novella's words, "chewable paper." Perhaps it is newsprint, the original source of the term "pulp," a composite of leftover materials, just like the hot dogs that Macabéa loves so much, or the yellowing butcher paper that will give birth to a novel in the context of the prison for Graciliano. Macabéa and her type have been used, Lispector suggests, as writing surfaces and as types: in this case, the impoverished northeasterner who was a blank page for the Brazilian artist-intellectual, often from the wealthier south, to inscribe a national dilemma.[51] But Macabéa responds to this lengthy history by stripping down paper to its bare materiality and swallowing it, a modest devouring that refracts the intellectual's labor back upon him/her, revealing the aporias of such attempts at identification.

By the mid- to late 1970s, when Lispector began to pen *Hour of the Star*, the very concept of lack and in particular of hunger had been resemanticized by various artists and intellectuals, most influentially in Glauber Rocha's manifesto for cinema, "An Esthetic of Hunger" (1968).[52] Influenced by Frantz Fanon, Rocha's postcolonial call to violence distinguished between the depiction of a suffering primitive, a legacy of the violence of the exoticizing outsider gaze, and the revolutionary potential of the subaltern. It is no coincidence, then, that *The Hour of the Star* abounds in discussions of hunger as a polysemic concept. Rather than the intellectual holding up a mirror to the misery of the suffering classes, as in Rocha's manifesto, Rodrigo fumbles through the asymmetries of power that produce art out of the raw material of the marginalized: "This story has no technique, nor style, it lives from hand to mouth. I who also wouldn't stain for anything in this world with shimmering and false words a life as meager as the typist's" (28). He wonders about using "succulent terms": "splendid adjectives, meaty nouns," but worries about the ill fit between such rich language and the poverty of his subject matter: "If I touch the girl's bread the bread will turn to gold—and the girl (she's nineteen) the girl wouldn't be able to bite it, dying of hunger" (7). Macabéa dreams of fancy skin creams, but not to layer on her skin; instead, she longs to eat them by the spoonful to satisfy her very literal hunger.

As the frequent recourse to images of hunger indicates, *The Hour of the Star* also brings Macabéa's marked body into the corpus of writing. Rodrigo draws connections between her subaltern status and typing itself: the corporeal punishment she experienced as a young girl, for example, is connected to her pounding away on the keyboard (the same verb, *bater*, is used). Macabéa has typing beaten into her. (In Benjamin Moser's clever translation: her aunt, who used to beat her, "gave her a crash course in typing" [7].) She marks up the pages she types with her greasy hands. She also makes mistakes, and her errors are the fruit of ignorance: she is a bad typist because she grew up uneducated and malnourished.

Over and over, these descriptions of an abused body puncture a well-known image: the seamless, professionalized work of the typing pool, familiar through advertising and the women's pictures that flooded the Brazilian market when Lispector first became a "working girl" in the 1940s. In contrast to these perky writing machines, Macabéa's shoulders are slumped, her chest caved in. Her body is poured into its *position*, in the double sense of "job" and "place in the world." And she is bad at what she does. The creation of units of words from abstract characters—the basic requirement of Taylorized typing—eludes her.

Kittler argues that "for mechanized writing to be optimized, one can no longer dream of writing as the expression of individuals or the trace of bodies."[53] For a typist's copying to be effective, the traces of his or her body and labor must not be made visible at the site of inscription. The ideal typist labors without a trace of signature or style that would betray her corporeal presence. She creates the illusion that there was no person between the machine and the page, or between original and reproduction. Typing schools and correspondence courses that debuted in the interwar period taught the omission of pauses and the internalization of words as nearly subconscious units.

But the "optimization" Kittler privileges is only one goal—and certainly only one possible outcome—of an encounter with the typewriter. Macabéa's clumsy interface with the medium opens up a different avenue of expression, leaving her own trace on the page, marking it up with her hot dog–stained hands. Lispector draws our attention to the dissonance between the machine's supposedly seamless flow and the interruptions and errors of the body that operates it. Typing, she shows, is shaped by a corporeal and mental concentration that channels or suppresses private or errant thoughts toward the automatized reproduction of words on the page. The fantasy of the dematerialized body corresponds to the fantasy of perfect mediation projected onto the typist, typesetter, or reproducer of the words of others: a labor that, like domestic labor, or the work of translation, is successful to the extent to which it is rendered invisible.[54] Macabéa copies—she doesn't produce—and she copies badly. Moreover, even her reproduction is flawed: she is barren, and her reproduction of the boss's words is also thwarted. Macabéa marvels at his "lovely" handwriting, a marveling that prevents her from performing her job seamlessly and efficiently, as it stops her typing short. The increasing separation of typing from reading/understanding as part of a process of administered rationality is also called into question. Nothing is less efficient than Macabéa's clumsy interface with the typewriter. Yet nothing is more compelling for Lispector than this slow approach to language.

The fiction of the typist as invisibilized, pure transmission can be maintained up until a certain point, the moment of error.[55] As with Graciliano's Luís da Silva, with the typographic error, the unseemliness of Macabéa's body seems to erupt on the page. If the typewriter exists to standardize, her errors introduce difference. And it is here where Lispector begins to experiment, in the late modernist sense of the term. Macabéa's errors become a fumbling inquiry into rather large philosophical problems: "Apparently, she didn't approve of two consonants together and copied from the lovely and round handwriting of her beloved boss the word 'designate' [*designar*] as she would have said it, 'desiginate' [*desiguinar*]" (7). Macabéa's love for the sounds of words, especially mispronounced ones, becomes a motif in the novella. On one hand, her errors underscore the quintessential problem of Brazilian modernism: the abyss between written and spoken language and the writer's capacity to traverse this divide, as epitomized by the work of Mário (as when Lispector writes "Marylin" to reflect Macabéa's pronunciation of the starlet's name). But there is more, because Macabéa also disturbs the boss's designation with her mistaken supplement. With that extra "ui" by which *desiginate* becomes *desiguinar*, she quite literally interrupts the word "sign"—and, by extension, a mark, design, or signature that bestows authority. Whether the lack of mastery of standardized grammar or the slippage of the tongue or the finger, the error stages an ephemeral alternative by exposing the conventions (or stereotypes) that the typewriter materializes.

Eschewing the authorial signature, the error indexes traces of the typist's labor that are also singular, unstandardized. As in the moments of error in *Anguish*, the error here also points us back to the modernist legacy, the trace or residue of the transformation that formal experimentation undergoes in late modernism, in the wake of the avant-garde typographic experiments of the 1910s and 1920s—from Dada to the surrealists to Oswald de Andrade's telegraphic writing to the covers of *Klaxon*. Late modernism absorbs this fascination with machine experiments but reroutes it toward the quotidian and proletarian. Lispector locates this now disenchanted form of the aura in Macabéa's wide-eyed approach to the materials and media of writing. Lacking access to the word's denotative function, Macabéa dwells in the grain of print.

Several of Lispector's late journalistic sketches are similarly engaged with typographic experiments that are less defamiliarizing ruptures than banal scenes of human-machine labor. In "Even the Machine?" (Até a máquina? 1972)—and this is the sketch in its entirety:

> I sent my typewriter to be fixed. Inserted around the cylinder (or however you call it; you all know what I mean) the repairman had left the paper where he had tried writing to test out its functions. On the paper was written: s d f g ç l k j a e v blessed be God p oy 3 thing.[56]

Here God is not in the machine; its technological enchantments are seemingly nonexistent. But in the repairman's revision of the domesticated object's basic operations, a strange ephemerality pushes the writer to reproduce its random letters. In an earlier sketch, "To the Typesetter" (1968), she connects such errors to her own style. She directs a plea to the typesetter but publishes it for all her readers to experience: "Forgive all my errors on the typewriter. First it is because my right hand was burnt. Second, I'm not sure why. Now a request: don't correct me. Punctuation is the breath of a sentence, and my sentence breathes in that way."[57] Punctuation requires a break in the flow of writing, a parceling out of meaning. As Lispector states here, deviating from standardized punctuation is also a way of inserting different rhythms into prose. Incorrect punctuation tweaks convention and becomes a different sort of authorial signature, an almost biorhythm of her prose.

Lispector and the typewriter repairman engage in experimentation through errors, accidents, and banal interruptions, like the subaltern typist Macabéa. In *The Hour of the Star*, both the error and the pause, as modes of interrupting efficiency, materialize as modest possibilities within the office space:

> There were things she didn't know what they meant. One was "ephemerides." And didn't Mr. Raimundo ask her to copy from his lovely handwriting the word ephemerides or ephemeris? She thought the term ephemerides was absolutely mysterious. When she copied it she paid attention to every letter. [Her colleague] Glória could do shorthand and not only earned more but didn't even miss a beat with all those difficult words the boss loved so much. Meanwhile the girl [Macabéa] had fallen in love with the word "ephemerides." (31)

Macabéa copies "letter by letter," indicating that she has not fully internalized many of these words as units; they are foreign to her, and she finds them estranging. She also types with love. The very sound of the word thrills her. At various points in the novella, Lispector teases us to decipher the moments where Macabéa interrupts typing or other forms of transmission to wonder at the sound of words, their sonic materiality. Rather than efficiently transmitting, Macabéa lingers on those words eccentric to the office setting: *ephemer-ides*, related to ephemera, a temporary possibility.[58] Macabéa pauses—something the typist, unlike the reader, is not supposed to do. In this sense, her pauses are examples of De Certeau's notion of *la perruque*, his term for the practice by which workers occupy with ephemeral tactics what they cannot occupy in space, usurping their labor power from the employer by stealing back a little of their own time. One of his examples is, precisely, a secretary writing a love letter on company time, creating something "gratuitous" in the space "where the machine he [*sic*] must serve reigns supreme."[59] Macabéa's love letters are directed toward *letters* themselves. She affectionately reproduces and recodes the boss's directives, wasting time, exploring. In these moments, Macabéa becomes, through her typewriter, a user.

Yet, at the same time as we are invited into this play of misplaced letters, we are keenly aware of the primacy of the boss's hand and the structural inequalities that make possible Macabéa's surprising errors. While she types anonymously, after all, her boss possesses a unique penmanship. The boss's hand writes and has a signature, while she types, ideally anonymously, without a style or proper name that would betray her corporeal presence.

This encounter between the hand's connection to auratic authorship and the ostensibly anonymous standardization of typing is one way of approaching the novella's unusual title page. All editions of *The Hour of the Star* list thirteen possible titles—or subtitles—for the book, each of which will resonate with moments in the text. Set in typescript to form a long column, broken up by the perfectly aligned repartition of "OU" ("or"), they are juxtaposed with Lispector's bold, thick signature. With the title page, the reader is asked to enter the text through this nonhierarchical list and to wonder about the location of the author's signature within it. As in Mário's poem "Typewriter" (1926), "All that is left of the lyrical subject is 'the handwritten signature.'"[60] Along with the typewriter's standardized letters, this mechanically reproduced signature displays the graphic materiality of literary texts. But this "all that is left" is not merely a supplement or remainder of a Romantic illusion of the author-subject, displayed as a corpse. It underscores the traffic between a series of typists—Lispector the author, Rodrigo the narrator, and Macabéa the protagonist.

There is an additional relationship alluded to in this title page: Lispector's experiences with her own typist-scribe. After her writing hand had been badly damaged in a fire in 1966, she turned to her new friend Olga Borelli, a constant companion during her final years.[61] Borelli typed and took dictation and also helped compile the intensely fragmentary work Lispector wrote toward the end of her life. Confidante, scribe, typist, and compiler, Borelli is also a prosthesis, an extension of Lispector's writing body. Not coincidentally, as she came into Lispector's life, the renowned author began to experiment most explicitly with different materialities of writing. The title page thus becomes what N. Katherine Hayles calls a "material metaphor": one that stages the circuits between words and their material supports.[62] The effect is one of various hands converging on the page—an image that evokes the constitutively uneven collaboration of writer, scribe, character, narrator, and machine itself—the multiple hands that make possible the authority of this signature.

Late modernist typewriters render bodily a series of tensions that become increasingly prominent in the wake of the first waves of Brazilian modernism: art versus labor, creation versus service, public versus private. Writing, after all, is a labor done both within and without sanctioned professional spaces: for every clerk's office, there is a typewriter purring on the lap of a writer; for every writer, there is a maid or scribe. Hunched over the machine, habituated to the act of writing, the late modernist author finds in the typist an extension of his or her own body, shifting from the fantasies of creation to the experience of a habituated usership.

For Kittler, the typewriter ushered in a democratic opening up to women, in stark opposition to the Romantic writer of the nineteenth century, who privileged and subjected women by making them a source of oral expressiveness—the mother tongue, harnessed and produced by the written word, gendered male. Poets, secretaries, and typesetters were almost exclusively male before the typewriter, Kittler notes; women could only appear in the guise of men, through the pseudonym. The typist interrupted this circuit and set into motion a new one, a revolution that would continue as the twentieth century progressed, finding its fruition in the computer. Canonical modernists like Proust, Nietzsche, Kafka, and Henry James (with his "Remington priestess," Theodora Bosanquet) owed a debt to these often invisibilized figures of women scribes and typists.[63] In Kittler's genealogy, women arrive too late to be real authors; the price women paid for entering into the world of authorship is precisely the devaluation of the category itself. Their compensation is the dubious distinction of being the heralds of authorship's death.[64]

Writing under her own masculine pseudonym of Tao Lao, Alfonsina Storni imagined her "perfect typist" prostrating herself before a king who can fix the typewriter and use it perfectly. The machine appears to the typist as a black box, while to him it is a seamless instrument: "Each of his fingers a faithful soldier who never misses a command, and even the pinky finger remembers perfectly the precise and invariable labor assigned to him" (909). (Interestingly, this "king" is described as "North American," suggesting the typewriter's doubly foreign nature to the typist.) In contrast, the typist labors with great difficulty "with the index and middle fingers"; enthralled by this prowess with the machine, "her mouth shapes a formidable O" (910): perhaps like the perfect "O" of the typewriter itself, which her fingers can produce with a good deal of effort. Behind the entrance of women into the lettered sphere as writing machines is the outsourcing of masculine labor to a new class of women workers, but under very certain conditions: the woman typist exists uncomfortably here as proletarian of letters and continues to be linked to orality—that round "O" of the typist's little mouth.

During the early twentieth century, Storni presented something of an exceptional type herself: a woman writer, making a living through her own journalistic sketches, commenting upon the emergence of this new class. If the journalistic sketch, as many scholars have shown, is central to modern Latin American literary production, the question of its circulation, its publicness, is gendered in specific ways. Despite the great prestige her literature would eventually afford her, Lispector was never immune to these obstacles.[65]

The Hour of the Star interrogates this Western tradition, including its Brazilian variant, with its legacy of prominent male authors drafting an enigmatic female subjectivity, most famously in Machado de Assis's Capitu in *Dom Casmurro* (1899) and Graciliano's Madalena in *São Bernardo* (1934). In *Anguish*, Luís's desire is split between two women: the bad reader, Marina, and the anonymous typist, the noble proletarian. With her promiscuity and love of film clichés and trashy novels, along with her explicit inability to type, Marina more closely approximates Huyssen's analysis of "woman as mass culture" and it is almost as if the novel needs her to sketch the contours of this other figure, encountered only ephemerally, of the typist.[66] For her part, the nameless typist in *Anguish* also reveals Luís's gendered fantasies: the fact that he imagines her as midwife to his work, rather than a furtive writer like himself.

The Hour of the Star gathers up these threads and foregrounds them. "Is this a melodrama?" Rodrigo asks as he drafts Macabéa's story. Invoking depictions of sentimentality, he marshals misogyny:

"because a woman would make it all weepy and maudlin" (6). Yet Macabéa is neither Marina nor the anonymous typist of *Anguish*, neither mass or popular, subject or object, but some very different amalgamation, a vulnerable, unwitting parasite with a penchant for hot dogs, Marilyn Monroe, clock radio, and language's nearly mystical properties. A strange new force, she begins to take over Rodrigo's life, his very body. One of the few female writers in Brazil whose proper name and signature were already a form of authority writes a novella in which a male writer abuses and loves an impoverished woman, a bad writer, and a worse reader-spectator: the position to which women were often consigned in the lettered sphere.[67] Through this troubling relationship, Lispector interrogates the knotted relationships of gender and class through the materialities of modern writing and its machines. Marrying, not without difficulty, aesthetic creation's immaterial labor with manual labor, her last work shows how the typist becomes an extension of the writer's body during late modernism's *longue durée*, an extension that continues authorship's shift from demiurgic creation to the bodily practices and habits of the fumbling, tactical user.

CHAPTER 4

The Residual Haptic

Feelership in Felisberto Hernández

This chapter opens with a return to an earlier text. In Chapter 2, Felisberto Hernández's microfiction "Lovebird Furniture" (1947) functioned as a parable of the mass media's continual encroachment onto interiority. Injected with a radio station's shifting formats, the unnamed narrator finds tangos, serialized novels, and sonnets for a furniture store alternating nightmarishly in his head. But when we follow the story to its unexpected ending, something in the parable shifts. The man supplying the injections lets the narrator in on a secret: he should stick his feet into a bucket of hot water to rid himself of these sounds.[1] To interpret the story as merely an allegory of mass culture invasion or entrapment requires overlooking this strange interruption. With the single closing sentence, folk wisdom and the black market converge on a note at once banal and absurd, throwing off our reading of radio as contagion. Through a sleight of hand, the older remedy temporarily trumps the anaesthetics induced by the medium. The radio's assaulting noise is transformed through the subject's skin, abruptly cut off by the apparition of a new sensory dimension. Although the story ends before we discover if the remedy is effective, the potential of the haptic—of skin submerged in water—shocks us right out of the radio's sinister presence.

Reading Hernández, we learn to brace ourselves for such interruptions. Marked by riffing or meandering, lacking an architecture, his works feature beginnings, endings, and middles that often seem to correspond to different registers or genres. Comic interludes constantly reroute the narratives of his short stories so that any attempt to summarize them tends to fall flat.[2] A light switch turns on suddenly, an ostrich appears wandering amid café tables, a musical instrument springs out of its case, seemingly of its own volition. As with Lispector's Macabéa in the previous chapter, the interruption becomes a way of reflecting on the aleatory in the wake of the avant-gardes—in this case, of surrealism, the movement that most interested Hernández. But it also poses a particular challenge to literary criticism, implicitly asking us to cultivate alternative, non-masterful approaches to his often inassimilable works.

This chapter analyzes interruptions in Hernández that transform authorship into a particular variant of usership that I call feelership. The defining feature of this usership is curiosity and receptivity, even vulnerability, to the sensations produced by residual media, specifically silent film. Authorship becomes a process of enacting a haptic ritual rather than inaugurating a new world. This transformation into feelership occurs not in spite but because of the massification that Hernández believed to be encroaching upon notions of the interior, during a period in which Uruguay experienced both rapid modernization and the aftermath, or hangover, of such changes. As an improvisatory accompanist to silent film might punctuate or corporealize a film image, Hernández's texts cull up alternatives to the anaesthetics of mass media by rerouting them through the newly anachronistic practices of silent film. This privileging of the residual corresponds to a specific, sensorial dimension in his works: that of the haptic. Despite his well-documented obsession with vision and voyeurism, we also find interwoven in his stories a doubled sense of touch—of giving and receiving, of the body's skin as organ and the hands as tools—as both an instantiation and allegory of earlier experiences of spectatorship. As in the unexpected ending of "Lovebird Furniture," his protagonists immerse themselves in haptic experiences that invoke, even as they disturb, the modernist anxiety of the passive spectator.[3] At the same time, the haptic indicates a transformation from the spectator's seemingly agentic gaze to the user's own vulnerable body. First, I sketch the terms for the residual haptic across a variety of short and rather minor texts, where we can see him essaying his feelership. Subsequently, I zero in on three of his better-known works where the haptic functions as the motivating principal.

HAND-WRITING (PIANIST, WRITER, USER)

Having begun his career as an accompanist to silent film, Hernández invokes untimely reader-spectators, long after they had disappeared from even most peripheral cinemas of midcentury Uruguay. Like their counterparts in Rio de Janeiro and Buenos Aires, spectators in Hernández's hometown of Montevideo had the opportunity to see cinema for the first time very early in the medium's history when, on July 18, 1896, moving pictures debuted at the Sálon Rouge in the city center. Cinema spectatorship would be an important part of the city's cultural fabric from this moment on. When the first (foreign) sound film made its appearance in Montevideo in 1929, cinema had already begun to separate out from other spectacles, such as circuses, sporting events, and lectures; synchronized sound continued this process of specialization, industrialization, and professionalization of exhibition practices. While some venues continued to play silent films—such as the early Chaplin shorts used as filler material in neighborhood cinemas during the 1930s—many theaters closed in the transition, which would be complete by the beginning of the decade in downtown Montevideo and its outlying barrios.[4]

In 1935, the first cinematheque was inaugurated in Montevideo, showcasing early/silent film and avant-garde films. This year is a proto origin for Uruguayan cinephilia, a beginning of the auratization of the silent and experimental eras that persists to this day—as eulogized recently in Federico Veiroj's acclaimed *The Useful Life* (*La vida útil*, 2012), a film that echoes Hernández in some respects. As in many parts of the world, however, it will be in the postwar period that cinephilia reaches its apex, particularly in institutional form: film cycles in state-sponsored institutions, specialized art-house film periodicals, and the proliferation of what is known more broadly as *cineclubismo* and the legitimation of cinema as an object of artistic exploration.[5] In Uruguay, a key moment in the history occurs through the founding of a branch devoted to "Cine Art" in 1943 as part of the SODRE (Servicio Oficial de Difusión, Radiotelevisión y Espectáculos), the national public broadcasting system; during the following decades, its efforts would increase through the creation of film festivals.[6] Cinema had to age before certain films could be consecrated as classics and before spaces could be created to cultivate an enraptured gaze.

I offer this brief sketch of national film reception to situate the alternative grammars of Hernández's haptic perception. The period from his childhood to the publication of his late work coincides with a series of changes in the medium's reception: first, its emergence out of popular spectacles, followed by its coexistence with them; then the waning of silent film, and the arrival and consolidation of synchronized sound. Yet in his works film history is not seamlessly reproduced as developmental stages but productively entangled through the practices of feelership. In some respects, for example, Hernández's user exhibits features of the cinephilia described by film theorists. His interest in multiple and often anachronistic forms calls to mind Thomas Elsaesser's definition that links cinephilia to "retroactive temporalities" and modes of affect like disappointment and disenchantment.[7] Similarly, Dudley Andrew's "Time Zones and Jetlag" connects cinephilia to the "delay and slippage," and the "discrepancy in space and deferral or jump in time," proper to cinema, marked by temporal loops and delays, an experience he labels *décalage* or "jetlag."[8] In addition to these kinds of temporal slippages, theorists of cinephilia also underscore the centrality of the body: its location and position within the cinema and, more obviously, the focused gaze, the fetishistic retrieval of particular, often eccentric moments or details.[9] All of these resonate with Hernández's relationship to cinema. Yet his cinephilia is very different from the impassioned versions we find with increasing intensity in the 1960s. Proper names (*auteurs*) and film titles are entirely absent from his works, and there is nothing like a fan culture or devotion to a cosmopolitan community of filmgoers that we find in postwar cinephilia. Instead, his fiction conjures up the sensation of a residual, somatic approach to cinema that had ostensibly disappeared.

Several years after his first story was published on pulp paper and bound by hand with discarded wire, Hernández had begun his own, non-linear transformation into a writer. Up until this point, he was principally a composer and, earlier still, an accompanist to silent film, tracing with his fingers "the madcap scenes of Buster Keaton, the seductions of Valentino, the sins of Theda Bara." As in Brazil and Argentina, film had a very close relationship to live musical performance, from its origins through the silent-to-sound transition in Uruguay. Throughout the 1910s and 1920s, Hernández had a more direct connection to this phenomenon than most of his contemporaries. As a young man, he traveled through the provincial towns of Uruguay and Argentina in "Chaplinesque tours" that took place in café-concerts, school auditoria, town halls in the provinces, and other peripheral spaces.[10] (A concert he offered in November 1934 in the small town of Mercedes is titled "Recital for the Benefit of the Commission of Ladies in the Struggle Against Tuberculosis.")[11] These improvisational experiences at concerts and silent film screenings, in turn, implied a unique, embodied response to reception.

In silent film accompaniment, to play was to watch, and to watch was to actualize. In this sense, the practice of playing the piano superimposed seemingly opposing realms, including watching and performing, reception and production, spectatorship and usership.[12] Film accompaniment would be echoed in Hernández's later obsession with stenography, a practice he fervently hoped would save him from his eternal struggle against poverty and unemployment. His manuscripts from the 1940s include pages and pages onto which he hammered out stenographic code. Chirography—handwriting, penmanship—was part of Hernández's broader interest in activities of the hands which, through the movements of copying and annotating secret codes, participate in registering the world. Piano playing and stenography serve as counterpoints to one another, as he writes in his journal from the small Argentine town of Bahia Blanca in 1940: "I went to a café, somewhat depressed, and I thought about stenography [*la taqui*, his "shorthand" for it]. When the piano goes poorly I think about it, and when it goes well, I shift away from it with an astonishing facility. Each of these tendencies—stenography and the piano—I defend formidably, depending on the moment in which I find myself."[13] The notational code of piano playing alternates with the different notational code of stenography. Both gloss authorship as a form of "manual" labor—yet, in contrast to the proletarian typist-writer of the previous chapter, Hernández invokes the craft-based work of the artisan.

In the shift from one labor of the hand (piano playing) to another (writing, stenography), the pivotal year was 1942, twenty years after the zenith of modernism in Latin America as well as Europe. That year, he sold his piano and published the autobiographical narrative "Around the Time of Clemente Colling." Fittingly, "Clemente Colling" recounts his experiences with the eccentric, abject piano teacher of his childhood. For the childhood narrator, the eponymous character suggests the possibility of "a secret of life we could forever be reaching toward with hidden delight in further surprises—the kind of surprises that largely depend on our own hands."[14] Providing cues for Hernández's major works of his subsequent period, Colling's blindness, his synesthesia, and his abject, fascinating hands, which the narrator dwells on as he watches his teacher read Braille (55), are examples of the fingertips becoming organs of visuality in Hernández's texts and foreshadow his later interest in surrealism. (They also recall the synesthetic inventions of his Argentine contemporary Xul Solar, who designed a piano for the blind with rugged surfaces and colors to correspond to the instrument's tones.) "Around the Time of Clemente Colling" became a fragmentary epitaph for the pianist-composer and a birth certificate for the writer.

Yet his past experiences with piano playing never disappeared entirely. Instead, they were subsumed into his later work through the experience and labors of the hand. Writing about another piano teacher:

> Celina would make me spread my hands on the keys and, with her fingers, she bent mine back, as if she were teaching a spider to move its legs. She was more closely in touch with my hands than I was myself. When she made them crawl like slow crabs over white and black pebbles, suddenly the hands came upon sounds that cast a spell on everything in the circle of lamplight, giving each object a new charm.[15]

Here, giving himself over to the tactile directives of his teacher, his hands begin to "suddenly" take on their own agency and pick up sounds, bestowing life onto the domestic objects that surround them. In passages such as this one, it is difficult to tease out who is acting upon what, or where the hands' agency resides, as in this description of piano playing from a late, autobiographical short story:

> In no time I was plunging my hands into the mass of sound and shaping it as if I were molding warm clay. At moments I would draw it out, lengthening the tempo, trying to give the mass a different shape, until it started going cold, and then I worked faster and felt it warm up again. It was like being in a magician's den. I couldn't guess what substances the magician had combined to start the fire, but I followed his every inspiration.[16]

Shifts from artistic production to spectatorship to usership take place in the brief span of this passage. All three modes are superimposed through the hand. The process is simultaneous, or nearly so. The hand makes and receives seemingly in the same instant—thus, like the skin more broadly, it is the ideal organ for usership. Hands play and hands applaud, they labor and seek pleasure. Disembodied hands with pianos or pencils become seeking animals, attempting to decipher the world involuntarily. The mind has fingers that grope for experiences, but in order to perceive submerged experiences, these fingers need to "br[ea]k off from the mind that was guiding them and continu[e] the search on their own."[17]

Hernández's works are structured around these experiences, and as such seem to invite phenomenological approaches.[18] His autobiographical narrators—almost always unnamed and first person—are less coherent characters, with backgrounds and motives, than bundles of affects and sensations, intersubjective nodes. Tangled circuits, sensory cross-pollination, and subject-object mimesis abound, producing experiences at once pleasurable and perplexing. Viewer and image, user and apparatus, mutually constitute one another. The haptic, in particular, bridges multiple sensory experiences and leaves synesthetic effects in its wake: one can touch with the eyes and ears ("Except Julia") or taste tactile experiences such as fabrics ("The Stray Horse"). The gaze itself can become a kind of touch: "I stole a look at her gaze: she'd placed it on me, as if laying a hand on my shoulder" ("My First Concert").[19] He often experiments with the double meaning of the verb *tocar*: "to touch" and "to play" (as in an instrument), to brush up against and to riff.[20]

The word "haptic" was coined in the late nineteenth century; like the term "nostalgia," its Greek pedigree belies a modernist lineage. *Haptikos* means "able to come into contact with": the haptic thus implies proximity, contiguity. ("Contiguous" comes from the Latin word meaning "to touch.") It is the perception of the skin as surface of contact between the perceiving subject and the perceived object. In contrast, the proprioception that anchored the typist in the previous chapter "folds tactility into the body" and is therefore less invested in subject-object mimesis.[21] In the haptic, the perceiving hand—a privileged, although not exclusive, medium for the haptic—cedes its control over the objects it encounters.[22] But this is not a zero-sum game; paradoxically, the user gains something for himself in the process. In the process, the hand's peculiar agency recasts authorship as a receptive feelership.

Theoretical reflections on haptic visuality can be found in the early film theory of Eisenstein, Benjamin, and Kracauer. At the end of his "Work of Art" essay, for example, Benjamin emphasizes the tactile over the optical, reflecting his own interest in earlier, untimely film practices; Eisenstein was indebted to the circus and other spectacles that also demanded tactile engagement on the part of the viewer.[23]

These modernists are themselves untimely, for their theories are deeply indebted to cinema's pre-history, its origins in the circus, and other late nineteenth-century experiences of spectacle as well as the immersive experiences of panorama and the stereoscope. The haptic's resistance to fixed attention also pops up in more recent interpretations of various modes of early cinematic reception: the cinema of attractions over classical narrative, the glance over the gaze, and the privileging of distraction and bodily identification.[24] For theorists of the haptic, the sense often seems to act in meta-fashion, activating and productively contaminating the boundaries of other senses in its wake.

If the spectator crystallized in 1970s film theory was both captive and disembodied, Hernández's is a distracted and embodied user, oriented toward the haptic dimensions of silent film.[25] By "silent film" I refer to the entire apparatus, including those modes of attention, distraction, and narrative that would be transformed with the arrival of synchronized sound. In silent cinema and proto-cinematic spectacles, the competition between different sensory modes was central. These spectacles were performance based, punctuated by the pianist and lector who would accompany the projection of images with music, voice, and gesture. With more than a hint of nostalgia for the polyvalent and chaotic world of early filmgoing, Jacques Polet notes of early film sounds: "Their *heterogeneity*, but most of all their *plural-localization*, are remarkable—sound could issue from virtually everywhere, from beside the screen, behind it, below it, backstage, outside the theater."[26] Thus, while the gaze was being centered through the filmic image, the viewer's sense of sound and the orientation of his or her body presented multiple vectors. Through their emphasis on distraction and crisscrossed sensory networks, Hernández's texts similarly appear to channel this "topological swarming" of early filmgoing,[27] an experience with which he was deeply familiar. In the title story of his collection *No One Lit a Lamp*, for example, the narrator reads aloud to an audience as he registers all their manifold bodily responses; the content of his story takes a back seat to the detailed descriptions of postures, faces, tricks of light, rustles, murmurs, and displays of distraction.

While critics have frequently noted the influence of cinema on Hernández, their analyses have tended to be both analogical and visual, highlighting the formal techniques he borrowed from film, such as framed close-ups or detail shots.[28] In contrast, I am interested in his experiences with accompanying images, his "glossing" of them through improvisation, which is also a very particular, and active, mode of reception. His works are not (or not just) structured *like* a film but activate pointedly residual elements of cinema. Take his unpublished fragment "In the Cinema." The first-person narrator arrives late to a movie theater and is guided by an usher into the darkened space, thinking to himself, "He did not know that I used to play piano in movie theaters when I was young, and that I'd grown accustomed to watching the movie at the foot of the screen. . . . Along with sitting up front, I like to be alone and slightly to the left."[29] In addition to the lateral gaze—that intriguing "slightly to the left"—Hernández's narrator enjoys dwelling in the period of adjustment required by a belated arrival such as this one, when images initially refuse to cohere into narrative and in which they have to compete with other stimuli. Elsewhere, Hernández describes his "mania" for attending spectacles early, when "the spirit, without knowing it, works as it waits, works almost as if in a dream, letting things come, waiting for them and watching them with profound, childlike distraction . . . when you lose all common sense and dream a future that makes your scalp tingle."[30] The narrators of Hernández's short stories repeatedly emphasize the liminal stages of anticipation before a spectacle begins: the practices and sensations that we could call the paratexts of the spectacle. They mine the multiple time lags, thresholds, or hazy moments in reception where the visual fails, blurs, or deviates from its path to comingle with other senses, like the haptic in that tingling scalp.

In the process, authorship becomes feelership. Watching the images unfold on the screen, the narrator of "In the Cinema" begins to identify with a woman who appears in them, not in narrative terms but through corporeal sensation, lingering once he departs the theater: "I felt sympathy for her, I put myself a bit inside of her skin, imagining the brushing [*roce*] of her dress in the slowness of her steps." The narrator speaks not of an afterimage but an after-touch: "All the luxury and slow steps of that film remained in my blood and when I left the theater . . . I walked slowly and my skin prickled imagining that I brushed up against [*rozaba*] worlds of greatness" (233). The key verb here is *rozar*: to brush up against, to move close to, to trip up against, to scrape. *Rozar*, like *tocar*, invokes the reciprocity of the tactile. This is not a scene that can be folded into Laura Mulvey's understanding of narrative cinema and visual pleasure, in which a male viewer congeals fragments of a female body. We "see" nothing; the body of the starlet is not the object of the voyeur's gaze.[31] Instead, he describes a process of becoming one, rather than devouring or consuming her, a process that lingers after the film is over.

Running through both his minor and well-known texts is an emphasis on haptic perception precisely at the moment when the classic modernist film spectator was ostensibly being formed. If Hernández's works imply in this way an interactive user, however, it is not because he looks forward to new media but instead looks back to older forms. In other words, I want to resist the temptation to position Hernández as a prophet for interactive technologies that have become, in their own way, bureaucratized in our present moment. I say this not only because of the dangers of facilely equating oppositional readings with interactivity but also because of the historical telos that such a reading would imply. Residual media, after all, can leave their effects, traces, or echoes even when the technology itself is no longer present. Hernández's works thus nudge us back into the recesses of film history in order to explore occluded utopian dimensions of participation. They are not nostalgic, for there is no lament for a lost time; rather, his works operate on the oppositional edge that Raymond Williams identified as the residual's potential, the difference that separates it from both the archaic and the dominant.[32] Writing and silent film (spectatorship, accompaniment) thus function in tandem: functional equivalents, they are media that are just this shy of the contemporary.

"EXCEPT JULIA"

The historical avant-gardes had their own reflections on the sense of touch. In Marinetti's "Manifesto of Tactilism" (1921), the Futurist designs a taxonomy to account for the different sensations produced by haptic encounters with variegated objects—sandpaper, marabou, "peach fuzz," "spongy cloth," "wool from the Pyrenees." As he states, touch has been overlooked in the dominance of sight and sound. The solution lies in "training" to make the skin an organ as apt as any medium, transforming it from a "mediocre conductor" to a "continuous transmission" of thought.[33] This pedagogical emphasis shores up against the queerness of the textures in his manifesto; it subsumes the tactile into the purview of Marinetti's celebrated modernity. Tactilism's inauguration occurs near a street named after Amerigo Vespucci; like the explorer, the Futurist will encounter new worlds and bring them into his reign, managing the vulnerability inherent in feelership through a *machista* appropriation. While Hernández will echo Marinetti in his lingering on the skin as an organ of communication through an attention to texture, his approach privileges receptivity over virility.

Hernández's short story "Except Julia" offers a counterpoint to Marinetti's dream of touch training sessions. An unnamed, first-person narrator happens upon a childhood friend who invites him to participate in a very peculiar ritual: the touching of objects in a dark tunnel. The touch chamber requires a separation from daily life: the country house, "deep in the garden"; the mouth of the tunnel hidden in a closed shed (90). Pleasure requires a surrendering to the controlled circumstances that someone has set up: "In an hour it's [the tunnel] swallowed us up and digested us" (91). As the two men grope their way through this space, touching and guessing, their sense of sight is suspended. Ultimately, the inexplicable magic of the tunnel sessions ends with a visual interruption: an intrusive light that renders the touch sessions banally visible, interrupting the series.

The arbitrary and strictly codified rules of the tunnel game at first appear to aim at identification (*what is this object I'm touching?*), but the narrator soon gives himself over to pure sensation.[34] When the lights dim, the hands come out. With touch, the objects in the tunnel grow strange. Their identities cannot be made out without the intervening hand, and even then with difficulty: "I placed divining hands on a small square box with a round surface bulging out the top. I couldn't tell how hard the bulge was and I didn't dare stick my nail in it" (94). In turn, the hand itself is affected by this non-epistemological search—a defining feature of the haptic, which privileges texture over unified figure, grain over coherence. While the guessing game thus appears to aim at discerning, the story emphasizes the relishing of the tactile before the object is identified. Although the translation of the above passage reads "divining hands," the original connects the experience to an initiation (*me inicié*) rather than a revelation.[35]

In the tunnel's haptic chamber, there is reciprocity between objects and hands. Hands are at once emancipated from the body, pursuing their own experiences, and vulnerable to the experiences of the objects in the tunnel, especially their texture. We are reminded of Merleau-Ponty's analysis of the hand touching itself, a philosophical fable that illustrates the reciprocity of touch, demonstrating the limitations of the subject-object opposition in apprehending the haptic. The hand that touches itself occupies both opposing categories in a kind of pendulum of "touch" and "being touched."[36] In the repeated sessions in the tunnel, the hands pursue sensations that do not ostensibly interest the protagonist: touching glass, or trying on gloves.

The gloves have a special significance in the context of feelership, as they stand out from the other objects in the tunnel. They acquire their own agency: "I wondered what the gloves meant to my hands: the surprise, I decided, was for them, not for me" (100). They eventually reappear in his dreams, the afterimage or aftertouch of the haptic. When he encounters chicken flesh in the tunnel, for example, the narrator finds the discomfort of recognition, and his skin responds mimetically, becoming that which it is touching. (*Piel de gallina*, literally "chicken skin," means "goose bumps.") "I felt a smooth ridge, a grainy area, and bumps—or warts—on one side, near the edge of the box. It made my skin crawl and I drew my hands back" (94). Touch is thus related to abjection, a recoiling of the body and the hand as its instrument and interface, as in Walter Benjamin's aphoristic "Gloves": "The horror that stirs deep in man is an obscure awareness that in him something lives so akin to the animal that it might be recognized. All disgust is originally disgust at touching."[37] But touch in Hernández is also often a source of pleasure in becoming one with objects: "The next thing I touched felt like a mound of flour. I enjoyed sinking my hands in it" (94). The flour also allows for an ephemeral imprint, a momentary tracking or tracing that recalls the improvisational and temporary inscription of both writing and piano playing. Like the hands and skin more broadly, gloves throw into relief the subject-object, interior/exterior distinctions that the tunnel game both invites and troubles.[38]

In the process of exposing and yielding to the hand, everyday objects are transformed, albeit temporarily. In this sense, the haptic guessing games in "Except Julia" are a miniature of Hernández's work more broadly, of its strange interface between the everyday and the fantastic. Indeed, the objects in the tunnel, presumably cut off from the outside world, are none other than those of the friend's *bazar*, a term for a local shop in which various products, often domestic, are arranged rather haphazardly. The *bazar*'s nonhierarchical accumulation of objects reappears in the tunnel's space of profane illumination:[39] "a pumpkin rind, a mound of flour, a cage without a bird, some baby boots, a tomato, a lorgnette, a woman's stocking, a typewriter, an egg, a burner grate from a Primus stove, a football bladder, an open book, a pair of handcuffs, and a shoebox with a plucked chicken inside" (95–96). Here simple, heterogeneous objects achieve their power when they are removed from circulation in the store and reframed through combinations.

Significantly, however, this same process is also reversible: the objects can be taken out of circulation within the tunnel, have a tag stuck on them, and return to their original use value in the store or on the kitchen table. For dinner, they eat the chicken whose flesh he had groped in the tunnel—a sinister experience, given the reciprocity he had just experienced with the animal's skin in the chamber. In this way, the tunnel's subterranean experiences are mirrored, object by object, in the mundane space of everyday life that takes place aboveground, in the kitchen and at the shop. The last line of the story returns us full circle to the story's defamiliarizing opening, with the description of the friend as a tiny lamb's face: "I reached out to put a hand on his shoulder and inadvertently touched his curly head. It felt like one of the objects in the tunnel" (105).

Two circuits or feedback loops thus emerge in "Except Julia." The first connects, through a seemingly infinite circle until the story's end, the everyday world of petit-bourgeois consumption with the tunnel, whose siphoned-off space and ephemeral rituals recall that privileged avant-garde experience, the encounter.[40] The tunnel game might find itself in the surrealist archive, with its desire to re-enchant the experiences of everyday life—or, reduced to its rules and typed up, the conceptual art wing of a museum: "Take a raw chicken, a baby boot, and the guts of a squash. Place them in boxes. Have some young women in blind-folds hold the boxes in a tunnel. Have the participant guess the contents of the box."[41] The second circuit links the subject of reception and its object: the man in the tunnel becomes, through the narrator's observation of his haptic rituals, one and the same. In this sense, "Except Julia" is a story about temporary inversions, the mobilizing and rechanneling of mundane objects. The novelty derives not from the aleatory per se but from how the user encounters the objects, and the temporary magic of his touch. Such haptic rituals in Hernández's fictions, I would argue, emerge as the utopic other face of mass culture and commodity fetishism that they invoke. The tunnel delivers objects from their exchange value and turns only on the user's sensations to grant them meaning. These objects operate at once in both sites: the store (or petit-bourgeois capitalism) and the tunnel-chamber, an artistic "other space." Like other Felisbertian fictions, "Except Julia" asks us to keep this tension present, rather than resolving it. There is no flight outside of the repetitive rhythms of daily, capitalist life, only ephemeral rituals of suspensions, the user's temporarily giving himself over to the haptic experience.

"THE DAISY DOLLS": SHOWCASING THE HAPTIC

Hernández's most well-known work, "The Daisy Dolls" (*Las Hortensias*, 1949), also traces a shift from haptic visuality to haptic perception. The protagonist of this novella is unique in the context of his oeuvre, for he is quite wealthy and possesses a proper name; the story is also recounted in the third person, instead of Hernández's customary first-person narrator. Combined with its unusual length, "The Daisy Dolls" stands out in these respects. It also underscores a dimension only implicit in many of his other stories—the relationship between haptic perception, on one hand, and the twinned experience of cinema spectatorship and shopping, on the other. "The Daisy Dolls" is Hernández's most elaborated approach to the relationship among feelership, artistic creation, and the processes of massification and consumption that often run surreptitiously through many of his works.

Horacio lives off the profits of a lucrative family business. He is a more ostentatious version of the man in the tunnel in "Except Julia," spending his evenings indulging in an eccentric, all-consuming hobby. In his private home his servants stage enigmatic scenes in glass cases with dolls "a bit taller than real women" (175).[42] Rather than the guessing games of identification in "Julia," these scenes are based around narrative enigmas. Horacio must solve the riddle by creating a narrative to fill in the tableau of dolls and the objects that surround them: a bride who has poisoned herself; a woman who removes herself from the world to raise her child, fruit of an illicit relationship with a sailor. Once he has fashioned his narrative/guess, he opens a small drawer with a brief description that either confirms or negates his hypothesis.

Even more than the tunnel ritual, Horacio's sessions invite a comparison to silent film spectatorship.[43] The dolls wait to be chosen for scenes in the glass cases; various workers (caption writers, costume designers, doll makers) create the invisibilized labor of the spectacles. The captions in the drawers themselves recall silent film titles; a pianist accompanies the static scenes, his back to Horacio. The cases are three-dimensional versions of the two-dimensional screen and allude to cinema's pre-history in the shop window: "a tableau, framed and inaccessible, not behind glass, but on the screen."[44] In this site of attractions, spectator and spectacle appear abstracted from the rest of the world. As in "Except Julia," the action can only occur in a space ostensibly separated out from daily life that, for its part, recalls the cinematic apparatus: "the black house," or "house of dark patina," as it is called in the opening sentences (173), and the darkness of the showroom. Horacio prepares himself for these scenes by separating out his body and the time of day: "The dark room would divide the day's worries from the pleasures he expected of the night" (174); "he had to feel completely isolated before going in to see the dolls" (176). These conditions seem to replicate the position of the classic film spectator, who leaves his world behind in order to enter the immersive experience of the cinema house.

And yet, despite this setup, even this ostensibly sovereign spectator does not remain in a purely voyeuristic state. The novella instead charts his erosion. When it opens, Horacio has already begun the process of wanting to break the frame of these spectacles, to transform spectatorship into something more tactile. He opens up the cases, and not just the stipulated drawers, to walk among the scenes, ostensibly to have a closer look but also to touch the dolls. His desire to break the tableaus he himself has carefully ordered to be constructed increases. He decides to fill his beloved Daisy doll with hot water, bring her to bed, and begins to stage extra, unscripted scenes with her.

If in "Except Julia" the glove and hands suggested the user's vulnerable relinquishing to subject-object mimesis, here it is the dolls that provide the concrete embodiment of that desire. More than any other of Hernández's works, "The Daisy Dolls" conjures the ghost of Auguste Villiers de l'Isle-Adam's *The Future Eve* (1886), also an ancestor of many of the texts I analyze here. In this foundational work of science fiction and ur-example of womb envy, the promise of giving birth to new life through technology is routed through a woman's body.[45] Yet in stark contrast to their predecessors—machine-women animated with life by scientist demiurges—Horacio's daisy dolls are explicitly not fabricated by him.[46] In fact, the novella eschews metaphors of birth and origin. The dolls multiply and replicate themselves in spite of Horacio. Through the cinematic rituals, he is yoked into a circuit that grants him both pleasure and anxiety: "[He] had reached the conclusion that she was one of those changeable dolls who could transmit warnings or receive signals from other dolls" (184). His sole purpose is to wire himself—often clumsily—into this network.[47]

Increasingly, Horacio turns toward moments of subject-object mimesis that curtail his agency but also increase this "networked" state. He begins to believe that the dolls are able to return his gaze and that their skin is a source of sensation not only for him but for them. In a Hans Bellmer–like inspiration, he requests extra doll limbs for the creation of alternative scenes: "As he dropped off to sleep, Horacio felt himself sinking into a warm pond where all their legs tangled, like the roots of trees planted so close together he was too lazy to find out which ones belonged to him" (192).[48] As in this image of (literal) erotic entanglement in the marital bed, Daisy and the other dolls are often described as though their very plasticity endowed them with a slippery, flexible resistance. They are activated not by the forces of electricity and mechanics but by those of texture and the haptic. Their plasticity is multiple and also multidirectional, at once malleable and resistant. While the dolls' malleability indicates that anything can be projected onto them, they themselves seem capable of doing the same in return. "I'd also like her to be softer, nicer to touch, not so stiff," he tells his employee (186), who expresses concern that Daisy will become dented through the process of making her tactile. Horacio responds that he would not mind, for he wants to make a literal impression that would register a trace of his contact with her. While this impression appears on the one hand as a brand of his ownership, it also implies recognition that this ostensibly inanimate object might itself register the world through its ("her") skin. While recalling here the ephemeral flour imprint that appears in the tunnel game of "Except Julia," the doll ups the ante: her skin registers more, but she also marks him in return. This variant of authorship as a feelership means that Horacio will not remain unscathed—and "scathe" has its origin in the word "scar," underscoring the importance of skin—from his increasingly intense encounters with these objects.

In this sense, "The Daisy Dolls" is not so much a warning against the dangers of the immobile, omnipotent spectator in the age of mechanical reproduction but a staging of his impossibility. While the novella teases us to read it as an allegory of this anxiety, as with "Lovebird Furniture," to end here is to overlook the impact of usership on the protagonist's body that runs throughout the work like its own electrical current, or the crisscrossed wires that seem to brush against Horacio's skin and haunt his sense of a monadic self. The separation that Horacio so jealously guards heightens his bodily identification, and the use of dolls makes his experiences "more real."

While the first half of the novella focuses on Horacio's growing connection to one particular doll, Daisy, the second half spins away from this locus and toward the reception of the dolls in the semipublic space of the shop window. This shift in focalization should give us pause, as it is unusual in Hernández's work. With this movement, "The

Daisy Dolls" traces a process of massification and of marketing that extends Horacio's own haptic perception and underscores the relationship between filmgoing and modern consumption in their shared origin in the late nineteenth century.[49] As the novella migrates in the second half from his gaze to a mobile or roaming subjectivity that includes his wife, anonymous men, and girls who gaze into shop windows at their own dolls, this process is experienced in radically different fashion by all those who look by touching or touch by looking. The shift in focus coincides with the dolls' entry into the circuits of mass consumption; how they fulfill the fantasies of not just Horacio but every man and woman who encounter them in the store or in advertising leaflets that decorate the city. Zooming out from the privatized rituals of a sovereign spectator, the dolls' invitation to feelership is depicted in increasingly wider concentric circles or networks. The novella even suggests its transnational extension, for Horacio's employee begins to advertise his blonde dolls as originating with "a manufacturer in a northern country"—an allusion to the global dimension of the dolls' prestige (205).

"The Daisy Dolls" posits a feedback loop wherein consumption and the intervention of feelership cannot be neatly siphoned off from one another or depicted in causal terms. Just as the objects in the tunnel spoke to an earlier iteration in the bazaar in "Except Julia," the dolls are linked, both materially and formally, to sites of consumption. Beginning as store mannequins, reproduced in the private home, they end up as massified conduits of individual usership. Finally, Horacio becomes increasingly automaton-like: he ends up, like Daisy, a puppet who receives injections to become more human. The process of the spectator becoming a user has come full circle: Horacio has become the object he longed to couple with; the subject-object mimesis reaches its apex. Neither granter of life nor passive spectator, Horacio embodies the uneasy transformation into feelership that is no longer contained within the private chamber.

"THE USHER": HAPTIC VISUALITY AFTER SURREALISM

Hernández's narrators are so scopophilic that many critics have understandably focused on the visual dimension of his fiction. His works overflow with ocular metaphors, "a whole orgy and lechery of sight," a phrase from "Around the Time of Clemente Colling" (29), along with scenes of peepholes and other images of voyeurism. Frank Graziano borrows the phrase "the lust of seeing" (*la lujuria de ver*) for the title of the only English-language monograph devoted to Hernández from the short story "The Usher" (El acomodador, 1946). The narrator employs this "craving to see" to describe his desire to possess objects through a mysterious light emanating from his own eyes.[50] However, even in "The Usher"—arguably the most voyeuristic of Hernández's stories—the haptic is central. Here it also serves to interrupt and reroute an ocular regime. In contrast to the rituals of "Except Julia" and "The Daisy Dolls," however, this user is explicitly connected to cinema through his subaltern status. He is able to momentarily invert the producer/spectator opposition of cinema through recourse to a fantastic haptic visuality.

"The Usher" invokes a topos of Latin American literature: the impoverished immigrant writer or "anti-flâneur" adrift in a city that resembles Paris, an experience Hernández knew all too well, and one he shared with fellow modernist travelers.[51] A brief excursus into his relationship with Paris and with French surrealism will clarify what is at stake in the setting of this story, one of the only times when a large cosmopolitan city makes an appearance in Hernández's work. Surrealism represents his most sustained, albeit ambivalent, engagement with the avant-gardes. South America has a lengthy relationship to surrealism in both its literary and painterly iterations (less so its cinematic variants); South Americans often consider their own the surrealists' elected origin, *Les Chants de Maldoror* (1869) by the Comte de Lautréamont, aka Isidore Ducasse, born in Hernández's Montevideo. While Latin American writers have disputed surrealism's origins and at times laid claim to them—echoing in this way Breton's own assertion that in Mexico he found the "real" surrealism—there is an equally powerful thread of writing from the region that rejected what was seen as the movement's colonial gestures, its mining of the continent as well as Africa and Oceania for treasures to reinvigorate a moribund European culture.[52]

Hernández's own experiences with surrealism relate more to the problems of literal and symbolic capital than to national patrimony or its appropriation. In 1946, he traveled to Paris at the encouragement of the Franco-Uruguayan surrealist Jules Supervielle and lived in the Latin Quarter, only to fail at making an artistic mark, as his letters home reveal. One exception to this failure would be his connection with Roger Caillois, whose intervention eventually led to his publication in Buenos Aires, as well as the support he received from Susana Soca, an Uruguayan poet and founder of the surrealist journal *La Licorne* (1947–48), along with an invitation by Supervielle to present at the PEN Club.[53] Hernández returned home to Montevideo in the late 1940s, deeply disappointed. It was then that he took his first job programming radio slots and, while he continued to write, his most intense period lay behind him; he would die without becoming particularly well-known or financially solvent, only to resurface in the 1960s and later as a cult figure in and beyond Latin America.

Hernández's stories certainly contain elements that we can link to this uneasy traffic with surrealism: a privileging of the quotidian, an erosion of the subject as a coherent entity, and an interest in dreamscapes and in the *démodé*, the outmoded or even kitschy, understood not merely as an attribute of objects but also in terms of practices.[54] Yet in "The Usher," Paris, the surrealist site of secret corners and improbable connections—of sphinxes, sirens, and bohemians, of Breton's *Nadja* (1928) and Aragon's *Paris Peasant* (1926)—has been stripped of its patina. Aesthetic experience is forged within and through these experiences of poverty, and in this sense he approximates Olivari's unnamed narrator in "Starstruck," the melancholic tenement-dweller who mobilizes the scraps of others' dream factories.[55] Immersed in the afterlives of surrealism, Hernández, along with his protagonists, finds no sublimation, no implicit celebration of tenement life like that found in Breton's *Nadja*. (In "The Usher," for example, the narrator goes to sleep each night with the sound of a butcher sawing soup bones, an image at once terrifying and mundane.) Hernández's take is neither Bretonian, with its affirmative charge of liberation, nor Bataillean, with its privileging of transgression through the abject. (I would liken him to a subaltern Magritte.) Even more than Caillois, the early champion of his work, he resides on surrealism's outermost edge.[56]

"The Usher" thematizes this disappointment and even *ressentiment* in surrealism's promises for the Latin American subaltern and reroutes them toward the problem of haptic usership. The (once again unnamed first-person) narrator works as an usher in a movie theater. One night, after his economic situation has become especially precarious, he discovers he has the power to see in the dark. This power at first seems a kind of afterimage, a side effect of his job. The light is an interiorized appendage: it clearly recalls the flashlight, his usher's tool of the trade, but also a camera eye, framing the world around him. Sinister but strangely empowering, it allows his "lust of seeing" to roam. In many ways, we could see the strangely debilitating power of his light as a banalization of the surrealists' profane illuminations.

A similar phenomenon occurs with respect to the narrator's relationship to the cinema, whose role here is more explicit than in either "Except Julia" or "The Daisy Dolls." No longer a source of magic otherworldliness, it has become bureaucratized, part of the meager sustenance the narrator receives in exchange for his labor. As an usher, the narrator is merely an ornamental conduit for the spectatorship of others who refuse to acknowledge his presence. Yet, as in "Lovebird Furniture," this sense of powerlessness does not produce merely pessimism. Instead, it spurs on his desire to (modestly) cannibalize the technology's possibilities. "The Usher" charts a possession made possible with and through the narrator's precariousness. When he gains his own interior light, he momentarily "ushers" things into being with the haptic gaze.

In many respects, the protagonist's interior light seems to literalize the phenomenon that Jean Epstein, working from Louis Delluc, described in his 1923 lecture, "On Certain Characteristics of *Photogénie*." In one of multiple attempts at defining the medium's specificity, Epstein wonders if cinema constitutes "an extension of our sense of sight, a sort of telepathy of the eye."[57] Epstein's gesture will be reflected in avant-garde writers throughout the 1920s, who celebrated the medium's potential to see the world anew, to endow objects with life. Epstein calls this cinema's animism: "Through the cinema, a revolver in a drawer, a broken bottle on the ground, an eye isolated by an iris, are elevated to the status of characters in the drama. Being dramatic, they seem alive, as though involved in the evolution of emotion" (54). Cinema grants life to objects, fashioning a new reality.

Hernández's work flirts with the medium specificity central to *photogénie* in particular, as well as the idea of animating objects that links Epstein to the surrealists despite their differences. Yet his emphasis lies elsewhere: not the medium of cinema, personified in "On Certain Characteristics of *Photogénie*," or the power of the director, clearly important for Epstein the filmmaker. Instead, it is uniquely the spectator, refashioned as a user, who confers life to objects. The focalization we find in "The Usher" underscores how his gaze activates the medium's potential. The narrator begins this power to animate by scanning his bare apartment with its few humble objects, transforming it into a private screening room. He will go on to practice his special power outside of his own flat and in other, more luxurious spaces. In these ritualized possessions of objects, the narrator's gaze lingers on texture: filigree, "a tortoise-shell binding with a streaked surface like burnt sugar" (77). In such descriptions, "the eyes themselves function like organs of touch." Per Marks, "Haptic looking tends to rest on the surface of its object rather than to plunge into depth, not to distinguish form so much as to discern texture. It is a labile, plastic sort of look, more inclined to move than to focus."[58] As in "Except Julia," the narrator privileges texture over identity and here his flashlight-like gaze (rather than his hands) also allows him to encounter objects without mastering them.

Eventually, as always in Hernández, these episodes are interrupted by unforeseen events. The narrator's light will lead him to a seductive, sleepwalking woman. He then initiates what he refers to as the "sessions," in which he lies prone while she walks toward him. These sessions recall the liminal space between dreaming and waking—he is prone, she walks without acknowledging him—that has long characterized the cinema. As the story progresses, the haptic continually encroaches upon the scopic: the sleepwalking woman physically intrudes on his body, stepping on him, first his knees ("which shuddered and parted"), then his stomach and throat. This contact produces a startling skin-to-skin encounter that implicates his entire body, radiating beyond the locus of contemplation and running like currents through different nodal points: "Spasms started in my temples and immediately became sleepy rivers running down my cheeks, then these same spasms wrapped round my head like a turban. Finally, the sensation climbed down my legs and formed a knot at my knees."[59] Haptic visuality cedes to haptic perception. As in the narrator's tingling scalp in "In the Cinema," the crossed wires in "The Daisy Dolls," or the hand-glove of "Except Julia," an exterior object infects and implicates the body's boundaries and sense of itself. The body becomes a live wire of sensation that migrates and implicates spaces far beyond the gaze or even the hands.

Later, as the narrator is racing through the Parisian streets in search of this woman, the optical spell experiences a final interruption. Desperate for the mysterious woman's attention, he tosses a hat at her, making direct contact with her body and definitively eliminating the fourth wall of the voyeuristic regime. The desire to cannibalize cinematic technology literalized in his gaze cannot be maintained in the ocular but spreads out from that nucleus. Thus, while critics have read

"The Usher" as a metaphor of writing itself,[60] we must ask then why writing feels the need to assert itself through practices of spectatorship and usership. For the narrator of "The Usher," "Everything happened just as before . . . and yet each night had been different" (79). This phrase applies equally to the shop windows and showcases of "The Daisy Dolls," the haptic chambers of "Except Julia," and many other examples from Hernández's corpus. Via haptic interruption, repetition breeds variation, seriality fosters its ostensible opposite, the tangential, itinerant, or interruptive. Feelership names the process by which the author, through his narrator, privileges experiences that transform the knowing I or the productive hand into agents of receptivity of literature's mediatic others, even or precisely at the moment when these seem bureaucratized.

Like many of the authors in this study, Hernández began his career in dialogue with the historical avant-gardes. His earliest writings approach the modern city with enthusiasm, as in the brief sketch "Things to Read on the Streetcar" (Cosas para leer en el tranvía).[61] Yet in his later and most influential works this enthusiasm is conspicuously absent. Despite some attempts to label him through familiar categories like surrealism, fantastic literature, or the avant-gardes, most careful readers of Hernández instead seek out unique and paradoxical formulations such as "a one-man avant-garde" (a phrase that recalls the attribution to Graciliano Ramos of a "modernist of ill-will").[62] These kinds of descriptions signal the difficulty of accounting for what happens to experimentation in the wake of the avant-gardes, when their collective and celebratory projects give way to the disenchanted experimentation of late modernism.

As Hernández moved away from the historical avant-gardes, traces of his interest in them linger: the revisionist approach to surrealism, or the return to cinema's origins as a way of defamiliarizing its consolidation. In "Around the Time of Clemente Colling," "the new" is deemed a "sales pitch"[63]—as it was for Hernández himself, drawn into the increasingly repetitive rhythms of capitalism through advertising, cinema, and the radio, the perceived failure of novelty unhinged from capitalism, its unfulfilled promises and aura. Yet this same frustration also allowed the older medium of silent film to become subtly defamiliarized and, more broadly, for experiences of momentary agency that would occur in and through processes of massification, consumption, and automatization.

We could certainly parse Hernández's remediation of silent film as an allegory of uneven technological development, of Latin America's hybrid modernity. This argument would follow a familiar line of scholarship on its "underdevelopment": earlier modes persist alongside what is seen as contemporary in the centers of global capital, a definitive feature of the continent's modernity. Yet insisting on the belatedness in Hernández's fiction as a symptom of a more generalized regional belatedness occludes an important dimension of his writing. His interest in newly obsolete practices and media instead pushes us to consider how the afterimage of a technology is incorporated, becoming something other than what it was intended to be. In Hernández's late modernist laboratories, teleological histories of both modernist literature and modern media, focusing on the "almost-but-not quite" modernity of the region, come up short. Reading with him, we are pushed to bracket the causality implicit even in recent appeals to globalize modernism, often undergirded by implicitly developmental or diffusionist accounts (for example, the requirement for a certain relationship to capitalism or the state for modernism to flourish).

Hernández's non-narrative and interruptive texts, with their crisscrossed haptic circuits, require another critical approach. We have seen how both haptic perception and haptic visuality mark the experience of authorship as feelership in his texts. A third haptic dimension, I would argue, also comes into play when we read Hernández: that of haptic criticism. This approach demands a close and even loving attention to the surface and materiality of texts. It is "mimetic: it presses up to the object and takes its shape. Mimesis is a form of representation based on getting close enough to the other thing to become it."[64] Like the skin that finds itself becoming one with the chicken flesh it encounters in "Except Julia," the reader of Hernández seems impelled to mimetize his work, to be willing to bracket mastery and distance when we immerse ourselves in his strange, banal worlds, worlds both iterative and eruptive. In this sense, Hernández's protagonists—even or perhaps especially his foolish bourgeois king, Horacio—are themselves unlikely models for approaching objects that productively contaminate the objectivity of the critical intervention.

Haptic criticism shares with other contemporary turns toward both surface reading and an "ethics of making" a desire to question the hermeneutics of suspicion and, in turn, the critic as an ideological unmasker. In its place, they posit receptivity toward the erotic dimensions of textual production. Perhaps for this reason one of the most compelling approaches to Hernández's works can be found in the hands of other artists. In the films of the retromodernist filmmakers the Quay Brothers, Hernández's intense half-lives are rendered visible, audible, and tactile.[65] His labors of the hand, activating immersive experiences of feelership, are manifested in their residual worlds. Populated by silent film practices and haptic perception, by objects like nineteenth-century toys animated in their obsolescence, the Quays' films pay homage to Hernández's ethos of interruption by dwelling in the distance opened up between the promises of the past and the bureaucratized present, in which cinema itself has now become a late medium.

CHAPTER 5

Imaginary Media

Usership and the World's Networks

A solitary man cannot create machines or capture visions, except in the truncated form of writing or drawing them for others, more fortunate than he.
—Adolfo Bioy Casares, *The Invention of Morel*

Imaginary media—sketches, drafts, or conjectures of media that might be or might-have-been—appear with surprising frequency in modernist texts from South America. In one well-known example, Horacio Quiroga's short story "The Vampire" (Argentina, 1927), a device transforms the two-dimensional image of a Hollywood starlet into a presence who haunts her inventor in Buenos Aires. Similarly, in Clemente Palma's science fiction novel *XYZ* (Peru, 1934), a scientist converts a desert island into a testing ground for transforming his favorite Hollywood stars into flesh-and-blood women. In these elaborate but ultimately pessimistic fantasies (the outcome in each case is fatal), eccentric inventors dream up new technologies that appropriate and expand upon an extant mass culture apparatus. Their imaginary media attempt "symbolic victories," rerouting and privatizing mass experiences of listening, viewing, and feeling, and eliminating the material boundaries that separate Hollywood from Latin America, and producers from consumers.[1]

The study of imaginary media is an eccentric subset of the antidiscipline of media archaeology, which seeks to trouble the narrative and developmental focus of media history.[2] Imaginary media reveal in pronounced ways the frustrated desires, utopian possibilities, and anxieties surrounding actual (or "realized") media as modes of connection. Janus-faced, they posit counterfactuals (*what if a medium had developed an alternate trajectory?*). If media often house within them the promise to traverse spatial-temporal boundaries, or to eliminate the distance between self and other, their imaginary counterparts underscore these utopic dimensions, while at the same time pointing to the sociohistorical, political, and economic conditions that act as their limits.[3] As such, they are ideal sites to conclude this study of authorship's transformation under late modernism, when the perceived technical bureaucratization of formerly new media prompted a different approach to their potential. Late modernist imaginary media are responses to increasingly pronounced asymmetries in the production, circulation, and theorization of actual media on a worldwide scale, asymmetries that located the United States at the center and Latin America on the outskirts.[4] In fact, imaginary media become more prevalent as emergent technologies give way to dominant ones, and as media's democratizing potential appears to recede or evaporate.

This chapter explores three prominent examples of imaginary media, Adolfo Bioy Casares's novella *The Invention of Morel* (*La invención de Morel*, 1940) and Jorge Luis Borges's stories "Funes, the Memorious" (Funes, el memorioso, 1942) and "The Aleph" (El Aleph, 1945). Like Felisberto Hernández, Borges and Bioy are interested in usership, but where Hernández's works posited feelership activated by the residual experiences of silent film, they focus on writing itself. Their fictional works stage a repeated encounter, a fable of usership: in each, a rather infelicitous writer comes across a fantastic medium whose capaciousness enthralls him. Ultimately, he is able to rechannel the medium's all-consuming scope through commentaries, notations, and partial interventions. On one hand, an imaginary medium, invented by a demiurge, with a metaphorical, subsuming thrust; on the other, writing, metonymical and partial, an ostensibly demoted and out-of-fashion medium running alongside the other, commenting on it, mocking it, fragmenting it: in this way, writing obliquely intervenes into what Vilém Flusser would call "the universe of technical images."[5]

THE BLACK BOX AND THE USER

Bioy Casares's *The Invention of Morel* recasts the desert island topos that runs through two genres that fascinated him as well as Borges, the adventure tale and science fiction. The novel depicts a parodic, pathetic version of Robinson Crusoe, who mastered space and time on the barbaric blank page of the desert island, and especially the eponymous scientist of H. G.

Wells's *The Island of Dr. Moreau*, who multiplied life through sinister experiments. Throughout, we find tropes from the anonymous pulpy paperbacks that spoke of "exotic" lands (such as South America) that began to be published in mass in Argentina during Bioy's adolescence.

To these source texts *The Invention of Morel* adds a new dimension, that of modern media.[6] The narrator is an unnamed Venezuelan criminal who flees the law and finds himself on an island in the Pacific. At first, he believes the island to be deserted and considers himself a solitary castaway. But soon after his arrival, he encounters the figures he calls "the others." After many frustrated attempts at making contact with these enigmatic people, he gradually comes to understand that they are simulacra in a machine produced by the title character. Morel has captured and archived their movements in order to preserve his love for the beautiful Faustine (whose name evokes the modern fantasies of Goethe's *Faust*); the human originals who visited the island have perished, and the gestures he had recorded now persist in an eternal return of a single week. Throughout, the narrator struggles to understand the strange habits of Faustine and Morel. His struggles are recorded, Crusoe-like, in the diary that gives the novella its form. The figure of the diary is a constant presence in the novella, inseparable from the events that unfold. I will return to it and other figures of writing in the novella shortly; for now, I will focus on the narrator-writer's shifting relationship to the imaginary medium.

Morel's invention is an all-encompassing machine. It combines several features of preexisting communications technologies into a device that subsumes and trumps them all. It receives, records, and stores life in all of its sensory particulars, not merely those of hearing (as in phonography) or seeing (as in photography) but extending into the realms of touch, taste, and smell. At the same time, it transmits and projects this data, animating it outside of the apparatus. Recalling the imaginary media of both Palma and Quiroga, Morel's invention thus converts shadowy projections into multidimensional, "living" objects. As he explains it, his goal was to eradicate any distance between an image and its original. He sought to "counteract absences" (*contrarrestar ausencias*): to eliminate death, distance, and other forms of separation from his love object.[7] He pursued an immediacy (the abolishing of mediation) that would put an end to the need for "screens or pages" (59), cinema and literature's supports.[8]

As readers we encounter this imaginary medium along with the narrator, from the outside looking in. In the course of the novella, he moves through different stages as he stumbles toward an understanding: from initial puzzlement, to semi-enlightenment, to participation in and cannibalization of the technology. In the process, he embarks on a series of inquiries: into the people whom he encounters (*who/what are they*?); into Morel's machine (*how does it work*?); and into his relationship to the machine (*what does it mean to me*?). These inquiries are often transmitted in his diary through lists of possible explanations, making us privy to a constant process of trial and error, of narratives picked up and discarded. In the process, each of these stages also reveals itself as a transformation in his own agency, drawing him closer to usership.

At first, he is a spectator to the others, whom he believes to be real. The opening pages of the novella underscore his passive position through the repetition of the verb *mirar* (to watch). In stark opposition to Crusoe, his initial position is non-agentic; the "others" tower above him, a "race of giants," victors in what he sees as a "dangerous game" of watching (4, 3; my translation.) Even as their lack of response to his attempts at communication humiliates and frustrates him, he is fascinated. Upon discovering the existence of Morel's invention and thus the identity of the others, the narrator's initial exasperation at being unacknowledged morphs into a different kind of frustration, one directed at the imaginary medium. At first, it too stubbornly resists the intervention of his gaze. It is "hermetic," like the sealed scientific or alchemical device of the word's etymology, a closed-off chamber that prohibits entry, comprised of "secret machines."[9] Its opacity is underscored by the novella's striking and frequent descriptions of trompe l'oeil architectures that serve as obstacles to unraveling the device's enigma. Unlocked doors remain shut to him, mirrors duplicate and falsify originals, aquariums are embedded in floors, immobile curtains can't be drawn back, keyholes peep only at blank walls, chambers appear in which distinctions between inner and outer are confounded. At one point, the narrator perforates a wall in a chamber and enters a porcelain blue cavern that mimics the open sky. But when he glances at the hole he has made, he encounters only the wall that Morel has built against intruders. As he struggles to break off chunks of it, the wall renews itself under his desperate gaze.

Scholars have often read these descriptions as signs of the novella's self-reflexivity, rendering literature a fun house of mirrors. Yet I would argue that these trickster architectural motifs do not point to writing as a closed chamber, tautologically insisting upon itself, and that it would be a mistake to equate Bioy's writing with Morel's invention. The latter loops back on itself in a hermetically sealed, autoerotic circuit; a device of perpetual repetition, its functioning depends upon its divorce from the world. Morel's device is a bachelor machine, a subset of imaginary media that "transform[s] love into a technique of death," joining other prominent modernist examples, including Duchamp's "The Bride Stripped Bare by Her Bachelors, Even" (1915–23), Kafka's "In the Penal Colony" (1919), and Raymond Roussel's *Locus Solus* (1914). (Roussel's novel likely influenced Bioy.)[10]

The bachelor machine also makes a brief appearance in Oswald de Andrade's *Seraphim Grosse Point*, the novel that acts as a swan song for the Brazilian avant-gardes (introduction). Like Morel's invention, this imaginary medium plays with the notion of a machine that is "more than" extant media:

> It works like a phonograph, also like a radio! And like virile Paris . . . Professor Freud, from Vienna, ordered seven dozen! It runs on dry cells. In cars, in buses, on airplanes, in the water closet! Resolves irresoluteness! Strikes lack of will at its root! Entertains, rejuvenates, enlivens!

The protagonist of *Seraphim* purchases the medium on a trip to France, "unwraps the machine, connects the wires, pulls out the antennas, replaces the fuses. Next, in its slot he puts in his name, age, sex, and an Indian-head penny. Finally, he listens like an electric lamp. There ensues a confusion of logarithms and hisses, a bellowing of Klaxons and various peepholes" (59). The Klaxon, metonymy of avant-garde production in Brazil, is here mobilized as part of a Rube Goldberg machine of spectatorship and desire for the age of modern media: bells and whistles, wires and antennae, are displayed, however, parodically yet proudly. Almost immediately after receiving its erotic transmission, the narrator "stops the immoral machine" and returns to his ludic experiments in the outside world. The imaginary medium is described in euphoric detail only to be set aside in favor of the avant-garde's privileged art-life sublation. It can be taken up or discarded at will. After this brief anecdote, the protagonist goes off in search of immediate (unmediated) pleasure in the bodies of live women, unscathed after this episode of hypermodernity.

No such freedom—no such immediacy—exists for the narrator of Bioy's novella. Instead he struggles, by means of his diary and a series of failed experiments, to understand the nightmarish capaciousness of the invention. Like many bachelor machines, Morel's is also a black box. Its opacity captivates the user even as it occludes his intervention, even as his participation is foreclosed through the hermeticism of the technology.[11] The black box spatializes—renders visible—the process by which technical operations are removed from the user's grasp. (In a scene from Danny Boyle's recent film *Steve Jobs* [2015], the eponymous character takes the decisive step to eliminate the user's ability to tinker with the personal computer he is developing, signaling the medium's domestication.) In this sense, the black box, like a blind spot, encloses operations that remain opaque to their users precisely because they have succeeded. Per Latour, "paradoxically, the more science and technology succeed, the more opaque and obscure they become."[12] The black box thus also speaks to the processes of automatization and consolidation of technologies: the repressed dimensions of miscalculations, occlusions, and counterfactuals that all technologies house within them, the histories and alternate histories of their production.

For Latour, the process of blackboxing is interrupted when a crack is discovered in the apparatus, revealing the clusters of actants (both human and nonhuman) that undergird the system. In the last part of *The Invention of Morel*, the narrator finally manages to activate the cracks in Morel's blackboxed medium. He opens up and reveals its multiple components, its history of failed experiments, the frustrated desires that lie at its origins. The pivotal moment comes when he disconnects the imaginary medium. This act is significant, for if the on switch embodies the demiurgic power of the inventor—a machine powers up and a new world emerges—the narrator's "powering down" draws our attention to a different kind of actor. While Morel resembles life-granting inventors like Thomas Edison and Nikola Tesla, fathers of electric modernity, the narrator's activity is precisely the opposite: tactical, a ruse of the weak.[13] Lacking the support of those "industrial magnates" who allowed Morel access to the resources that fueled his experiments (58), he likewise lacks his own space for experimenting. Instead, his laboratory lies in the temporary gaps opened up within the other's space, and in his own vulnerable body.

The narrator's ruse or tactic produces a new figure, the user. Up until he touches the off-switch, he has experienced what he describes as "un desdoblamiento en actor y espectador" (a splitting into actor and spectator) (89). It is when the spectator powers down and begins to insert himself into Morel's device that the two figures are superimposed. Entering Morel's invention at the novella's end, he violates the bachelor machine's closed circuit. By stitching himself into the archive of that eternal week, he recuts his own movie; he temporarily misappropriates the machine's intent, "splicing" himself into someone else's creation.[14] Now the other's novum must accommodate his experiences. In the last phase of this continuum from spectatorship to usership, the narrator begins to dream his own dreams, contributing to the invention's altered afterlife.[15]

The narrator's changing relationship to Morel and his black box provides us with a map of approaches for users who encounter all-encompassing media. A spectator approaches the distancing and obfuscating tendency of a medium. The opacity of this medium elicits two contradictory phenomena: on one hand, frustration and humiliation; on the other, a provocation to tinker, elaborate, splice. The narrator is drawn to its black box as an enigma and provocation. Not content to merely describe this bachelor machine, he "activates" it by first observing and then revealing its constitutive elements; in the process, he is also activated by cracks in the imaginary medium's hermeticism. As I explore further below, this form of usership operates via a far-from-novel medium: that of writing.

MEDIA, PARTIAL AND ABSOLUTE

The act of writing is foregrounded throughout *The Invention of Morel*, as it will be in Borges's "Funes, the Memorious" and "The Aleph." The unnamed narrators of both "Funes" and *Morel* describe their texts as *testimonios*—the genre of witnessing, central to Latin American literature beginning with the sixteenth-century *relación* and continuing to the present; "The Aleph" is similarly structured as an eyewitness account of a marvel. Yet all three narrator-writers are fumbling, unsuccessful, and even bathetic in their attempts at either mastery or seamless transmission. Their writers are users not because they exhibit the "firm hand" of the *letrado* but precisely because they see writing as a partial intervention, even a necessary failure.

In *The Invention of Morel*, the moment in which the narrator grafts his own presence onto the other's medium is only the last of many instances of writing that appear throughout the novella. (I read this "splicing" as a form of writing, one that is not generative but rather metonymic and minor.) Before entering into the machine, the narrator is a veritable storehouse of inscriptions, nearly all of which miss the mark of the experience or explanation he is attempting to pin down:

"Writing helps me control myself" (91); "Perhaps writing down my idea will make it lose its force" (93). If Morel's machine abolishes the distance between things and their representation, the narrator's writing exacerbates differences, relinquishing all claims to immediacy. In the epigraph that opens this chapter, he laments that, unlike Morel, he cannot "create machines or capture visions, except in the truncated form of writing or drawing." Like the protagonist of Virgilio Piñera's "The Dummy" (Chapter 2), "if he consents to write, it is precisely because he has been unable to design the device" (79). Truncated, mutilated, or incomplete: this is writing's function in the desert island media ecology that Morel has founded and into which the narrator is cast.

The diary, after all, tracks the evidence of time's passing, precisely that which Morel's machine is designed to interrupt and abolish. As though pointing back to the origins of writing—per Flusser, it has its origins in tracks and traces: *graph* means to dig; *scriber* to scratch[16]—the narrator makes gashes in a tree to record the passing of days, just as he will later attempt to make gashes in Morel's wall, in an effort to inscribe his presence onto its smooth, endlessly renewable blue surface. A similar confrontation between writing and Morel's machine comes to the fore in the episode of the flowers. The narrator, still unaware that Faustine is a projection, attempts to express his love by creating a message, via caption and words, using the island's raw materials, its vegetation. As the tropical fecundity asserts its power, his sentimental attempt to shatter her silence withers and decays. Meanwhile, Morel's machine plugs along in its hermetic repetition. Writing—whether in dying flowers, impermanent gashes, or the slippages foregrounded in his omnipresent diary—is repeatedly depicted as fragmentary and precarious.

It is worth pointing out that this depiction of writing is not inevitable. Robert Brown's imaginary medium, "The Readies" (United States, 1930–31), for example, has recently attracted attention from scholars seeking to understand the status of print culture and of writing more broadly in our digital present. Brown imagined a machine that would transform typewritten letters into an experience that paralleled moviegoing. Print would be animated in front of the reader's eyes, transforming reading into a mobile, dynamic experience. "The Readies" situates writing in healthy competition with the ever-denser presence of aural and visual media during the interwar period.[17]

In contrast to Brown's sanguine vision, Bioy and Borges position writing as a "truncated" response to all-encompassing imaginary media. In "Funes, the Memorious" and "The Aleph," Borges divests from the novum to query writing's residual potential. Like the protagonist of *Morel*, the narrators of both of these stories are writers who observe, rather than create, hyperbolically capacious media. The Aleph is a world picture that displays the entire universe in a small sphere, a miniature in which everything in space and time coexists, where "all the places in the world are found, seen from every angle."[18] It renders visible everything on the planet with crystalline detail. In this miniature prison house, nothing can be new or exterior: "In that gigantic instant I saw millions of delightful and atrocious acts; none astonished me more than the fact that all of them together occupied the same point" (150). In a gesture typical of late modernist exhaustion, after witnessing the Aleph, the narrator, here named "Borges," fears nothing will ever be new to him again.

The Aleph shares several key features with Morel's invention. Both texts are named for imaginary figures of absolute storage and transmission. The Aleph staunches the flow of loss and the passing time: a constant preoccupation in Borges's work.[19] It is also a black box and a bachelor machine. As in Bioy's novella, moreover, encountering the Aleph inspires in the narrator an admixture of humiliation and fascination. He, too, approaches the imaginary medium in a position of spectatorship that emphasizes his passivity: in order to access its paradoxical plenitude, he must remain lying down, immobile and in darkness, staring into a fixed point in space (665). In a near caricature of the spectator as theorized in classical film theory—and in contrast to Hernández's haptic chambers—the narrator enters into the voluntary imprisonment of the peephole. A lack of bodily agency is the price for immersion in its universe.[20] In the course of the story, this spectatorship will also be transformed, via writing, into a kind of usership.

"Funes, the Memorious" also recounts a brief encounter between a writer and an Aleph-like medium (who happens to be a person) whose boundlessness elicits both awe and fear. The unnamed first-person narrator begins by describing the eponymous character, whom he meets as an adolescent, for the purposes of a volume being written on him. Funes—less a man than a medium—perceives the world around him with a level of detail unavailable to the rest of humanity. This "chronometer" (109) records all minutiae and contingencies, "the solitary and lucid spectator of a multiform world which was instantaneously and almost intolerably exact" (114). Funes thus exhibits perception that resembles various storage media. His memory recalls the stop-motion photography and chronophotography of cinema's pre-history (Eadweard Muybridge and Étienne-Jules Marey), for example, breaking down what is perceived as flux into innumerable parts: "the tempestuous mane of a stallion, a herd of cattle in a pass, the changing flame and the innumerable ash, the many faces of a dead man during a long wake."[21] This memory is exhaustive, and exhausting.[22]

On one hand, his strange gift grants Funes superhuman powers that anticipate modern media's orientation to register and archive the world in all its detail. (The story is pointedly set in the 1880s: "In those days neither the cinema nor phonograph yet existed" [132].) Yet even as he clings proudly to his strange ability, it also traps him. At once a fantastic medium and an impotent witness to his own freakishness, Funes is enthralled, literally paralyzed by his own condition. He describes his mind as a *vaciadero de basuras*—a garbage dump, an abundance of detail paradoxically resulting in a wasteland.[23] He lacks access to the specific images that would punctuate this ceaseless storage. In this sense, his mind-medium functions in ways that also recall the preoccupation of cinema since its origins: "If everything is recordable, nothing matters except the act of recording itself."[24] Thus, although critics have linked Funes's experiences to literary realism (a favorite target of Borges's), this reading overlooks the stark contrast between the unnamed narrator-writer and the subsuming qualities of Funes's brain.[25] Like the reading of *The Invention of Morel* as a bachelor machine of literature, the interpretation of Funes as an allegory for literary realism fails to satisfy, as it encloses writing in its own hermetic circle, whereas Bioy and Borges open it up in confrontation, exploring its strengths and limitations vis-à-vis its others. Even realism can only dream of the capaciousness of this imaginary medium.

Rather than intervene directly in the apparatus, as Bioy's narrator does with his splicing at the end of *The Invention of Morel*, Borges's writer-users remain exterior to the imaginary media, deflating their pretentions through contrast, juxtaposition, and metonymy. The similarity in the language employed to describe the encounters with the Aleph and Funes, and to translate them into writing, is striking. Each writer-narrator must first pass through darkness before bearing witness, as though clearing his mind for a spectacle of unfathomable proportions. This space-clearing gesture underscores the dilemma with which both are burdened: how does one medium (the imaginary one) interface with another (writing), when the former appears to trump or subsume, with its very capaciousness, the latter? The fragments that follow from these two scenes of encounter are my own translations, which hew more closely toward the original, in which the Latinate roots underscore writing's specificity in this encounter. As the narrator approaches Funes-the-medium:

> I reach, now, the most difficult point in my tale. Which has no other story (let the reader be aware at this point) than this dialogue half a century ago. I will not attempt to reproduce his words, now irrecoverable. I prefer instead to summarize succinctly the many things Ireneo [Funes] told me. Indirect discourse is remote and weak; I know that I sacrifice my tale's efficacy. My readers may imagine the labored periods which burdened that night.[26]

When approaching the Aleph:

> I reach, now, the ineffable core of my story; now begins my writerly despair. All language is an alphabet of symbols whose exercise presupposes a past that its readers share—how can I transmit to others the infinite Aleph, which my frightened memory can scarcely encompass? . . . Apart from all this, the central problem remains irreducible: the enumeration, even partial, of an infinite set. In that colossal instant, I have seen millions of acts, delightful and horrifying; none has astounded me as much as the fact that they all occupied the same point, without superimposition and without transparency. What my eyes saw was simultaneous: what I will write, successive, because language is. Yet I will capture something of it.[27]

Each passage underscores the limits of writing when it encounters the imaginary medium. In the original, each opens with *arribo*, "to arrive or dock." After venturing through different phases—multiple interior patios, in the case of Funes, nineteen rungs on a ladder, in the case of the Aleph—the narrator reaches his shore, or his limit (*orilla*),[28] one that takes places within language. Writing requires succession as opposed to simultaneity ("The Aleph") and abstraction as opposed to infinite detail ("Funes").

Yet is in the "writerly despair" (149) spawned within the Aleph where we counterintuitively find writing's value as a nondemiurgic alternative to the imaginary medium. The Aleph explores the problem of registering, through writing, an experience triggered by a word prominent in the writing of the medieval Spanish mystics: *inefable* ("non-utterable," "inexpressible"). Yet this very inexpressibility inspires a lengthy display. The description of the Aleph unfolds in a single paragraph of approximately one page, but this feels at once excessive and incomplete in light of the medium's simultaneity. Tiny but infinite, the Aleph shares features with Susan Stewart's analysis of the miniature: "writing about the miniature achieves a delirium of description," she observes. The miniature threatens to spawn *verborragia* (excessive language; language like Funes's brain).[29] As in *The Invention of Morel*, writing's productive limitations are made apparent only when it encounters these imaginary media, when it carves out temporary tactics in relation to the other. The "I remember . . . I remember" (107) that opens "Funes" and the "I saw . . . I saw" (140) associated with the Aleph are one such tactic: anaphora, like enumeration, is one of writing's tools to gesture at an ineffable experience while simultaneously indicating the impossibility of capturing it. The repetition here intones writing's clear limitations, its stylized failures.

Writing was among the earliest inscription technologies and storage media, and at one point spawned its own anxieties as a purported threat to memory, orality, lived experience. The phonograph, cinematograph, photograph, telegraph—media that undergird Morel's invention, are foreshadowed in Funes's memory, and are the reference points for the Aleph—originally borrowed from writing's attributes to legitimize themselves, as the suffix *graph* reveals. Modern media write with movement, light, sounds; the hologram or holograph, which Morel's invention anticipates, writes wholeness, the wholeness of the figure it captures. Humans, Bioy and Borges remind us, have always employed a variety of technologies to store our memories, transmit them to others, and "counteract absences," through what Bernard Stiegler calls *mnemotechniques*.[30] What shifts over time is the emergence of *mnemotechnologies*, "large-scale technological systems or networks that organize memories." We now "displace" our memories onto these mnemotechnologies; we also outsource our cognitive functions in the process.[31]

Like *The Invention of Morel*, "The Aleph" and "Funes" thus suggest that the difference between the imaginary medium and writing is one of degree that has been transformed, over time, into a difference of kind. In the context of omnipresent mnemotechnologies, they counterintuitively position writing as a technology of excision and forgetting. Borges's narrators "summarize" (*resumir*) or "retrieve" (*recoger*) rather than produce or even reproduce.[32] They cling to writing as a slippery life raft. As contemporary science fiction often suggests, as the memories of our machines become ever more capacious, forgetting is increasingly positioned as irreducibly human. Thus, while on the first page of "The Aleph," the narrator mourns oblivion, by the story's conclusion he will embrace it. Like forgetting, writing does not bring about new life but functions as a net whose very porousness makes the vast archive of the world legible, manageable, inhabitable.

PLOTTING LATE MODERNIST AUTHORSHIP

Repositioning writing, Bioy and Borges similarly recast authorship. This recasting occurs in relation to formerly new media but also to those who often championed them, the historical avant-gardes, targets that allow Bioy and Borges to posit a different figure for the author. Virgilio Piñera offers a trenchant early observation of Borges's late modernist authorship. In his "A Note on Contemporary Argentine Literature" (Nota sobre literatura argentina de hoy, 1947), he describes the experience of reading the Argentine author: "The reader is left with the outline [*plano*] of the thing but not the thing itself." These outlines or "formulae" "are repeated ad infinitum," "they become mechanized." And, in the process "the writer enjoys [*goza*] them and they provide him enjoyment in return."[33] In Piñera's account, the reader is ultimately frustrated because it appears that the writer has occupied his role, leaving him bereft of a purpose. It is as if the writer had set up operations in order to immerse himself within them.

Piñera suggests how in Borges's works authorship becomes usership, even a kind of gaming, a ludic exploration of or intervention into what ostensibly already exists "out there," activating it and claiming it as his own. (Borges was apparently taken with the essay after Piñera read it aloud on a local radio show and sought permission to publish it in his journal *Anales de Buenos Aires*.) His interpretation resonates with a favorite Borgesean exercise, the staging of different plots for possible books that will never be written, as in the stories "An Examination of the Work of Herbert Quain," "Pierre Menard, Author of the Quixote," and "The Garden of Forking Paths," among others. In his prologue to *Ficciones*, Borges posits an author who annotates, streamlines, or glosses: "A laborious and impoverishing delirium governs the composition of lengthy books—expounding for five hundred pages an idea whose perfect oral exposition fits within a few minutes. Much preferable is to proceed as if such books already exist, offering a synthesis, a commentary, of them."[34] As in "Funes" and "The Aleph," Borges privileges writing as an excising or winnowing down. (The "delirium" in this passage recalls at once the Aleph, Funes, and Morel's invention.) The synthetic reduction—the blueprint, the sharp relief of a plot's skeleton, the taxonomy, plots for imaginary books—allows the writer to stage multiple routes without obligating him to fully fashion corresponding worlds.[35] Borges's author-user creates the book that he would like to read, in synthetic, skeletal, abbreviated fashion. He lays out different combinations or permutations, sometimes explicitly, and chooses the one that most succinctly and unexpectedly presents the most pleasurable solution.

In his prologue to *The Invention of Morel*, Borges's praise of the novella's intervention into contemporary literature hinges on one word: *trama* (plot). Etymologically linked to weaving, the *trama* is the construction of threads or events to form a coherent unit that is sustained by mutually dependent parts. For Borges, *tramas* are anti-expressionist, anti-romantic, anti-Proust (a frequent target of his), and anti-experimental, at least in the avant-garde sense of the term. They are a temporary abstraction from daily life, of indeterminate logic.[36] Literature that displays its plot proudly foregrounds the necessary illusion of order, which both art and science, as opposed to the messy particulars that take place outside of the laboratory, are uniquely poised to do. While the writer creates the *trama*, he does not do so as an inventor/demiurge but rather, as Piñera suggests, the protagonist of the choose-your-own-adventure stories he himself creates. In contrast to the bachelor machine that is Morel's invention, or the all-encompassing thrust of the Aleph or Funes, writing has no womb envy under this definition. Usership, as we have seen, is explicitly non-generative.

The resultant figure of authorship also differs from Quiroga's technical imagination, or that of his avant-garde contemporaries, including the earlier Borges and Bioy. It is in this sense that I read the prologues to both *Morel* and *Ficciones*, along with the important essay "Narrative Art and Magic" (El arte narrativo y la magia, 1932), as both backdoor *ars poetica* and anti-manifestos. I would also include Bioy's Prologue to the *Anthology of Fantastic Literature* in this subset of statements eschewing the oppositional logic of novelty, whether literary or technological. All reject, as Borges proclaims in his prologue to *Morel*, "every superstition of modernity, of any illusion that yesterday differs intimately from today or will differ from tomorrow."[37] Borges's rejection of the avant-garde movements that nurtured his first experiences as a writer began in the late 1920s and early 1930s and were honed in his first work of citational fiction, *A Universal History of Infamy*, in response to cinema; during these same years, he began to tinker with this shifting definition of authorship in "Narrative Art and Magic," a purgative for the last vestiges of his younger self.[38] Authorship would now be willfully stripped of any of the patina of inspiration or expressivity. The collections *The Garden of Forking Paths* (1941), *Ficciones* (1944), and *The Aleph* (1949) would continue to pursue the magic of narrative play over the expressivity of literary invention, while also staging an anti-avant-garde author figure.[39]

In "The Aleph," the narrator's object of desire, Beatriz, dies in 1929—a turning point for the Argentine avant-gardes, and one that inaugurates his own melancholic, schmaltzy ritual: every year he returns to her family home to gaze at her photograph. Beatriz's death thus precipitates a lengthy, nostalgic incubation until the story's present in 1951. This incubation, I would suggest, is precisely the time required for the avant-gardes and their restless enthusiasm for rupture in its technological and aesthetic guises to transmutate. In *Morel*, the island is detained and enshrined by Morel's machine in 1924—the year of the founding of *Martín Fierro*, Argentina's most important avant-garde journal, in which Borges participated. Like 1929 in "The Aleph," this date rubricates a moment from the immediate past that the late modernist text revisits only to overturn. Morel's island is replete with ornaments of avant-garde consumption: paintings of Picasso, clothes that had once been fashionable, a certain modern style detained at the moment of its decadence. If his invention allows the character on the island "to live a life that is always new" (94), the narrator juts up against the newly aged quality of these formerly avant-garde manifestations. *The Invention of Morel* inaugurates Bioy's anti-rupture stance. He would later credit Borges with helping him out of the "anarchy" of his earlier experimental phase.

Consider an intriguing episode in *The Invention of Morel*: in one of his initial attempts at intervening in the imaginary medium, the narrator reproduces his own hand (81). There is no mistaking this choice: the hand, as I have explored in the previous chapter, is at once the user's medium and the writer's tool. It indexes the partial intervention of the narrator in the eponymous device. Yet this metonymic hand, the first part of the narrator's body that he gives over to Morel's machine, also participates in a larger commentary on the break between the avant-gardes and the late modernist moment. In particular, it recalls Bioy's own earlier fascination with surrealism, one he shared with Felisberto Hernández, although with less direct engagement with the movement's French practitioners. In *Morel* he both parodies and abandons this inheritance (for example, with his staging of his *l'amour fou* for Faustine, apparently modeled after the silent-film star and "It Girl" Louise Brooks, an erotic obsession for both Bioy and his surrealist precursors).[40] Writhing grotesquely, the hand is thus at once the user's first, hesitant appropriation of the machine and a reminder, dissonant and uncanny, of Bioy's own recent avant-garde past.

IMAGINARY MEDIA'S GLOBAL NETWORKS

The distance that separates Bioy and Borges from their earlier, avant-garde selves is mirrored in their fictions through the distance between the protagonists and the representatives of the imaginary media they encounter: Morel versus the narrator, Funes versus his narrator, and "Borges" versus Carlos Argentino Daneri in "The Aleph." The narrator of "The Aleph" encounters the imaginary medium inadvertently, through his reluctant relationship with the pompous, fatuous poet; both were deeply attached to Beatriz Viterbo, the woman whose death sets into motion the *trama* of his story. It is easy to forget how much energy "The Aleph" devotes to his ridiculous words; what remains in our minds is often the novum, the Aleph itself. But Daneri receives an extensive amount of page time in the story: before we can reach the Aleph's queasy enchantment we must wade through a lot of *verborragia*.[41] The narrator is especially sardonic in his descriptions of Daneri's pompous paean to modernity, a "vindication of modern man," "as though perched in the watchtower of a city, equipped with telephones, telegraphs, phonographs, radiotelephonic apparatuses, cinematographs, magic lanterns, glossaries, schedules, memos, bulletins" (659).[42]

With his simultaneous interest in cataloging the world and in celebrating the metonymies of modernity, Daneri is a doubled target of Borges's wrath. First, his obligatory shout-outs to modernity are exactly what does not make this writer modern. Picking up on Gibbon's (inaccurate) assertion that in the Koran there are no camels, Borges will famously argue in "The Argentine Writer and Tradition" that Argentines "can emulate Mohammed, can believe in the possibility of being

Argentine without abounding in local color."[43] Daneri is the mouthpiece of what Borges saw as a certain modernist equivalent: the belief in the totemic power of those ethnographic tags or conventions that signify technological modernity (as in the telephone, telegraph, phonograph, and cinematograph of Daneri's poem) and, in turn, in the author as vanguard that exalts them with his language. In addition to the "superstition of modernity" that Borges denigrated in the Prologue to *Morel*, Daneri also has worldwide ambitions. His project, a lengthy poem ambitiously titled *The Earth* (or *The World*), purports to "versify the roundness of the globe," which echoes Borges's parodic title in *A Universal History of Infamy*.[44] Daneri's is an especially pretentious form of "world" literature. Both he and "Borges" are writers, yet their understanding of writing's scope is diametrically opposed. Borges the narrator mocks Daneri because he refuses to embrace what Borges the author was fashioning as writing's strategic partiality.

Daneri's ambition also mirrors the Aleph's spatial plenitude, its capturing of the world's particulars in a single sphere. South American imaginary media are especially preoccupied with the global scope of their real-world counterparts. In *Morel* and "The Aleph," imaginary media draw our attention to the doubled nature of modern media networks. If on one hand they suggest the fantasies of abolishing distance between peoples separated by space and spatialized by time[45]—as when Borges posited cinema as a means of making the Americas known to one another in "The Other Whitman" (Chapter 1)—they also highlight the failure of this exchange, the asymmetries and uneven distributions of resources implicit in the desires to network the world.

The term "networking" is a global project made possible by modern technologies of the late nineteenth century.[46] On one hand, discourses of science, technology, and science fiction appeared to offer the possibility of a transnational exchange among the world's diverse producers and consumers. These possibilities speak to the desire to foster connections that would supersede the economic and political sphere of narrow nationalisms and linguistic groupings, as in the promise of a universal language that subtended modern phenomena such as Esperanto or, earlier, the telegraph. On the other hand, the utopian impulse behind these projects also contained, from the outset, dystopian dimensions (as in the telegraph's rapid transformation into a military tool, or photography and cinema's close-knit relationship to war).[47] This dual potential is embodied in the figure of the "world project" and its executor, the "projector," which Markus Krajewski has identified with the late nineteenth and early twentieth centuries. Their goal was to stitch the world together along spatial and temporal axes, connecting it through cables, railroads, timetables, and other media. As Krajewski shows, the world projector operates on a new premise, that the world can and should be completely connected. This impulse finds—or produces—increasingly smaller gaps to fill in, ostensibly blank spaces on the world map: "A network constantly promises the ability to be more finely spun, to fill . . . the void" (25). The world projector is positioned between potentiality and realization; he operates under the sign of the technical aura. Morel, with his capitalist backers and designs on eliminating distance, is a kind of world projector.

During the interwar period, the optimism embodied in the world projector began to show its seams and the fantasy of a truly global project of technology was increasingly thrown into doubt.[48] This doubt was exacerbated in the Americas, where a language of "networks" and "circulation" was mobilized by a United States looking to develop markets outside of its borders, and when the term "telecommunication" was coined, as the United States established news and advertising agencies across Latin America.[49] A large panel from the Westinghouse headquarters, exhibited at the 1933 World's Fair in Chicago, shows a map of the world with concentric circles radiating out from a center in the U.S. mid-Atlantic region; as the circles become farther flung—incorporating Africa, Latin America, and Asia—the icons representing the regions become more exoticized and less elaborate, reflecting the raw materials (palm trees, elephants, etc.) that apparently define their contribution to the world. "Radio Broadcasting Has Made the Whole World a Neighborhood," it reads, anticipating the trope of the "global village."[50] Westinghouse inaugurated the world's first commercial radio station, and it is clear that its map imagined connectivity as a means of shoring up, rather than undercutting, global asymmetries.

Like the imaginary media of Quiroga and Palma, Borges and Bioy allude to this problem of an asymmetrical interconnectivity. Their imaginary media are pointedly displaced, positioned in peripheral locations: in *The Invention of Morel*, a desert island where a fragment of life is archived and abetted from the ravages of time. In each text, the peripheral site is not simply an extension of a center located elsewhere—a pale reflection or copy of designs inaugurated off-stage—but rather the precondition for the medium to operate. In *Morel*, the narrator's story suggests superimposed imperialist fantasies: he is Venezuelan; he heard about the island in the Pacific while living in India, where Columbus believed he was headed when he discovered the Americas (deemed "las Indias" in the early colonial period). The fountain of youth, the Ciudad de los Césares, William Walker's new southern kingdom within Nicaragua: Latin America in particular has been continually produced as a space for reinscribing, centuries later, fantasies of starting anew in a place devoid of history.[51] These fantasies will be found, in distorted and parodic echoes, in seminal Latin American novels of the twentieth century, most famously in the "marvel" of cinema arriving to the jungles of Macondo in *One Hundred Years of Solitude* (1967). Bioy's troping of blank nature alludes to the ways in which the colonization of time and outer space of twentieth-century science fiction, a tradition in which he inscribes, revamps and reflects upon these earlier iterations.[52] When the novella opens, the narrator is hounded by technologies of global surveillance in which radio broadcasting, fingerprinting technologies, and systems of bureaucratic documentation interpellate him as a fugitive. From the outset, his desert island is not a refuge but rather refracts globalization, or the shrinking of the globe.[53]

In contrast to his friend's desert island, Borges's imaginary media are miniature or, to use his privileged adjective, "modest" (*pudorosos*). An infinitesimal world is found in the cramped basement of a soon-to-be-torn-down apartment of a mediocre poet in an unremarkable Buenos Aires neighborhood; a humble shack in a provincial Uruguayan town houses a brain that anticipates the globalizing medium of the cinema. If Bioy's world is that of the dystopian projection screen of the desert island, Borges's is the contiguous, the hither side of a broader elsewhere: "Babylon, London, and New York have overwhelmed with fierce splendor the imagination of men; no one in their populous towers or on their urgent avenues has felt the heat and pressure of a reality as tireless as that which day and night converged on the unhappy Ireneo in his humble South American backwater [*arrabal*]."[54] Anchored around an imaginary medium with its global pretentions, the media laboratories of Bioy and Borges also urge us to question all models of literary and mediatic "plenitude." Rather than seeking out, like the world projector, holes in a map, only to fill them in through incorporation, compilation, or dialectical resolution, we can examine the frustrated desires that underscore modernism's quest to produce difference—in the form of exotic locations or alternative modernities—only to subsume it.

Borges and Bioy are often privileged exceptions in the realm of media theory and media studies, with its almost exclusive focus on the United States and western Europe. Borges opens Lev Manovich's influential "New Media from Borges to HTML," and he appears frequently in the work of theorists such as N. Katherine Hayles and Jay Bolter. Often he is seen as "prescient" with respect to computational technology, especially in "The Garden of Forking Paths."[55] For his part, with *The Invention of Morel*, Bioy Casares has often been read as anticipating both media theory (for example, the Baudrillardian simulacra) and new media themselves (holography, virtual reality).[56] *The Invention of Morel* is also a unique apprehension of the desires of cinema to be "more than,"[57] and perhaps for this reason it has become a source for various filmic and televisual adventures: Alain Resnais's cinematic repetition machine, *Last Year at Marienbad* (France, 1961); the desert island paranoid idealism of the television hit *Lost* (United States, 2004–10); and the filmic adaptations of Claude-Jean Bonnardot (*L'Invention de Morel*, France, 1967), Emidio Greco (*L'Invenzione di Morel*, Italy, 1974), and Eliseo Subiela (*Man Facing Southeast/El hombre mirando al sudeste*, Argentina, 1986), as well as the retromodernism of the Quay Brothers' *Piano Tuner of Earthquakes* (U.K./France/Germany, 2005).[58]

Rather than reassert once again the exceptional status of Borges and Bioy as proto media theorists, however, I would suggest something else—that this very exceptionalism is a symptom of a deficit of imagination. Borges and Bioy are, in fact, in good company in the late modernist moment in South America.[59] Their imaginary media form part of a broader project of submitting technologies to strange experiments and potential critiques that parodically inflate their scope to the point of explosion or exhaustion or, alternatively, miniaturize them in order to probe their limits. In underscoring geopolitical dimensions often missing from modernist accounts of media, they suggest that modern media's promises and perils can arguably be analyzed most intensely from the periphery—because their contradictions are felt more keenly. If, as Trotsky suggested, futurism took faster in what he called "backward countries"—and if it is in the "inconsequential part of the world" where time, per Borges, is experienced more keenly, "is more profuse"—then we might extend this argument to the media that "invented modern life."[60] On this view, media change and transformation are thrown into relief in South American late modernism, along with the tenants of media archaeology.

Josefina Ludmer has argued that Manuel Puig's novels of the 1960s inaugurated a shift in Argentine literature, from the art of the *library* to the art of the *media*.[61] In Ludmer's pithy formulation, Borges epitomizes the former: he transformed libraries into characters ("The Library of Babel") and displayed his own library at every turn, in a virtuoso intertextuality in which literature endlessly points back to itself. Yet is Borges the last librarian, per Ludmer and others, or the first programmer, per Manovich and company? A third Borges—neither the adherent to book culture nor the prescient precursor to contemporary "new" media—emerges if we bracket the emphases on origins and deaths that undergird many histories of both literature and media. Pressing upon Ludmer's periodization, I aim equally to press upon the language of "belated," on one hand, and "prescient" or "anticipatory," on the other. Both imply a narrative that late modernist writers, and Borges in particular, rejected. One way to problematize Ludmer's assertion, then, is to read the art of the library as itself an art of the media. But the use that writing makes of other media during a given context is less a historical inevitability than a specific provocation, from the sidelines, margins, or the sting of the residual, that I have called the media laboratory.

Like Ludmer, other scholars of Latin American literature have offered us compelling analyses of literature's intense engagement with mass media beginning in the 1960s–1970s.[62] This book has explored how the anxiety surrounding increasingly powerful media and their implications for authorship can be mapped earlier. This "earlier," however, comes with a caveat, for it is not a question of establishing an ever-receding origin but of questioning the shift that relegates one term, author, or text to pre-history. This is not to say, of course, that nothing changed in the mediatic landscape between 1930 and the 1960s–1970s, when the prevalence of advertising, youth culture, the televisual, and the verticalization of multinational media industries become dominant modes. With her typist, Clarice Lispector reflects upon these very historical transformations (Chapter 3). Yet when artists and intellectuals began to probe this altered media landscape in the post-1968 period, it was to the recent past of late modernism that they returned.

Like Lispector, who both paid homage to and troubled the gendered, proletarianized body of Graciliano Ramos's typist, other artists returned to his work to grapple with the specificities of their present. Brazil's first generation of leftist auteur filmmakers, for example, began to reread Graciliano under the rubric of Cinema Novo, or "New

Cinema."[63] In the wake of the failed developmental projects and agrarian reform of Juscelino Kubitschek (1956–61), culminating in first one and then another military dictatorship, they revealed the photographic negative of the slogan "Brazil, nation of the future" and found in Graciliano's disenchanted approach to modernism a cue for their own projects. Outside of Brazil, perhaps no author stages this return to mid-century modernism with as much energy as Manuel Puig, who remediated the radio melodramas and women's films of the 1930s–1950s of his provincial childhood in novels like *Betrayed by Rita Hayworth* (1968) and *Heartbreak Tango* (*Boquitas pintadas*, 1969). A return to the radio melodrama also appears in Mario Vargas Llosa's *Aunt Julia and the Scriptwriter* (Peru, 1977). The same year, in his late short story "We Love Glenda So Much," Julio Cortázar will rewrite Olivari's "Starstruck" in a more sinister vein, imagining a group of obsessed fans violently stitching alternative narrative endings to the filmography of a beloved international star.

Critical theory of this later period will also pay its debts to late modernism. Like their novelistic contemporaries, Latin American scholars, newly in dialogue with the Frankfurt School, joined their Euro-American colleagues in returning to the scene of the avant-gardes in order to offer an interpretation of modernism's promises, failures, and blind spots.[64] With pessimism and at times despair, they reflected on this legacy: the incorporation of the avant-gardes into the language of advertising and, in the South American case, the ways in which technological modernity and modernist intellectual projects had been subsumed into current or impending military dictatorships. In this sense, thinkers as diverse as Peter Bürger, Hans Enzensberger, Fredric Jameson, Ángel Rama, Alfredo Bosi, Silviano Santiago, and Roberto Schwarz are all theorists of late modernism. Enzensberger's assertion that "the historical avant-garde perished by its aporias," for example, is markedly similar to the position of writers I have analyzed in this study, including Borges, Galvão, and Graciliano; so is his understanding of the wearing-down of the term "experiment," now "threadbare and unelucidated."[65] In Roberto Schwarz's Adornian reading of the first wave of Brazilian modernism, "The Cart, the Tram, and the Modernist Poet" (1977), the movement's later incorporation into the technocratic, market-friendly modernization associated with the dictatorship is an opportunity to reread these texts as speaking to the automatized present: "Present-day success on the grand scale, in the media, has to do with its integration into the discourse of conservative modernization.

In part this happened in spite of itself, in part it was the logical consequence of its own internal propensities."[66]

Not all of these returns to the late modernist scene embraced skepticism. A bit later on, a more hopeful iteration surfaced in the first Benjaminian Latin Americanist writings, in the work of Jesús Martín-Barbero, whose *From the Media to the Mediation: Communication, Culture, Hegemony* (1987) provided an account of mass culture not through the lens of negative classicism but as a new kind of pact between working classes and elites that emerged, precisely, in the 1930s.[67] And, just as later filmmakers would take up Graciliano's work, so too would writers and audiovisual artists discover the audacious figure of Galvão and her Cannibalist precursors. *Industrial Park* gave a hint of what the filmmaker Glauber Rocha will baptize three decades later an "aesthetics of hunger": the privileging of smeared, imperfect visual effects as a response and antidote to the slippery smoothness of Hollywood, the reauratization of the imperfect and impoverished as the site of an aesthetic-political praxis.[68]

Read in this light, the post-1968 period—the moment in which Latin American art and literature finally begins to receive global recognition, most notably in the Boom—was less a "first contact" with mass media than an interpretation and reworking of late modernist tendencies that often appear within these texts as crystallizations of a recent past.[69] In these disparate examples from later artistic and critical practice, late modernist writing reappears to critique the sense of having moved on, mobilizing artists and intellectuals frustrated by the confluence of market logic, technocratic modernization, and the multinational mass media industries whose presence was especially prominent in the consolidating medium of television. As our own contemporary experience with media change becomes ever more central to our lives as scholars, writers, readers, and users, and as the velocity of technological transformation (whether or not as engineered obsolescence) only increases, the late modernist media laboratories of South America offer us compelling alternatives from the residual, yet endlessly transforming, practice of authorship.

Epilogue

Fragment of a Diary in the Alps (2002), an essay/novella by Argentine author César Aira, features a series of appendices that reflect upon art and media change.[1] As he stages these reflections, the narrator holds in his hands a thaumatrope, an early nineteenth-century optical toy and precursor to the cinema. When he tilts the object, the image at its center, a bird, changes to another, a cage; sometimes the bird appears inside of the cage. The thaumatrope, or "wonder-turner," depends upon the afterimage imprinted on the retina, which creates the illusion of superimposition.[2] But it also depends upon the intervention of the user's body, and more specifically his hand, an intervention that would disappear in its successor, cinema.

As he plays with it, the narrator speculates on what might have happened had specific media followed alternate paths. Similar to the thaumatrope, cinema "could have had remain[ed] a charming toy, closed-off, with a whiff of a by-gone era" or "the nostalgic aftertaste" of an epoch (76–77). Like the thaumatrope, Aira's narrator spins around, circles back, and pendulums back and forth between media origins and deaths, possible pasts and futures, between what constitutes a medium's success, its consolidation, and what is lost in the process. A medium becomes an art, he supposes, when a "providential man" is

> able to capture in all its freshness the novelty of the medium, its magic: to feel the contrast between the medium's existence and

> its inexistence. And not to let this moment pass by: for, without the artist, the medium would take a functional path; it would begin to fulfill certain expectations. (75)

What the narrator sees as the gap or "contrast" between what is not yet and what already is—a gap that he supposes is fundamental to that bifurcating path where a medium becomes an art—recalls nothing so much as Beatriz Sarlo's "technical aura," a motivating concept for this study. Throughout this book, I have inquired into what happens next, and what remains possible, in that zone where "freshness" and "novelty" have been evacuated, when media have "fulfilled certain expectations" and, in the process, blackboxed different paths or outcomes.

Aira's essay provides us with a clue, for it is the nineteenth-century optical toy that spawns his musings on rupture. In the hands of the user, the thaumatrope is a trigger for a media archaeology, and not just for that of the cinema. Its role in the pre-history of cinema also leads the narrator to reflect upon a different medium, his own: "Which marvelous, coarse, imperfect toys presaged the arrival of literature? What I wouldn't give to see them, to have them! And perhaps I do have them, and I don't know it, and that makes my nostalgia incurable" (86). Literature's pre-history is so far back as to be irrecoverable for the contemporary writer. Yet it is also possible that literature's pre-history exists, occluded ("perhaps I do have them, and I don't know it"). Significantly, the narrator comes across the thaumatrope inside a friend's workshop in the Alps, an exotic site, far away from his native Argentina. (Perhaps not incidentally, considering Borges's influence on Aira, the place where his precursor spent time as an adolescent.) Like Bioy's island and Borges's basement, Felisberto Hernández's touch chambers, Olivari's impoverished screening room, and many other sites explored in this study, the workshop in the Alps allows for withdrawing from the world and makes possible the ephemeral setting-up of a media laboratory.

Activated by the user's hand inside this temporary site, the thaumatrope, for its part, makes possible the experience both of movement and of the lingering and persistent. Its anachronistic and residual nature troubles our narratives of technological development, spawning a reflection on authorship itself—for it, like the thaumatrope, persistently finds its energy not in the sting of the new but in the residual, the untimely, the out-of-place.

Notes

PREFACE

1. Nicolás Olivari, *El hombre de la baraja y la puñalada y otros escritos sobre cine* (Buenos Aires: Adriana Hidalgo, 2000), 164, 171, 172, my translation throughout. On Olivari, see Jason Borge, *Latin American Writers and the Rise of Hollywood Cinema* (New York: Routledge, 2008), 1–3, 119–20. The "modest apparatus" is perhaps a homegrown, or stolen, version of the small home film projectors by Pathé Baby that began to be advertised in periodicals during the period, for it is unlikely this protagonist would have been able to afford the real thing.

2. W. J. T. Mitchell, "There Are No Visual Media," *Journal of Visual Culture* 4.2 (2005): 257–66. See also Brian Massumi, *Parables for the Virtual: Movement, Affect, Sensation* (Durham, N.C.: Duke University Press, 2002), 145–58.

3. Olivari, for example, breaches the avant-garde/social realist divide of the 1920s–1930s in Buenos Aires known as Florida/Boedo. On these divisions, see Graciela Montaldo, ed., *Yrigoyen entre Borges y Arlt (1916–1930)* (Buenos Aires: Paradiso, 2006); Francine Masiello, *Lenguaje e ideología: Las escuelas argentinas de vanguardia* (Buenos Aires: Hachette, 1986).

4. The borders between late modernism and postmodernism are fuzzy. See, for example, Tyrus Miller, *Late Modernism: Politics, Fiction and the Arts between the World Wars* (Berkeley: University of California Press, 1999), 9–11; Fredric Jameson, *Postmodernism, or the Cultural Logic of Late Capitalism* (Durham, N.C.: Duke University Press, 1991), ix; Fredric Jameson, *A Singular Modernity: Essay on the Ontology of the Present* (London: Verso, 2013), 150–51; Jed Esty, *A Shrinking Island: Modernism and National Culture in*

England (Princeton, N.J.: Princeton University Press, 2004), 4; Brian McHale, *Postmodernist Fiction* (New York: Methuen, 1987), 8–10.

INTRODUCTION

1. See Maite Conde, *Consuming Visions: Cinema, Writing, and Modernity in Rio de Janeiro* (Charlottesville: University of Virginia Press, 2012); Ester Gabara, *Errant Modernism: The Ethos of Photography in Brazil and Mexico* (Durham, N.C.: Duke University Press, 2008); Borge, *Latin American Writers and the Rise of Hollywood Cinema.*

2. See Susan Buck-Morss, "Aesthetics and Anaesthetics: Walter Benjamin's Artwork Essay Reconsidered," *October* 62 (Autumn 1992): 3–41; Miriam Hansen, "The Mass Production of the Senses: Classical Cinema as Vernacular Modernism," *Modernism/Modernity* 6.2 (1999): 59–77.

3. In Argentina, Perón's first term begins in 1946, although, as Matthew Karush has persuasively argued, populist narratives of radio and cinema prepared the terrain beginning in the 1930s. See Karush, *The Culture of Class: Radio and Cinema in the Making of a Divided Argentina* (Durham, N.C.: Duke University Press, 2012).

4. On the Latin American masses, see Jesús Martín-Barbero, *De los medios a las mediaciones: Comunicación, cultura, hegemonía* (Mexico City: Ediciones G. Gili, 1987). On populism, see Michael L. Conniff, ed., *Populism in Latin America* (Tuscaloosa: University of Alabama Press, 2012), especially 1–70.

5. While Roland Barthes stresses that neither Work nor Text lines up along a historical continuum—and, indeed, expresses a distaste for "History" (64)—it is nonetheless useful to compare the "process of filiation" he identifies with the Work (e.g., paternity, legal rights) to the author who circulates "like a guest" in the Text: "his inscription is no longer privileged, paternal, alethic, but ludic: he becomes, one can say, a paper author" (61). Written in 1971, this seminal essay forms part of a motley group of French contemporaries (Genette, Foucault, de Certeau) marked by the sign of Borges. Barthes, "From Work to Text," in *The Rustle of Language*, trans. Richard Howard (New York: Hill and Wang, 1987), 56–64.

6. Ángel Rama, *La ciudad letrada* (Hanover, N.H.: Ediciones del Norte, 1984).

7. The "great divide" of modernism and the avant-gardes becomes increasingly precarious when modernism travels; therefore, I use the terms interchangeably, as many Latin Americanists do. See, for example, Jean Franco, "Vallejo and the Crisis of the Thirties," *Hispania* 72 (March 1989): 42.

8. See Nicolau Sevcenko, *Orfeu Extático na Metrópole: São Paulo, cultura e sociedade nos frementes anos 20* (São Paulo: Companhia das Letras, 1992).

9. Mário de Andrade, *O empalhador de passarinho* (São Paulo: Livraria Martins Editôra, 1972), 237. *Revista de Antropofagia* was cofounded by Oswald de Andrade (no relation), Raul Bopp, and Antônio de Alcântara Machado. See also António Cândido and José Aderaldo Castello, *Presença da literatura brasileira: Modernismo* (São Paulo: Difel, 1982), 24. For a defense of *antropofagia*'s postcolonial thrust, despite the violence of the rupture it proposes, see Luís Madureira, *Cannibal Modernities: Postcoloniality and the Avant-Garde in Caribbean and Brazilian Literature* (Charlottesville:

University of Virginia Press, 2005), especially 46. Brazilian modernism, per Madureira, constituted "a quest for a national childhood" (26–27, 30).

10. António Cândido, "Literature and Underdevelopment," in *On Literature and Society* (Princeton, N.J.: Princeton University Press, 1995), 119–21. On the reassertion of Romantic ideals in the Latin American avant-gardes, see Mário de Andrade, "O movimento modernista," in *Aspectos da literatura brasileira* (São Paulo: Livraria Martins Editora, 1972), 21–46; Octavio Paz, *Los hijos del limo: Del Romanticismo a la Vanguardia* (Barcelona: Seix Barral, 1974). Ángel Rama ("Las dos vanguardias latinoamericanas," in *La riesgosa navegación del escritor exiliado* [Montevideo: Arca, 1993], 135–48) also invokes the striving for a "cultural independence" (a break with the Spanish tradition) that begins in the 1820s as a precursor for the historic avant-gardes. Rosalind Krauss suggests an unacknowledged debt to Romantic originality in the avant-gardes in "The Originality of the Avant-Gardes and Other Modernist Myths," *October* (1985): 151–70.

11. On the emergence of the new as a criterion of value in nineteenth-century Latin America, see Víctor Goldgel, *Cuando lo nuevo conquistó América: Literatura, prensa y moda en el siglo XIX* (Buenos Aires: Siglo XXI, 2013).

12. João Luíz Lafetá, *1930, a crítica, e o modernismo* (São Paulo: Livraria Duas Cidades, 1974), 19. Jed Esty's *A Shrinking Island*, a study of British literature of the 1930s, makes similar arguments for this context; the question of the national in particular suggests intriguing parallels with contemporaneous Brazil. See also Luís Bueno, *Uma história do romance de 30* (São Paulo: EDUSP, 2006).

13. De Andrade, "O movimento modernista."

14. Felisberto Hernández, "Around the Time of Clemente Colling," in *Lands of Memory*, trans. Esther Allen (New York: New Directions, 2002), 6.

15. Alceu Amoroso Lima (Tristão Athayde), "Idade Nova," *Lanterna Verde* 3 (February 1935): 97; Luis Franco, "América Inicial," *La vida literaria* (October 4, 1931): 33.

16. See Rosalind Krauss, *The Originality of the Avant-Gardes and Other Modernist Myths* (Cambridge, Mass.: MIT Press, 1985). My argument here also resonates with Peter Bürger's now classic formulation about the automatization of the avant-gardes—a perspective he shared with many of his contemporaries across the Americas—but underscores not only the logic of the market but more specifically those media (cinema, the typewriter, and the radio) that threatened to usurp literature and the figure of the author.

17. Roberto Arlt, "Recordando el Eclesiastés" (1940), in *Notas sobre el cinematógrafo* (Buenos Aires: Ediciones Simurg, 1997), 18–22.

18. As quoted in Conde, *Consuming Visions*, 186. See also Flora Süssekind's seminal *Cinematograph of Words: Literature, Technique and Modernization in Brazil*, trans. Paulo Henriques Britto (Stanford, Calif.: Stanford University Press, 1997), 96. An important account of the arrival of cinema to the region from a film studies perspective can be found in Ana López, "Early Cinema and Modernity in Latin America," *Cinema Journal* 40.1 (Fall 2000): 48–78.

19. Leo Charney and Vanessa Schwartz, eds., *Cinema: The Invention of Modern Life* (Berkeley: University of California Press, 1995).

20. Borge, *Latin American Writers and the Rise of Hollywood Cinema,* 20.

21. On Quiroga, see especially Beatriz Sarlo, *La imaginación técnica: Sueños modernos de la cultura argentina* (Buenos Aires: Nueva Visión, 1992); Carlos Dámaso Martínez, "Horacio Quiroga: La industria editorial, sus relatos y la literatura fantástica," in Horacio Quiroga, *Todos los cuentos* (Madrid: Fondo de Cultura Económica, 1993), 1293–1303.

22. See Francesco Casetti, *The Eye of the Century: Film, Experience, Modernity* (New York: Columbia University Press, 2008), 11.

23. Mário da Silva Brito, "O Alegre Combate de Klaxon," facsimile edition of *Klaxon—Mensário de Arte Moderna* (São Paulo: Martins; Secretaria da Cultura, Ciência e Tecnologia do Estado de São Paulo, 1976), 5; *Klaxon* 3 (July 15, 1922): 11.

24. As quoted in Laura Marcus, "Film," in *A Companion to Modernist Literature and Culture*, ed. David Bradshaw and Kevin J. H. Dettmar (London: Blackwell, 2006), 252. On the metaphor of seeing with new eyes in the Argentine literary avant-gardes, see Masiello, *Lenguaje e ideología*; in European cinema during the first decades of the twentieth century, Casetti, *The Eye of the Century.*

25. Examples include Antônio de Alcântara Machado's camera-eye in *Pathé-Baby* (1926), Oswald de Andrade's *Memórias Sentimentais de João Miramar* (1924), Mário de Andrade's *Paulicéia Desvairada* (Hallucinated City, 1922); and the films *Rien que les Heures* (Alberto Cavalcanti, 1926), *Fragmentos da vida* (José Medina, 1929), and *São Paulo, Sinfonia da metrópole* (Adalberto Kemeny and Rudolf Rex Lustig, 1929). On the formal influence of cinema on Brazilian writing during the 1920s, see Conde, *Consuming Visions*, especially 2–3, 179; Süssekind, *Cinematograph of Words*, 95. Critics often make reference to, if not fully developing, the "cinematic" quality of avant-garde poetry. See, for example, Alfredo Bosi, *Céu, inferno: Ensaios de crítica literária e ideológica* (São Paulo: Editora Atica, 1988), 118–19.

26. Horacio Quiroga, "Espectros que hablan," *La Nación* (March 17, 1929): 365, my translation.

27. Jean Epstein, "On Certain Characteristics of *Photogénie*," in *Film Theory: Critical Concepts in Media and Cultural Studies*, vol. 1, ed. Philip Simpson, Andrew Utterson, and Karen Shepherdson (London: Routledge, 2003), 52.

28. Olympio Guilherme, "Questão de gosto . . . ," *Cinearte* 202 (January 8, 1930): 10. On late modernist laughter in the Anglo-American context, see Miller, *Late Modernism*, 47–54.

29. Silviano Santiago, "Literature and Mass Culture," in *The Space In-Between: Essays on Latin American Culture*, ed. Ana Lúcia Gazzola (Durham, N.C.: Duke University Press, 2001), 121.

30. On Brazil, see Randal Johnson, *The Film Industry in Brazil: Culture and the State* (Pittsburgh: University of Pittsburgh Press, 1987), 19–63; Stephanie Dennison and Lisa Shaw, *Popular Cinema in Brazil, 1930–2001* (New York: Palgrave, 2004), 9–58; Lia Calabre, "Políticas públicas culturais de 1924 a 1945: O rádio em destaque," *Estudos históricos* 31 (2003): 1–21; Daryl Williams, *Culture Wars in Brazil: The First Vargas Regime,*

1930–1945 (Durham, N.C.: Duke University Press, 2001); Anita Simis, "Movies and Moviemakers under Vargas," *Latin American Perspectives* 29.1 (January 2002): 106–14. On Argentina, see Karush, *The Culture of Class*; Mariano Calistro, *Reportaje al cine argentino: Los pioneros del sonoro* (Buenos Aires: ANESA, 1978); Emilio Daniel Díaz, César Maranghell, and Elina Mercedes Tranchini, *El cine argentino y su aporte a la identidad nacional* (Buenos Aires: Federación Argentina de la Industria Gráfica y Afines, 1999); Fernando Martín Peña, *Cien años de cine argentino* (Buenos Aires: Editorial Biblios, 2012), 15–82. On Uruguay, see Owald Saratsola, *Función completa, por favor: Un siglo de cine en Montevideo* (Montevideo: Ediciones Trilce, 2005).

31. Adorno will point out in a late essay that the culture industry refers not only to the production process but also to the specific kinds of standardization and rationalization that occur all along the chain of distribution and reception. See Theodor W. Adorno and Anson G. Rabinbach, "Culture Industry Reconsidered," *New German Critique* 6 (Autumn 1975): 14. On the concept of the culture industry in Brazil, see Renato Ortiz, *A Moderna Tradicão Brasileira: Cultura brasileira e indústria cultural* (São Paulo: Editora Brasiliense, 1988), 13–37.

32. Jack Sampião, "Cinema," *Boletim de Ariel*, no. 1 (October 1931): 16.

33. Beatriz Sarlo, *The Technical Imagination: Argentine Culture's Modern Dreams*, trans. Xavier Callahan (Stanford, Calif.: Stanford University Press, 2008), 81. On the technical aura, see ibid., 124–27. Raymond Williams's study of television is his most direct engagement with the relationship between a medium, its intention, and its effects. See *Television: Technology and Cultural Form* (New York: Schocken Books, 1975).

34. On womb envy, see Mary Ann Doane, "Technophilia: Technology, Representation, and the Feminine," in *Liquid Metal: The Science Fiction Film Reader*, ed. Sean Redmond (London: Wallflower Press, 2004), 182–90; Andreas Huyssen, *After the Great Divide: Modernism, Mass Culture, Postmodernism* (Bloomington: Indiana University Press, 1986), 70–71.

35. See Bruno Latour, *Pandora's Hope: Essays on the Reality of Science Studies* (Cambridge, Mass.: Harvard University Press, 1999), 30; see also 43, 122–23; Jussi Parikka, *What Is Media Archaeology?* (Cambridge: Polity, 2012), 15.

36. Michel de Certeau, *The Practice of Everyday Life* (Berkeley: University of California Press, 1984), xi–xxiv, 29–42.

37. Ibid., 50. For a recent vindication of De Certeau, see Paula Amad, "*Visual Riposte*: Reconsidering the Return of the Gaze as Postcolonial Theory's Gift to Film Studies," *Cinema Journal* 52.3 (Spring 2013): 65–66.

38. Fernando Rosenberg's brilliant *The Avant-gardes and Geopolitics in Latin America* (Pittsburgh: University of Pittsburgh Press, 2006) explores the avant-gardes' approach to geopolitics in a model that challenges diffusionist approaches to modernity.

39. On global capitalism and media/technology, see especially Armand Mattelart, *Networking the World: 1794–2000*, trans. Liz Carey-Libbrecht and James A. Cohen (Minneapolis: University of Minnesota Press, 2000);

Ricardo Donato Salvatore, "Imperial Mechanics: South America's Hemispheric Integration in the Machine," *American Quarterly* 58.3 (September 2006): 662–91. On negative classicism, see Patrick Brantlinger, *Bread and Circuses: Theories of Mass Culture as Social Decay* (Ithaca, N.Y.: Cornell University Press, 1983).

40. In the words of Hamid Naficy, the third-world film spectator is not only hailed by the cinema but also "haggles," in a negotiation that occurs in public space through practices of reverse address. Naficy, "Theorizing 'Third World' Film Spectatorship," *Wide Angle* 18.4 (1996): 9; see also Ella Shohat and Robert Stam, *Unthinking Eurocentrism: Multiculturalism and the Media* (New York: Routledge, 1994), 350; Ron Eglash et al., eds., *Appropriating Technology: Vernacular Science and Social Power* (Minneapolis: University of Minnesota Press, 2004); Janet Staiger, *Perverse Spectators: The Practices of Film Reception* (New York: New York University Press, 2000); Beatriz Sarlo, *Tiempo Presente: Notas sobre el cambio de una cultura* (Buenos Aires: Siglo XXI, 2001), 217; and especially Travers Scott, "The Postfeminist User: Feminism and Media Theory in Two Interactive Media Properties," *Feminist Media Studies* 10.4 (2010): 457–75. On fandom, see Henry Jenkins, *Fans, Bloggers, and Gamers: Exploring Participatory Culture* (New York: New York University Press, 2006). Michele Aaron also challenges the equation of agency with activity in *Spectatorship: The Power of Looking On* (London: Wallflower, 2007).

41. Epstein, "On Certain Characteristics of *Photogénie*," 53; Laura Marks, *The Skin of the Film: Intercultural Cinema, Embodiment, and the Senses* (Durham, N.C.: Duke University Press, 2000).

42. Miriam Hansen, *Cinema and Experience: Siegfried Kracauer, Walter Benjamin, and Theodor W. Adorno* (Berkeley: University of California Press, 2011), 19–20.

43. On the sensory dimensions of modern media, see especially Epstein, "On Certain Characteristics of *Photogénie*"; Justus Nieland, *Feeling Modern: The Eccentricities of Public Life* (Urbana: University of Illinois Press, 2008); Vivian Sobchack, *Carnal Thoughts* (Berkeley: University of California Press, 2004); Sara Danius, *The Senses of Modernism: Technology, Perception, and Aesthetics* (Ithaca, N.Y.: Cornell University Press, 2002); Julian Murphet, *Multimedia Modernism: Literature and the Anglo-American Avant-garde* (Cambridge: Cambridge University Press, 2009); Michael North, *Camera Works* (Oxford: Oxford University Press, 2005); Mark Goble, *Beautiful Circuits: Modernism and the Mediated Life* (New York: Columbia University Press, 2010); and Michael Taussig, *Mimesis and Alterity: A Particular History of the Senses* (New York: Routledge, 1993).

44. See N. Katherine Hayles, *Writing Machines* (Cambridge, Mass.: MIT Press, 2002); Jay David Bolter and Richard Grusin, *Remediation: Understanding New Media* (Cambridge, Mass.: MIT Press, 2000); Friedrich A. Kittler, *Discourse Networks, 1800/1900* (Stanford, Calif.: Stanford University Press, 1990).

45. The whole-scale importation of Kittler's "discourse networks" into the Latin American context is problematic for several reasons; for one, the radical

break he finds in 1900 is premised on universal literacy, a phenomenon realized at best unevenly at the turn of the century.

46. "A medium is a medium is a medium" (Kittler, *Discourse Networks, 1800/1900*, 229). For Kittler, as for Marshall McLuhan before him, a medium is its own content. Both pointedly deemphasize the social in the production of its meaning, as in McLuhan's problematic example of the "railway medium," which opens itself up to a Latin Americanist critique. See *Understanding Media: The Extensions of Man* (Cambridge, Mass.: MIT Press, 1999), 8. Raymond Williams's critique of McLuhan offers us an early iteration of critiques that could also apply to Kittler. See *Television: Technology and Cultural Form*, especially 125–28.

47. In the tension between German media materialities and Anglo-American media cultural studies, I tip toward the latter, while drawing on the former. Broadly speaking, German media theory tends to explore the specificity of media through thick descriptions of their materialities over the more sociocultural analysis of Anglo-American media theory. See Jussi Parikka, "Media Theory and New Materialism," in *What Is Media Archaeology?* (Cambridge: Polity, 2012), 63–89.

48. On the novum, see especially Darko Suvin, "On the Poetics of SF Genre," *College English* 34.3 (December 1972): 373.

49. I share with Bruce Sterling's Dead Media Project, Charles Acland's edited volume *Residual Media*, and Siegfried Zielinski's "deep time of the media" a critique of capitalism's planned obsolescence and teleological media histories that implicitly affirm it. See Bruce Sterling, "Media Paleontology," in *The Book of Imaginary Media: Excavating the Dream of the Ultimate Communication Medium*, ed. Eric Kluitenberg (Rotterdam: NAi Publishers, 2006), 69; Siegfried Zielinski, *Deep Time of the Media: Towards an Archaeology of Seeing and Hearing by Technical Means* (Cambridge, Mass.: MIT Press, 2006). In thinking through problems of use in media history, the following have also been especially helpful for me: Rick Altman, "Crisis Historiography," in his *Silent Film Sound* (New York: Columbia University Press, 2004), 15–26; Lisa Gitelman, *Always Already New: Media, History, and the Data of Culture* (Cambridge, Mass.: MIT Press, 2008), especially 7–12; Timothy Druckrey, foreword to Zielinski, *Deep Time of the Media*, vii–xii.

50. David Trotter, *Cinema and Modernism* (London: Wiley, 2007). On "rehumanizing" in the Latin American avant-garde, see Vicky Unruh, *Latin American Vanguards: The Art of Contentious Encounters* (Berkeley: University of California Press, 1994), 23–26.

51. See Mary Ann Caws, *Manifesto: A Century of Isms* (Lincoln: University of Nebraska Press, 2000). On the specifically space-clearing language of the manifesto, see Martin Puchner, *Poetry of the Revolution: Marx, Manifestos, and the Avant-gardes* (Princeton, N.J.: Princeton University Press, 2006), especially part 1, 2–66; Vicky Unruh, "Constructing an Audience: Concrete and Illusory: Manifestos for Performing and Performance Manifestos," in *Latin American Vanguards*, 31–70.

52. César Vallejo, "Autopsia del superrealismo," in Jorge Schwartz, *Las vanguardias latinoamericanas: Textos programáticos y críticos* (Mexico City: Fondo de Cultura Económica 2002), 470.

53. Patrícia Galvão, *Industrial Park*, trans. Elizabeth Jackson and K. David Jackson (Lincoln: University of Nebraska Press, 1993), 24, 37. Unless otherwise indicated, I use this translation throughout.

54. See, for example, the early writings of Vicente Huidobro, Borges, or Mário de Andrade (e.g., "A escrava que não é Isaura"). On the Latin American avant-garde inflection through *mundonovismo*, see George Yúdice, "Rethinking the Theory of the Avant-Garde from the Periphery," in *Modernism and Its Margins: Reinscribing Modernity from Spain and Latin America*, ed. Anthony Geist and José Monleón (New York: Garland, 1999), 53; Unruh, *Latin American Vanguards*, 141–51. On the first wave of Brazilian *modernismo*, see especially Madureira, *Cannibal Modernities*, 21–51.

55. Jorge Amado, "Apontamentos sobre o moderno romance brasileiro," *Lanterna Verde* 2 (1933): 48–51.

56. Oswald de Andrade, *Seraphim Grosse Point*, trans. K. David Jackson and Albert Bork (Austin: New Latin Quarter Editions, 1979), 5.

57. Fernando Rosenberg, "Cosmopolitanism and Repentance: The Homecoming of the Avant-Garde Poet," in *The Avant-gardes and Geopolitics in Latin America*, 136–60. Such a homecoming is described at the end of *Seraphim*: "Tired / Of my travels on the earth / By camel and taxi / I seek you / The road home / In the stars / Atmospheric coasts of Brazil" (de Andrade, *Seraphim Grosse Point*, 102).

58. In 1939 Mário de Andrade will both disparagingly and wistfully refer to the earlier avant-gardes in which he participated as the "new ones" (*os novos*), those movements that privileged metaphors of infancy and childhood. "Noção de Responsibildiade" (first published March 19, 1939), in de Andrade, *O empalhador de passarinho*, 23.

59. See Enrique Mallea, "La crisis y el hombre actual," *Megáfono*, no. 11 (August 1933): 1–6, an article that coincidentally precedes a survey on the relevance of Borges to contemporary literature.

60. Rita Felski, "Context Stinks!" *New Literary History* 42.4 (Autumn 2011): 590. See also Eric Hayot, "Against Periodization; or, On Institutional Time," *New Literary History* 42.4 (Autumn 2011): 739–56.

61. See Michael North, *1922: A Return to the Scene of the Modern* (New York: Oxford University Press, 1999); in Latin America, 1922 also saw the founding of the Argentine avant-garde journal *Martín Fierro*, the publication of César Vallejo's *Trilce*, and Brazil's Modern Art Week. See also Hans Gumbrecht, *In 1926: Living on the Edge of Time* (Cambridge, Mass.: Harvard University Press, 2006), an "essay on historical simultaneity" (xi) that ludically yokes together Argentina and Brazil, the USSR and Germany around this pivotal, if arbitrary, date.

62. The uneven simultaneity applies to countries within Latin America as well, as a comparison of Argentina or Brazil to Ecuador or Bolivia makes immediately clear. The diversity of Latin America is another element of this non-simultaneously simultaneity, often overlooked in the tendency to "regionalize" very different national contexts. On simultaneity, see Carlos Blanco Aguinaga, "On Modernism from the Periphery," in *Modernism and Its Margins: Reinscribing Cultural Modernity from Spain and Latin America*, ed.

Anthony L. Geist and José B. Monleón (New York: Garland, 1999), 3–16; Rosenberg, *The Avant-gardes and Geopolitics in Latin America*, 37–38.

63. In *A Singular Modernity*, Jameson critiques the discourse of multiple modernities for overlooking the determining force of capitalism. On periodization, see Marshall Brown, "Introduction," *Modern Language Quarterly* (December 2001): 315.

64. Often, as it was for Anderson, this ostensible belatedness is read positively, as breathing new life into a moribund modernism. See Perry Anderson, "Modernity and Revolution," *New Left Review* 144 (March–April 1984): 109. There is often confusion for non–Latin Americanist scholars as to what constitutes modernism in the region. Scholars from other fields describing Latin American modernism may reference Rubén Darío (1867–1916), the experimental prose of the 1920–1930s, or, most strangely, as in Anderson, magical realism of the 1960s–1970s: three radically different moments and approaches to literature.

65. To give just a few examples, Borges translated the last page of *Ulysses* in *Proa* in 1925; in 1932, the Argentine journal *Sur* published portions of Heidegger's *Being and Time*; Eisenstein and Fritz Lang were relatively well-known figures in the same circles in the mid- to late 1920s. Alejandro Mejías-López has recently shown how the term "modernism" shifted from its origins in the Spanish-speaking world to a predominantly Anglophone one, arguing that the assertion of the region's belatedness is retrospective, and historically inaccurate, for the late nineteenth- and early twentieth-century period. See Alejandro Mejías-López, *The Inverted Conquest: The Myth of Modernity and the Transatlantic Onset of Modernism* (Nashville: Vanderbilt University Press, 2010), 3–4.

66. See Néstor García Canclini, *Hybrid Cultures: Strategies for Entering and Leaving Modernity* (Minneapolis: University of Minnesota Press, 2005), especially chapter 2; Ortiz, *A Moderna Tradicão Brasileira*; Sarlo, *La imaginación técnica*; Rama, "Las dos vanguardias latinoamericanas"; Martín-Barbero, *De los medios a las mediaciones*; Roberto Schwarz, *Misplaced Ideas: Essays on Brazilian Culture*, trans. John Gledson (London: Verso, 1992). For approaches to global modernism rooted in the Anglophone context, see Susan Stanford Friedman, "Definitional Excursions: The Meanings of Modern/ Modernity/ Modernism," *Modernism/Modernity* 8.3 (2001): 493–513 and her "Periodizing Modernism: Postcolonial Modernities and the Space/Time Borders of Modernist Studies," *Modernism/Modernity* 13.3 (2006): 425–43; Mark Wollaeger, introduction to *The Oxford Handbook to Global Modernisms*, ed. Mark Wollaeger (Oxford: Oxford University Press, 2012).

67. For compelling examples of criticism on non-English-language modernisms, see Hannah Freed-Thall, *Spoiled Distinctions: Aesthetics and the Ordinary in French Modernism* (Oxford: Oxford University Press, 2015); Allison Schachter, *Diasporic Modernisms: Hebrew and Yiddish Literature in the Twentieth Century* (Oxford: Oxford University Press, 2014); William Gardner, *Advertising Tower: Japanese Modernism and Modernity in the 1920s* (Cambridge, Mass.: Harvard University Press, 2006); Seiji Lippit, *Topographies of Japanese Modernism* (New York: Columbia University Press, 2002);

Shu-mei Shih, *The Lure of the Modern: Writing Modernism in Semi-Colonial China, 1917–1937* (Berkeley: University of California Press, 2001); Leo Lee, *Shanghai Modern: The Flowering of a New Urban Culture in China, 1930–1945* (Cambridge, Mass.: Harvard University Press, 1999). A pioneering and often overlooked work in this respect is Chana Kronfeld, *On the Margins of Modernism* (Berkeley: University of California Press, 1996), a study of Jewish modernism and critique of the Anglophone-centric model of modernist studies. As I was putting the final touches on this book, I read with great interest Janet Poole's *When the Future Disappears: The Modernist Imagination in Late Colonial Korea* (New York: Columbia University Press, 2014).

68. Jennifer Wicke, "Appreciation, Depreciation: Modernism's Speculative Bubble," *Modernism/Modernity* 8.3 (September 2001): 396.

69. Silviano Santiago, *Nas malhas da letra* (São Paulo: Companhia das Letras, 1989), 77, my translation.

70. Jameson, *A Singular Modernity*, 101, 104; see also Wollaeger, introduction. Jameson's references to Latin American modernism tend to be superficial—it is Asia, and Japan in particular, that has pride of place in his theories of non-Western modernisms—but his work encourages us to think through the global dimensions of the pairing modernism/modernity.

71. Graciliano Ramos, *Cartas inéditas: De Graciliano Ramos a seus tradutores argentinos*, ed. Pedro Moacir Maia and Fernando da Rocha Peres (Salvador: EDUFBA, 2008), 26, my translation. Garay translated his short stories "Dois dedos" and "Relógio" for the Buenos Aires periodical *La Prensa* in 1937.

72. See Raul Antelo's pioneering *Na ilha de Marapatá: Mário de Andrade lê os hispano-americanos* (São Paulo: Editora HUCITEC, 1986); later, Florencia Garramuño, *Primitive Modernities: Tango, Samba and Nation*, trans. Anna Kazumi Stahl (Stanford, Calif.: Stanford University Press, 2011); and the journal *Grumo*, published in Rio de Janeiro. Vicky Unruh's seminal *Latin American Vanguards*, the first book-length study of the Latin American avant-gardes in English, also incorporated Brazil, as did the equally pioneering work of Jorge Schwartz in *Las vanguardias latinoamericanas: Textos programáticos y críticos* (Mexico City: Fondo de Cultura Económica, 2002); first published in 1991.

73. Emir Rodriguez Monegal, *Jorge Luis Borges: A Literary Biography* (New York: Paragon House, 1988). For historical context, see Arnold J. Bauer, *Goods, Power, History: Latin America's Material Culture* (Cambridge: Cambridge University Press, 2001). In *The Contemporary History of Latin America*, Tulio Halperin Donghi periodizes 1930 as the end of the neocolonial period (Durham, N.C.: Duke University Press, 1993), 159.

74. See, for example, Otávio de Fária, "Mensagem post-modernista," as well as other essays in the special issue of *Lanterna Verde*, no. 4 (November 1936): 49–67; Guillermo Giucci, "Gilberto Freyre e o (Pós) Modernismo," in *Arquivos literários*, org. Eneida Maria de Souza and Wander Melo Miranda (Minas Gerais: Universidade Federal de Minas Gerais, Centro de Estudos Literários, 2003); Bueno, *Uma história do romance de 30*, 47–50.

75. The notion of failure is constitutive of the avant-garde's notion of experiment, contained within them, as "seeds of exhaustion" (*germes de*

caudicdade), per Mário de Andrade. See *O empalhador de passarinho*, 23. See also Matei Calinescu, *Five Faces of Modernity: Modernism, Avant-Garde, Decadence, Kitsch, Postmodernism* (Durham, N.C.: Duke University Press, 1987), 123–24; Jonathan P. Eburne and Rita Felski, "Introduction," *New Literary History* 41.4 (Autumn 2010): v–xv. I also discuss the figure of the failure briefly in Chapter 3.

76. Afonso Arinos de Mello Franco, "Poesia, 1936," *Lanterna Verde* 4 (November 1936): 4; Tristão de Athayde, "Síntese," *Lanterna Verde* 4 (November 1936): 94.

77. In stark contrast to Argentina, even those Brazilian intellectuals who were extremely critical of the state ended up participating in it. On the many different Brazilian modernists incorporated into the Vargas regime, see Randal Johnson, *Literature, Culture and Authoritarianism in Brazil, 1930–1945* (Washington, D.C.: Latin American Program, The Wilson Center, 1989); Williams, *Culture Wars in Brazil*.

78. See Susan Buck-Morss, *Dreamworld and Catastrophe: The Passing of Mass Utopia in East and West* (Cambridge, Mass.: MIT Press, 2000); Hansen, *Cinema and Experience*, 80; Boris Groys, *The Total Art of Stalinism: Avant-Garde, Aesthetic Dictatorship and Beyond* (New York: Verso, 2011); Katerina Clarke, *The Fourth Rome: Stalinism, Cosmopolitanism, and the Evolution of Soviet Culture, 1931–1941* (Cambridge, Mass.: Harvard University Press, 2011). On Argentina, see María Pía López, "30/43: Historia, Ensayo y Literatura," in *La década infame y los escritores suicidas (1930–1943)*, ed. David Viñas, Gabriela García Cedro, and María Pía López (Buenos Aires: Paradiso Ediciones, Fundación Crónica General, 2007), 11–39; David Viñas, "La historia excluida: Ubicación de Martínez Estrada," in *La década infame y los escritores suicidas (1930–1943)*, ed. David Viñas, Gabriela García Cedro, and María Pía López (Buenos Aires: Paradiso Ediciones, Fundación Crónica General, 2007); Rocco Corbone, "Erdosain entre Yrigoyen y Uriburu: *Los siete locos* y *Los lanzallamas* entre la república radical y el autoritarismo," in *La década infame y los escritores suicidas (1930–1943)*, ed. David Viñas, Gabriela García Cedro, and María Pía López (Buenos Aires: Paradiso Ediciones, Fundación Crónica General, 2007), 65; Tulio Halperin Donghi, *La república imposible (1930–1945)* (Buenos Aires: Ariel, 2004); Alejandro Cattaruzza, ed., *Crisis económica, avance del estado e incertidumbre política (1930–1943): Nueva historia de la nación argentina*, tomo IX (Buenos Aires: Planeta, 1999), 422–23. Gonzalo Aguilar argues that the 1930s marks a closing down of the possibilities of technology in the Argentine context, in particular because of how they were employed by the state. See Gonzalo Aguilar, "El motor y el cachivache (La vanguardia martinfierrista y las transformaciones tecnológicas)," in *Episodios cosmopolitas en la cultura argentina* (Buenos Aires: Santiago Arcos, 2009), 60. On Brazil, see Johnson, *Literature, Culture and Authoritarianism in Brazil, 1930–1945*; António Cândido, "A Revolução de 1930 e a cultura," *A educação pela noite* (São Paulo: Editora Atica, 1987); Ângela Maria de Castro Gomes, "A 'cultura histórica' do Estado Novo," *Luso-Brazilian Review* 36.2 (1999): 103–8; Boris Fausto, *A revolução de 1930: Historiografia e história* (São Paulo: Editôra Brasiliense, 1976); Lafetá,

1930; Vavy Pacheco Borges, "Anos trinta e política: Conceitos, imagens e temas," *Luso-Brazilian Review* 36.2 (Winter 1999): 109–26. On France, see Eugene Weber, *The Hollow Years: France in the 1930s* (New York: W. W. Norton, 1994). On the United States and U.K., see Miller, *Late Modernism*, especially 4–6. In *Advertising Tower*, Gardner explores the period of Japanese avant-gardes before their closing down in the 1930s (6).

79. Writers like Faulkner, Waldo Frank, and Countee Cullen, for example, arrived to South American readers first through French translation, as did the first writings of Eisenstein and other Soviet avant-garde filmmakers. The phrase "blindness of the center" comes from Fredric Jameson, "In the Mirror of Alternate Modernities," in *The Modernist Papers* (London: Verso, 2007), 292–93. Jameson's understanding here echoes, in a negative vein, Silviano Santiago's seminal concept of the "space in-between" and, more recently, "the cosmopolitanism of the poor." See Santiago, "Literature and Mass Culture"; Silviano Santiago, *O cosmopolitismo do pobre: Crítica literária e crítica cultural* (Belo Horizonte: Editora UFMG, 2004). Both Jennifer Wicke and Jameson have argued that the rebranding of modernism as increasingly expansive serves to secure the original prestige of a high modernist canon. See Wicke, "Appreciation, Depreciation"; Jameson, *A Singular Modernity*, 7. This canon is anchored in the dominance of Anglophone primary texts and scholarship, particularly those from the United States and the U.K.

80. For an intellectual historian's account of this critical interpretation of modernity in Latin America, see Nicola Miller, *Reinventing Modernity in Latin America: Intellectuals Imagine the Future, 1900–1930* (New York: Palgrave, 2007).

81. See Miller, *Late Modernism*; Esty, *A Shrinking Island*. Each of these scholars posits different periodizations of late modernism. Miller argues that it emerges in the Anglo-American context in 1926; whereas for Jameson in *A Singular Modernity* and, much earlier, in "Seriality in Modern Literature," it is a postwar phenomenon coinciding with the ideology of modernism, something like its co-optation. For Esty, writing about England, late modernism begins in the 1930s–1940s. See also Michael Denning, *The Cultural Front: The Laboring of American Culture in the Twentieth Century* (New York: Verso, 2011), 165; Rita Barnard, *The Great Depression and the Culture of Abundance: Kenneth Fearing, Nathanael West, and Mass Culture in the 1930s* (Cambridge: Cambridge University Press, 1995). A synthetic account of the periodization of the *vanguardias* (Brazilian and Spanish American) can be found in Schwartz, *Las vanguardias latinoamericanas*, 36–40.

82. G. W. F. Hegel, *Lectures on the Philosophy of World History* (New York: Cambridge University Press, 1975), especially 162–70; Conde Keyserling, "Perspectivas sudamericanas," *Sur* 2 (1931): 3–12. For Hegel, Latin America constituted one of the zones of the "peoples without history"—whereas the United States, albeit without history, represented futurity. Keyserling, who was admired by Argentine intellectuals of the 1930s, posited a telluric history of the world in which South America had not yet reached its potential. Ortega y Gasset delivered a series of lectures, among them "Hegel y la historia," in various institutions in Buenos Aires during the late 1920s; he

was close with Victoria Ocampo and had an influence on publications in *Sur*. See also José Luis Romero, "Introducción a un sudamericanismo esencial," *Sur* 8 (1933): 131–40.

83. In the words of the historian Dain Borge, "As always in Latin America, scholars find it hard to analyze the 1930s as a period in their own right, rather than as a breakpoint." Borge, "Review Essay: Brazilian Social Thought of the 1930s," *Luso-Brazilian Review* 31.2 (1994): 148. Scholars of Latin American literature in particular have been wary of positing the 1930s as a point of rupture, arguing instead for a different modernist periodization that links the decade to the previous one. In this context, Luís Bueno's monumental *Uma história do romance de 30* is a major contribution to the idea that 1930s literature has its own specificity, that it should not be elided as simply a continuation of earlier *modernista* discourse, and that these differences are related to transformations in the aesthetic, technological, political, and social spheres in Brazil.

84. After finishing this manuscript, I read with great interest Craig Epplin's *Late Book Culture in Argentina* (London: Bloomsbury Academic, 2014), which follows Jameson in this respect.

85. Raul Antelo, "Gilberto Freyre: Alteração e iteração," in *Gilberto Freyre e os estudos latino-americanos*, ed. Joshua Lund and Malcolm McNee (Pittsburgh: Instituto Internacional de Literatura Iberoamericana, 2006), 76.

86. *Pré-modernismo* is a term invented by Tristão de Athayde in 1939 (Conde, *Consuming Visions*, 11); *pós-modernismo* begins to circulate in little magazines in the mid-1930s.

87. André Gaudreault, "Showing and Telling: Image and Word in Early Cinema," in *Early Cinema: Space, Frame, Narrative*, ed. Thomas Elsaesser and Adam Barker (London: BFI Publishing, 1990), 68–75. See also Jameson, "Seriality and Modern Literature," *Bucknell Review* 18.1 (Spring 1970): 63–64; Jameson, "Periodizing the 1960s," *Social Text* 9/10 (Spring 1984): 178–209. In *Postmodernism, or the Cultural Logic of Late Capitalism* (Durham, N.C.: Duke University Press, 1991), Jameson offers another critique of rejections of periodization (3–5); see also his *A Singular Modernity*, especially 29, 102, 167.

88. Virgilio Piñera, "Grafomanía," in *Cuentos fríos & El que vino a salvarme* (Madrid: Cátedra, 2008), 293.

89. Santiago, "Literature and Mass Culture," 128. See also Ted Striphas, *The Late Age of Print: Everyday Book Culture from Consumerism to Control* (New York: Columbia University Press, 2011), especially p. x. More recently, Craig Epplin has analyzed the materiality of contemporary (twenty-first-century) Argentine book culture as a symptom or expression of its "lateness." See Epplin, *Late Book Culture in Argentina*, especially 3–4.

90. Santiago, *Nas malhas da letra*, 98, my translation.

91. Raymond Williams, "Dominant, Residual, and Emergent," in *Marxism and Literature* (Oxford: Oxford University Press, 1977), 121–27. See also Charles Acland, introduction to *Residual Media*, ed. Acland (Minneapolis: University of Minnesota Press, 2007), xxi, and Michelle Henning, "New Lamps for Old: Photography, Obsolescence, and Social Change," in *Residual*

Media, ed. Charles Acland (Minneapolis: University of Minnesota Press, 2007), 57–58.

CHAPTER 1

The epigraphs to this chapter are from the following: Jorge Luis Borges, "The Other Whitman," *La vida literaria* 14 (September 1929), my translation; Galvão, *Industrial Park*, 98.

1. See Calinescu, *Five Faces of Modernity*, 95–150.

2. See Leopoldo Hurtado, "Celuloide," *Martín Fierro* (November 1926), in Jason Borge, *Avances de Hollywood: Crítica cinematográfica en Latinoamérica* (Rosario, Argentina: Beatriz Viterbo, 2005), 68; Leopoldo Hurtado, *La vida literaria* (August 2, 1931).

3. See José Luis Romero, "Las ciudades masificadas," in *Latinoamérica: Las ciudades y las ideas* (Mexico City: Siglo Veintiuno Editores, 1986), 386–409; Francisco Foot Hardman, *Nem Pátria, nem Patrão! (Vida operária e cultura anarquista no Brasil)* (São Paulo: UNESP, 2002).

4. On the crowd and the masses, see Graciela Montaldo, *Zonas Ciegas: Populismos y experimentos culturales en Argentina* (Buenos Aires: Fondo de Cultura Económica, 2010), especially 61–110; López, "30/43," 29.

5. On publicness in Anglo-American modernism, Justus Nieland's *Feeling Modern: The Eccentricities of Public Life* is particularly illuminating.

6. See the facsimile edition, *Crítica: Revista multicolor de los sábados, 1933–1934*, ed. Nicolás Helft (Buenos Aires: Fondo Nacional de las Artes, 1999).

7. See Beatriz Sarlo, *Una modernidad periférica: Buenos Aires, 1920 y 1930* (Buenos Aires: Ediciones Nueva Visión, 1988); see also Sarlo, *La imaginación técnica*, 14; Sylvia Saítta, "Nuevo periodismo y literatura argentina," in *Historia crítica de la literatura argentina*, vol. 7, *Rupturas*, ed. Celina Manzoni (Buenos Aires: Emecé, 2009), 239–62.

8. On the incorporation of *martinfierristas* into *Crítica*, see Sylvia Saítta, ed., *Contra: La Revista de los franco-tiradores* (Buenos Aires: Universidad Nacional de Quilmes, 2005), 19–20.

9. On authorship in Borges, see especially Sylvia Molloy, *Las letras de Borges y otros ensayos* (Rosario, Argentina: Beatriz Viterbo Editora, 1999), 49–57. An English translation exists: *The Signs of Borges* (Durham, N.C.: Duke University Press, 1994).

10. Roland Christ, for example, describes the *Universal History of Infamy* as larval, declaring its aesthetic qualities "negligible," interesting only for developmental reasons. Christ, *The Narrow Act: Borges' Art of Allusion* (New York: Lumen, 1995), 85. See also Jaime Alazraki, "Génesis de un Estilo: *Historia Universal de la Infamia*," *Revista Iberoamericana* 123–24 (April–September 1983): 247.

11. Comics first appeared in Argentine publications during the 1920s and 1930s, influenced by syndicated U.S. strips.

12. Carlos Ulanovsky, *Paren las rotativas: Diarios, revistas, periodistas* (Buenos Aires: Emecé, 2005), 69.

13. On the contingency of modern print journalism, see Julio Ramos, *Desencuentros de la modernidad en América Latina* (Mexico City: Fondo de Cultura Económica, 2003); Roland Barthes, "The Structure of the *Fait-Divers*," in *Critical Essays*, trans. Richard Howard (Evanston, Ill.: Northwestern University Press, 1972), 187–96.

14. Ulyses Petit de Murat, *Borges* (Buenos Aires: Municipalidad de la Ciudad de Buenos Aires, Secretaría de Cultura, 1980), 140–41.

15. See Hayles, *Writing Machines*, 23. There is a precedent: the "mural" little magazine *Prisma* (1921–22), which Borges cofounded. Its experimental format was intended to paper the walls of the city.

16. Jorge Luis Borges, *A Universal History of Iniquity*, trans. Andrew Hurley (New York: Penguin Classics, 2004), 3. Unless otherwise indicated, I use this translation, although I refer to the book's title as *A Universal History of Infamy.*

17. While Borges will later express fear and abhorrence of the masses under Peronism, in the 1930s he is not yet afraid of the masses, and he laments the military coup that overthrew the democratically elected Yrigoyen in 1930.

18. For Benjamin, the increasing participation of the masses begins in periodicals, especially in the "letters to the editor" section, and finds its apex in film, where the masses go to recognize themselves on the screen. Walter Benjamin, "The Work of Art in the Age of Its Technological Reproducibility," in *The Work of Art in the Age of Its Technological Reproducibility and Other Writings on Media*, ed. Michael W. Jennings, Brigid Doherty, and Thomas Y. Levin (Cambridge, Mass.: Harvard University Press, 2008), 33–34.

19. See Edgardo Cozarinsky, *Borges in/and/on Cinema*, trans. Gloria Waldman and Roland Christ (New York: Lumen Books, 1988); José Eduardo González, *Borges and the Politics of Form* (New York: Garland, 1988); Christ, *The Narrow Act*, 69–70.

20. See López, "Early Cinema and Modernity in Latin America," 50–51. On Argentina's cosmopolitan, transnational taste in filmgoing, as well as on its film production during the period, see also Karush, *The Culture of Class*; Calistro, *Reportaje al cine argentino.*

21. H. P. Tew, "Cinema in the Argentine," *Close Up* 17.2 (February 1930): 140.

22. On this context, see Gonzalo Aguilar and Emiliano Jelicié, *Borges va al cine* (Buenos Aires: Libraria, 2010); Fernando Martín Peña, "Amigos del Cine," in *Amigos del Arte, 1924–1942*, ed. Patrícia Artundo and Marcelo Eduardo Pacheco (Buenos Aires: MALBA, 2008).

23. Jorge Luis Borges, "Dos Films," *Sur* 103 (April 1943): 104.

24. Cozarinsky, *Borges in/and/on Film*, 26–27. This reading of Vidor appears in Jorge Luis Borges, "Street Scene," *Sur* 5 (Summer 1932): 199.

25. Jorge Luis Borges, *Historia universal de la infamia* (Buenos Aires: Alianza Emecé, 1971), 68, my translation.

26. Cozarinsky, *Borges in/and/on Film*, especially 15–19. On film's fragmented continuity, see Friedrich Kittler, *Gramophone, Film, Typewriter*, trans. Geoffrey Winthrop-Young and Michael Wutz (Stanford, Calif.: Stanford University Press, 1999), 117–22; Hansen, *Cinema and Experience*, 274–75. Jean

Epstein's early reformulation of Zeno's paradox through film is developed in "On Certain Characteristics of *Photogénie*" (1923) and later, more fully, in his book *The Intelligence of a Machine*, trans. Christophe Wall-Romana (Minneapolis: Univocal, 2014).

27. Scenes of spectatorship also appear in several other stories in the *Universal History*: "Monk Eastman, Purveyor of Iniquities," "The Uncivil Master of Ceremonies Kotsuké no Suke," "The Improbable Impostor Tom Castro," and "The Terrifying Redeemer Lazarus Morell."

28. "Narrative proved to be a more effective and surer means of assimilating the inassimilable by conferring on death a meaning." Mary Ann Doane, *The Emergence of Cinematic Time: Modernity, Contingency, and the Archive* (Cambridge, Mass.: Harvard University Press, 2002), 164.

29. Paul Ricoeur, *Time and Narrative*, vol. 1, trans. Kathleen Blamey and David Pellauer (Chicago: University of Chicago Press, 1990), 10. On the resistance to emplotting history in modernist literature, see Hayden White, "The Modernist Event," in *The Persistence of History: Cinema, Television, and the Modern Event*, ed. Vivian Sobchack (New York: Routledge, 1996), 24–25.

30. Arthur Schopenhauer, *The World as Will and Representation*, vol. 2, trans. E. F. J. Payne (Clinton, Mass.: Falcon's Wing Press, 1958), 443.

31. As I noted above, Ortega y Gasset delivered a series of lectures, among them "Hegel y la historia," in various institutions in Buenos Aires during the late 1920s; he was close with Victoria Ocampo and had an influence on publications in *Sur.*

32. After completing this manuscript, I read with great interest Hernán Díaz's study on the chiasmatic relationship between history and eternity in Borges in his *Borges: Between History and Eternity* (New York: Continuum, 2012). Díaz offers an extensive analysis of Borges's long-running devotion to U.S. literature (rather than film), beginning with the *Universal History of Infamy.*

33. Ranajit Guha, *History at the Limit of World-History* (New York: Columbia University Press, 2000), 35. See also Daniel Balderston, *Out of Context: Historical Reference and the Representation of Reality in Borges* (Durham, N.C.: Duke University Press, 1993), 9–10.

34. See John King, *Magical Reels* (London: Verso, 2000), 11.

35. See Salvatore, "Imperial Mechanics"; Bauer, *Goods, Power, History.*

36. See especially Siegfried Kracauer, *The Mass Ornament: Weimar Essays* (Cambridge, Mass.: Harvard University Press, 2005), 78; Peter Wollen, "Modern Times: Cinema/Americanism/The Robot," in *Raiding the Icebox: Reflections on Twentieth-Century Culture* (Bloomington: Indiana University Press, 1993), 35–71.

37. On Ford's industrials, including their international sweep, see Lee Grieveson, "The Work of Film in the Age of Fordist Mechanization," *Cinema Journal* 51.3 (Spring 2012): 25–51. On Ford's Amazonian enclave, see Greg Grandin, *Fordlandia: The Rise and Fall of Henry Ford's Forgotten Jungle City* (New York: Picador, 2010). Anxiety over Fordlandia is palpable in Brazilian cultural journals of the 1930s. The afterlives of Ford in Latin

America persisted after his stock began to wane in the late 1920s in the United States.

38. *The Man of the People*, no. 1 (March 27, 1931): 17.

39. Abelardo de Araújo Jurema, "Sobre os campos do noite," *Revista Acadêmica* 10 (April 1935): 3.

40. See Jonathan Sterne, "Out with the Trash," in *Residual Media*, ed. Charles Acland (Minneapolis: University of Minnesota Press, 2007), 20–22.

41. Alfonso Junco, "El cinematógrafo y la invasión pacífica," *El Universal* (June 1, 1929), in Jason Borge, *Avances de Hollywood: Crítica cinematográfica en Latinoamérica* (Rosario, Argentina: Beatriz Viterbo, 2005), 116. Writers had also leveled a very similar critique at the "Americanization" of modern print journalism.

42. Abelardo de Araújo Jurema, "O Paraíso Norte Americano," *Momento*, no. 3 (March 1934): 14.

43. Miriam Hansen, "The Mass Production of the Senses" and "Vernacular Modernism: Tracking Cinema on a Global Scale," in *World Cinemas, Transnational Perspectives*, ed. Nataša Durovicová and Kathleen Newman (New York: Routledge, 2010).

44. On this broader process in Latin America during the 1930s, see Martín-Barbero, *De los medios a las mediaciones*, 177–93.

45. Borges may have been influenced by his experience watching King Vidor's *Hallelujah!* (1929), as well as by his recent translation, for the journal *Sur*, of Langston Hughes's poem "The Negro Speaks of Rivers."

46. Borges, *Universal History of Iniquity*, 8; Hansen, "Vernacular Modernism," 302.

47. Borges, *Historia universal de la infamia*, 53, my translation. Years later, in his neo-modernist *Hopscotch* (*Rayuela*, 1963), Julio Cortázar will create a similar game with his readers by dividing the novel into two halves that the reader can interlace by "jumping" (as in a game of hopscotch) between Paris and Buenos Aires. The halves are titled, respectively, "From the Side of There" (Paris) and "From the Side of Here" (Buenos Aires).

48. Beatriz Sarlo has argued instead that film implies a more mythologizing and ultimately passive role in 1920s–1930s Argentina, in contrast to the radio. See *La imaginación técnica*, 117–20.

49. On the problem of the copy and modernism in Borges, see A. J. Cascardi, "Mimesis and Modernism: The Case of Jorge Luis Borges," in *Literary Philosophers: Borges, Calvino, Eco* (New York: Routledge, 2002), 100–128. On the premise of literature's depletion as opportunity in Borges, see John Barth, "The Literature of Exhaustion," in *The Friday Book: Essays and Other Non-Fiction* (Baltimore: Johns Hopkins University Press, 1984), 62–76.

50. First published in 1933 in a very limited edition apparently financed by Oswald de Andrade, *Industrial Park* remained out of print until 1981. Elizabeth Jackson and K. David Jackson's translation into English, with a very helpful critical commentary, appeared in 1993.

51. On her life and work, see Eduardo de Assis Duarte, "Patrícia Galvão: Comunismo e Feminismo nos Anos 30," in *Mulher: Cinco séculos de desenvolvimento na América: Capítulo Brasil*, ed. Sylvia Maria von Atzingen

(Venturoli Aud. Belo Horizonte: Unicentro Newton Paiva, 1999), 371–77; Geraldo Galvão Ferraz, "A *pulp fiction* de Patrícia Galvão," in Patrícia Galvão, *Safra macabra: Contos policias* (Rio de Janeiro: José Olympio Editora, 1998); Thelma Guedes, *Pagu: Literatura e revolução: Um estudo sobre o romance "Parque industrial"* (São Paulo: Nankin Editorial, 2003); Flávio Loureiro Chaves, "Pagu e a experiência da linguagem," in Patrícia Galvão, *Parque industrial* (Porto Alegre: Mercado Aberto; São Paulo: Edufscar, 1994), 7–11; Luiz Fernando Valente, "Canonizando Pagu," *Letras de hoje* 33.3 (1998): 27–38; Patrícia Galvão, *Paixão Pagu: A autobiografia precoce de Patrícia Galvão* (Rio de Janeiro: Agir, 2005). On the gendered dimensions of the avant-garde muse in Argentina and Brazil, see Vicky Unruh, "Las ágiles musas de la modernidad: Patrícia Galvão y Norah Lange," *Revista Iberoamericana* 64.182–83 (January–June 1998): 271–86.

52. Galvão joined the Brazilian Communist Party in 1931, the year before she began to write *Industrial Park* and two years before the novel's publication, apparently inspired by a recent trip to Buenos Aires. See Galvão, *Paixão Pagu*; Jorge Schwartz, "De lo estético a lo ideológico: *Klaxon* y *Revista de Antropofagia*," in *La cultura de un siglo: América Latina en sus revistas*, ed. Saúl Sosnowski (Buenos Aires: Alianza, 1999), 63.

53. Hansen, "Vernacular Modernism," 293.

54. Romero, *Latinoamerica*, 156.

55. Andrade, *Seraphim Grosse Point*, 68.

56. Mário de Andrade, *O empalhador de passarinho* (São Paulo: Livraria Martins Editôra, 1972), 232, 222–23.

57. *O homem do povo* (São Paulo: Impr. Oficial do Estado, Divisão de Arquivo do Estado de São Paulo, 1985).

58. In one of the few contemporaneous accounts of the novel, Galvão was accused of artificially imposing the factory model imported from writers like Mike Gold, rather than representing the essence of Brazil, and *Industrial Park* was unfavorably contrasted with the paternalistic plantation setting of *Cacau*, Jorge Amado's novel published the same year. *Industrial Park* and *Cacau* vie for the title of the first proletarian novel in Brazil. See R. Magalhães Junior, "O romance proletário," *Correio da Manhã* (November 3, 1934): 6.

59. On the series versus the group, see Jean-Paul Sartre, "Collectivities," in *Critique of Dialectical Reason I: Theory of Practical Ensembles*, trans. Alan Sheridan-Smith (London: NLB, 1976), 256–344.

60. For example, in Brazil, Antônio de Alcântara Machado's camera-eye in *Pathé-Baby* (1926); Mário de Andrade's *Paulicéia Desvairada* (Hallucinated City, 1922); and the films *Rien que les Heures* (Alberto Cavalcanti, 1926), *Fragmentos da vida* (José Medina, 1929), and *São Paulo, Sinfonia da metrópole* (Adalberto Kemeny and Rudolf Rex Lustig, 1929); the quintessential city film is Walter Ruttmann's *Berlin: Symphony of a Great City* (1927).

61. See Roberto Schwarz, "A Carroça, o Bonde e o Poeta Modernista" (originally published in 1977), in *Que horas são?* (São Paulo: Companhia das Letras, 1987), 11–21. There is an English translation: "The Cart, the Tram, and the Modernist Poet," in *Misplaced Ideas: Essays on Brazilian Culture*, 108–25.

62. See, for example, Eisenstein, "Montage of Attractions," originally published in *Lef* in 1923, with its emphasis on a liberation from the hero-driven plot. In Sergei Eisenstein, *Film Form and Film Sense*, trans. and ed. Jay Leyda (New York: Meridian Books, 1960), 230–33.

63. Michael Denning, *Culture in the Age of Three Worlds* (London: Verso, 2004), 67. In *The Cultural Front*, Denning labels "radical modernists" those who took a leftward turn in the 1930s after creating their first modernist works previously (163). While outside of my scope here, there are many compelling parallels between *Industrial Park* and the *U.S.A.* trilogy in particular.

64. See Denning, *Culture in the Age of Three Worlds*, 67. On the proletariat in the Brazilian novel of the 1930s, see Bueno, *Uma história do romance de 30*, 243–82.

65. In "The Author as Producer" and in earlier texts such as "One-Way Street," Benjamin, like Galvão, had reflected on the ending of the traditional book form and the increasing turn toward graphic materiality.

66. For a critique of analogical readings of European modernist literature and cinematic montage, see Trotter, *Cinema and Modernism*; Murphet, *Multimedia Modernism*, 14–15.

67. Scholars have tended to overlook this presence, with the key exception of the Mexican context, where Eisenstein's influence on film production was direct. See Masha Salazkina, *In Excess: Sergei Eisenstein's Mexico* (Chicago: University of Chicago Press, 2009). Outside of Mexico, Soviet film would have a pronounced impact in Latin America in the work of auteurs of the 1960s–1970s. I analyze the early reception of Soviet film across the continent in "Parallel Modernities? The First Reception of Soviet Cinema in Latin America," in *Cosmopolitan Film Cultures in Latin America, 1896–1960*, ed. Rielle Navitski and Nicholas Poppe (Bloomington: University of Indiana Press, 2017).

68. *O homem do povo* 8 (April 13, 1931); *O homem do povo* 1 (March 27, 1931): 18; see also issue 3 (April 2, 1931): 4.

69. A similar construction of Garbo can be found in the articles "Em material de estrellas" and "Cinema sexual" in *The Man of the People*, which juxtapose Garbo's image with that of a British woman on strike.

70. See Roland Barthes, "The Face of Garbo," *Mythologies* (London: Vintage, 1993), 56–57. Throughout the 1920s and 1930s, Garbo functioned as a *denkbild*, or thought-image, crystallizing various debates about the conjunction of cinema and the modern woman (Hansen, *Cinema and Experience*, 24).

71. Note that I am describing a certain idea of Soviet montage as understood by Latin American readers and viewers at the time, rather than a strict description of Eisenstein's own constantly shifting thought.

72. See Sergei Eisenstein, "Montage Is Conflict," in *The Cinematic*, ed. David Campany (Cambridge, Mass.: MIT Press, 2007), 30–32. See also David Bordwell, *The Cinema of Eisenstein* (Cambridge, Mass.: Harvard University Press, 1993); Sergei Eisenstein, "A Dialectical Approach to Film Form" and "Methods of Montage," in *Film Form and Film Sense*, trans. and ed. Jay Leyda (New York: Meridian Books, 1963), 45–63, 72–83; Jay Leyda, *Kino: A History of the Russian and Soviet Film* (Princeton, N.J.: Princeton University

Press, 1983); Michael Tratner, *Crowd Scenes: Movies and Mass Politics* (New York: Fordham University Press, 2008).

73. Denning, *Culture in the Age of Three Worlds*, 66–67.

74. Eisenstein, *Film Form*, 16. See also Peter Giglin, "Aesthetics: History after Films," in *Mapping Benjamin: The Work of Art in the Digital Age*, ed. Hans Ulrich Gumbrecht and Michael Marrinan (Stanford, Calif.: Stanford University Press, 2003), 59–60.

75. Humberto Mauro, "Cinema falado no Brasil," *Cinearte* 324 (May 11, 1932): 10.

76. Cited in Siegfried Kracauer, *Theory of Film* (Princeton, N.J.: Princeton University Press, 1997), 160.

77. On dissensus, see Jacques Rancière, *The Emancipated Spectator* (London: Verso, 2011), 72–73. On "talking back" see Naficy, "Theorizing 'Third World' Film Spectatorship."

78. Galvão recounts this experience in the posthumously published *Paixão Pagu*, 98–99.

79. Romero, *Latinoamérica*, 409; see also 159–60, 409–16. Romero is writing in the wake of Peronism. Raymond Williams notes a similar tension for the English *masses*, which emerges in the modern period with a dual valence: see *Key Words: A Vocabulary of Culture and Society* (Oxford: Oxford University Press, 1985), 193–94.

80. Foot Hardman, *Nem pátria, nem patrão!* 27, my translation.

81. In "Eccentric Types," Justus Nieland uncovers this queer dimension of Eisenstein. See Nieland, *Feeling Modern*, 68–102; see also Salazkina, *In Excess*.

82. Galvão would be expelled shortly after the 1934 Soviet Writers Congress. See K. David Jackson and Elizabeth Jackson, afterword to Patrícia Galvão, *Industrial Park*, trans. Elizabeth Jackson and K. David Jackson (Lincoln: University of Nebraska Press, 1993), 140–54; Augusto de Campos, *Pagu-Vida-Obra* (São Paulo: Brasiliense, 1982), 9.

83. Borges, "Street Scene," 199, 198, my translation. For an English version, see Cozarinsky, *Borges in/and/on Film*, 25–26.

84. See Francesco Casetti, *Inside the Gaze: The Fiction Film and Its Spectator* (Bloomington: Indiana University Press, 1998), 2–3.

CHAPTER 2

1. Felisberto Hernández, "The Daisy Dolls," in *Piano Stories*, trans. Luis Harss (New York: New Directions, 2014), 178.

2. Mikhail Bakhtin, "Discourse in the Novel," in *The Dialogic Imagination: Four Essays*, trans. Michael Holquist (Austin: University of Texas Press, 1982).

3. See Mladen Dolar, *A Voice and Nothing More* (Cambridge, Mass.: MIT Press, 2006).

4. In "The Grain of the Voice," Barthes attributes signification to the very materiality of the body, "not . . . what it says, but the voluptuousness of its

sound-signifiers, of its letters," in *Image-Music-Text*, trans. Stephen Heath (New York: Hill and Wang, 1978), 182.

5. While the materialities of given media are certainly an important part of the experience of reception, it is also true that scholars and theorists of media have the tendency to overdetermine these particularities. These often matter less to the viewer, user, or listener—or creative writer—than to the specialist. The anxiety around the shift to digitality, for example, means more to filmmakers and film scholars than it does to many film viewers.

6. Marinetti's later poem "Drama of Distances" (1931) calls attention to the radio's transnational sweep. See "Radio Syntheses," *Modernism/Modernity* 16.2 (Spring 2010): 417. *Klaxon* declares itself "shrieking [*gritante*] like jazz music." Issue 3 (July 15): 10. Luigi Russolo's *The Art of Noise* (1913) is a particularly potent example of futurist sound. On the *estridentistas*, see Rubén Gallo, *Mexican Modernity: The Avant-garde and the Technical Revolution* (Cambridge, Mass.: MIT Press, 2010), especially 121–26.

7. See Douglas Kahn, *Noise Water Meat: A History of Sound in the Arts* (Cambridge, Mass.: MIT Press, 2001); Michael North, "International Media, International Modernism, and the Problem of Sound," in *Literature and Visual Technologies: Writing after Cinema*, ed. J. Murphet and L. Rainford (London: Palgrave, 2003). Kittler identifies the recording of all noise through the technological media with the Lacanian real (*Discourse Networks, 1800/1900*, 249).

8. "Antenna," *Nervio*, no. 1 (May 31, 1931): 1.

9. See Kittler, *Discourse Networks, 1800/1900*, 236–37; Süssekind, *Cinematograph of Words*, especially 36; Michel Chion, *The Voice in Cinema*, trans. Claudia Gorbman (New York: Columbia University Press, 1999), 27. The phrase "secondary orality" to refer to the electronic media of the twentieth century appears in Walter Ong, *Orality and Literacy: The Technologizing of the Word* (New York: Routledge, 2002), especially 3–11.

10. James Hamilton, "Unearthing Radio Broadcasting in the Anglophone World," in *Residual Media*, ed. Charles Acland (Minneapolis: University of Minnesota Press, 2007), 291.

11. On the radio as traversing exteriority and interiority, see Jason Loviglio, *Intimate Publics: Network Broadcasting and Mass-Mediated Democracy* (Minneapolis: University of Minnesota Press, 2005); Debra Rae Cohen, Michael Coyle, and Jane A. Lewty, *Broadcasting Modernism* (Gainesville: University Press of Florida, 2009); Anke Birkenmaier, *Alejo Carpentier y la cultura del surrealismo en América Latina* (Madrid: Vervuert-Iberoamericana, 2006).

12. Sartre, "Collectivities," 272. See also David Jenemann, "Flying Solo: The Charms of the Radio Body," in *Broadcasting Modernism*, ed. Debra Rae Cohen, Michael Coyle, and Jane A. Lewty (Gainesville: University Press of Florida, 2009), 89–103.

13. Bertolt Brecht, "The Radio as a Communications Apparatus," in *Bertolt Brecht on Film and Radio*, ed. Marc Silberman (London: Methuen, 2000), 41–42. For an alternative to Brechtian readings through a contemporary Argentine novel, see Tom McEnaney, "No Transmitter: Clandestine Radio

Listening Communities in Ricardo Piglia's *The Absent City*," *Cultural Critique* 91 (Fall 2015): 72–97.

14. Walter Benjamin, "Reflections on Radio," in *The Work of Art in the Age of Its Technological Reproducibility and Other Writings on Media*, ed. Michael W. Jennings, Brigid Doherty, and Thomas Y. Levin (Cambridge, Mass.: Harvard University Press, 2008), 391.

15. Sarlo, *La imaginación técnica*, 100–102.

16. Mário de Andrade, *Taxi e crônicas no Diário nacional*, ed. Telê Porto Ancona Lopez (São Paulo: Livraria Duas Cidades, Secretaria da Cultura, Ciência e Tecnologia, 1976), 303–4.

17. The *crônica* was published on February 3, 1940. Reprinted in Andrade, *O empalhador de passarinho*, my translation. The *Radio Hora*, Brazil's first state-based radio program to be emitted simultaneously across the country, was launched in 1934; from 1939 to 1945, under Vargas's New State, the control of radio and other activities was taken over by the DIP (Departamento de Impresa e Propaganda), whose earlier incarnation, the DPDC (Departamento de Propaganda e Difusão Cultural), also had a radio division. See Calabre, "Políticas públicas culturais," 4–6.

18. Focusing on the case of Argentina and the radio as preserving oral or folk culture, as in tales of the gaucho, Martín-Barbero argues that the radio produces the national-popular during the 1930s. *De los medios a las mediaciones*, 168–71.

19. By the late 1920s, multiple periodicals devoted to the radio were being published in Argentina. See Sarlo, *The Technical Imagination*; Christine Ehrick, "Radio Transvestism and the Gendered Soundscape in Buenos Aires, 1930s–1940s," in *Media, Sound, and Culture in Latin America and the Caribbean*, ed. Alejandra Brofman and Andrew Grant Wood (Pittsburgh: University of Pittsburgh Press, 2012), 18–36; and Karush, *The Culture of Class*. As in Argentina, in Brazil, 1930 marks the end of the "idea of experimental radio." See Calabre, "Políticas públicas culturais," 3; Renato Ortiz, "Popular Culture, Modernity and Nation," in *Through the Kaleidoscope: The Experience of Modernity in Latin America*, ed. Vivian Schelling (London: Verso, 2000), 127–47. For a less pessimistic interpretation, and one that emphasizes the transnational, see Bryan McCann, *Hello, Hello Brazil!: Popular Music in the Making of Modern Brazil* (Durham, N.C.: Duke University Press, 2004).

20. Roberto Arlt, *Aguafuertes porteñas: Buenos Aires, vida cotidiana* (Buenos Aires: Losada, 1999).

21. Felisberto Hernández, "Muebles 'El Canario,'" in *Nadie encendía las lámparas* (Montevideo: Arca, 1967), 101–4.

22. Tzvetan Todorov, *The Fantastic: A Structural Approach to a Literary Genre* (Ithaca, N.Y.: Cornell University Press, 1975), 79.

23. Jameson, "Seriality and Modern Literature," 73–74.

24. See Jonathan Crary, *24/7* (London: Verso, 2013).

25. *Modernismo* defines the late nineteenth-century Spanish American movement inspired by Symbolism, Romanticism, and the decadents, and should not be confused with the avant-gardes or *vanguardias* of the late 1910s through the 1920s. Darío is its central figure. Rubén Darío, "The Bourgeois

King," trans. Andrew Hurley, in *Selected Writings* (New York: Penguin, 2005), 221–25.

26. Tim Armstrong, "Film Finds a Tongue," in *Modernism, Technology and the Body: A Cultural Study* (Cambridge: Cambridge University Press, 1998), 220–48. In addition to Armstrong's study, the following have been particularly useful to me: Chion, *The Voice in Cinema*; Rick Altman, "Moving Lips: Cinema as Ventriloquism," *Yale French Studies* 60 (1980): 67–79; and Kaja Silverman, *The Acoustic Mirror: The Female Voice in Psychoanalysis and Cinema* (Bloomington: Indiana University Press, 1988).

27. Quiroga, "Espectros que hablan," 363.

28. Mauro, "Cinema falado no Brasil," 10. The film in question is *Ganga Bruta* (1933).

29. Per López ("Early Cinema and Modernity in Latin America"), the arrival of sound debilitated more precarious national industries in Latin America, but Argentina and Brazil managed, after an initial bump, to not be obliterated in the transition. On the transition to sound, see also King, *Magical Reels*, 67; Sarlo, *La imaginación técnica*, 123; Karush, *The Culture of Class*, 60–71; Timothy Barnard and Peter Rist, *South American Cinema: A Critical Filmography* (Austin: University of Texas Press, 1999), 10.

30. Rudolf Arnheim, "A New Laocoön: Artistic Composites and the Talking Film," in *Film as Art* (Berkeley: University of California Press, 1957), 227–28. The essay was originally published in 1938.

31. See Borge, *Latin American Writers and the Rise of Hollywood Cinema*, 11; on the British case, see Anne Friedburg, "Reading *Close Up*, 1927–1933," in *Close Up: Cinema and Modernism*, ed. James Donald, Anne Friedberg, and Laura Marcus (London: Bloomsburg, 2001), 26; Michael North on the Euro-American context (*Camera Works*, especially 63–65). Per North, 1927 is a "crisis" year for Euro-American avant-garde film because it signals the beginning of the end of intertitles and an aestheticized reading of written language in film; it coincides with a flourishing of experiments between avant-garde writing and film, as works by Man Ray, Jolas, and others sought to collapse the boundaries among European languages and between the visual and verbal codes (17–32, 65–67, 71–73). These possibilities seem to be truncated as the decade of the 1930s progresses.

32. Quiroga, "Espectros que hablan"; José María Podestá, "El film hablado," *La Pluma* (June 1929): 33–36.

33. See "A imagem e o som," *O Fan* 8 (June 1930): 37 (no author).

34. "La monstruosidad antiartística que se avecina." José María Podestá, "La evolución cinegráfica angloamericana," *La Pluma* (October 1930).

35. Guilherme, "Questão de gosto."

36. Arnheim, "A New Laocoön," 199.

37. See Aguilar and Jelicié, *Borges va al cine*, 77–86.

38. "'Our stuttering cinema'—as this stage was ironically deemed." In Calistro, *Reportaje al cine argentino*, 22.

39. Quiroga, "Espectros que hablan," 364.

40. See Armstrong, "Film Finds a Tongue," 221–26. Goat-glanding was invented by the Russian physician Voronoff and popularized in the United

States; it was also covered by the press in South America. Argentina experienced goat-glanding when variations on the Voronoff method were employed in Buenos Aires hospitals by both national and foreign physicians from 1926 to 1930, attracting frenzied coverage and medical outcries. See Sarlo, *The Technical Imagination*, 141–47.

41. *Revista Acadêmica* 23 (November 1936): 19.

42. Luz Alba, as cited in Borge, *Latin American Writers and the Rise of Hollywood Cinema*, 115; see also 117.

43. On the Anglo-American context, see especially North, *Camera Works*, 83–105; Armstrong, "Film Finds a Tongue"; Friedburg, "Reading *Close Up*," 26.

44. Nataša Durovicová, "Local Ghosts: Dubbing Bodies in Early Sound Cinema," in *Il film e I suoi multipli/Film and Its Multiples*, ed. Anna Antonini, IX Convegno Internazionale di Studi sul Cinema (Forum: Udine, 2003), 83–98.

45. Olivari, *El hombre de la baraja*, 65–67.

46. Chion, *The Voice in Cinema*, 9, 125–26.

47. Olivari, *El hombre de la baraja*, 163. Christine Ehrick shows how during this period Argentine radio was a "contested medium," registering both the possibility for greater opportunities for women and an anxiety over women's publicness as a marker of modernity. A plurality of women's voices in the early 1930s was followed by the closing off of these possibilities during the medium's consolidation or maturation ("'Savage Dissonance': Gender, Voice, and Women's Radio Speech in Argentina, 1930–1945," in *Radio and the Gendered Soundscape: Women and Broadcasting in Argentina and Uruguay, 1930–1950* [Cambridge: Cambridge University Press, 2015], 76). In general, radio programming became increasingly homogenous nationally in the latter part of the 1930s (Karush, *The Culture of Class*, 67–70).

48. See Silverman, *The Acoustic Mirror*, especially 68.

49. *The Jazz Singer* was also described by writers as a "strange, almost hermaphroditic form incorporating both silent and sound techniques" (as cited in Miller, *Late Modernism*, 108).

50. Sophie Treadwell, *Machinal* (London: Royal National Theater, 1995), xi.

51. Denning, *The Cultural Front*, 188; see also 175–80.

52. On Evita and the gender politics of radio during the 1930s, see Ehrick, "Savage Dissonance," 84–88. Radio would be shifted from the market to the state under Peronism in the latter part of the 1940s in Argentina (Karush, *The Culture of Class*, 177–214).

53. As Sylvia Molloy points out, the sources for the tale are themselves already "masked"—or, we could say, have their voices thrown—in a heterogeneous archive that includes corrected passages, revisions, and coins without faces (*Las letras de Borges y otros ensayos*, 43–47).

54. Borges, *Historia universal de la infamia*, 86, my translation.

55. On Borges's anti-populist anti-Peronism, see his short stories "El simulacro" (1957) and the ferocious "La fiesta del monstruo" (1947), a short story he coauthored with Adolfo Bioy Casares.

56. See Jorge Marturano, "Nuestro hombre en Buenos Aires: Una lectura cubana del peronismo a través de Virgilio Piñera," *MLN* 126.2 (March 2011): 323–43; Thomas Anderson, *Everything in Its Place: The Life and Works of Virgilio Piñera* (Lewisburg, Pa.: Bucknell University Press, 2006), 45–48.

57. Unless otherwise indicated, I use Mark Schafer's translation of *Cold Tales* here. Virgilio Piñera, *Cold Tales* (Hygiene, Colo.: Eridanos Press; New York: Rizzoli International, 1988), 81.

58. Virgilio Piñera, "El muñeco," in *Cuentos fríos & El que vino a salvarme* (Madrid: Cátedra, 2008), 255, my translation.

59. Ibid., 265, my translation.

60. Dolar, *A Voice and Nothing More*, 169. The phrase appears in a discussion of Kafka.

61. "Like other populist experiments, Peronism sought the 'noise' but not the 'signal' of the working and popular classes" (Ehrick, "Savage Dissonance," 90). See also Romero, *Latinoamérica*, 385, 409, 415–16.

62. Dolar, *A Voice and Nothing More*, 80–81.

63. On the polysemic quality of *artefacto* in this story, see Santiago Juan-Navarro, "Hiperrealidad y simulacro: La crisis de la modernidad en 'El Muñeco,' de Virgilio Piñera," in *Virgilio Piñera: El artificio del miedo*, ed. Humberto López Cruz (Madrid: Editorial Hispano Cubana, 2012), 155–56.

CHAPTER 3

The first epigraph comes from page 174 of Kittler's work; the second epigraph comes from Alfonsina Storni, "La perfecta dactilógrafa," in *Obras. Prosa. Narraciones, Periodismo, Teatro. Tomo II*, ed. Delfina Muschietti (Buenos Aires: Losada, 2002), 909, my translation throughout. An alternate translation appears in Viviane Mahieux, *Urban Chroniclers in Latin America: The Shared Intimacy of Everyday Life* (Austin: University of Texas Press, 2011), 179–82.

1. In modernizing, urban South America women's public visibility inspired polemics and censure. See Conde, *Consuming Visions*, 130–34, on the Brazilian *melindrosa*; on the Argentine context of women's circulation during modernism, see Mahieux, *Urban Chroniclers in Latin America*, 126–27, 156–57; Francine Masiello, *Between Civilization and Barbarism: Women, Nation, and Culture in Modern Argentina* (Lincoln: University of Nebraska Press, 1992), especially chapter 6; and Adriana J. Bergero, *Intersecting Tango: Cultural Geographies of Buenos Aires* (Pittsburgh: University of Pittsburgh Press, 2008). Focused on the Australian context, Liz Conor's *The Spectacular Modern Woman: Feminine Visibility in the 1920s* (Bloomington: Indiana University Press, 2006) offers an analysis of the modern woman during the period that resonates with the context I am analyzing.

2. Menotti del Picchia, "Arte Moderna," in *Vanguarda Europeia e Modernismo Brasileiro*, ed. Gilberto Mendonça Telles (Rio de Janeiro: José Olympio, 2012), 421, my translation.

3. Peregrino Junior, "Enigma da mulher moderna," *Estética* 2 (January–March 1925): 73–74. *Estética* is the successor of *Klaxon*, Brazil's first avant-garde little magazine.

4. In Kittler's riff on Lacan, the typewriter operates in the realm of the symbolic, while the cinema correlates to the imaginary and the gramophone to the real. See Kittler, *Discourse Networks, 1800/1900* and his *Gramophone, Film, Typewriter.*

5. On Mário's "Typewriter," see Süssekind, *Cinematograph of Words*, 105–7; Gallo, *Mexican Modernity*, 92–103.

6 Süssekind, *Cinematograph of Words*, 104.

7. Massumi, *Parables for the Virtual*, 59; see also 179, 186. I am clearly writing against the grain of Massumi's argument by combining his insights with arguments about social and political positionality. Proprioception is related, but not equivalent, to kinesthesia, the sensory registering of movement.

8. Graciliano Ramos, *Angústia* (São Paulo: Editora Record, 1985). Unless otherwise indicated, all translations of the novel are mine. There is a published English translation: *Anguish*, trans. L. C. Kaplan (New York: Alfred A. Knopf, 1946).

9. See Silviano Santiago, "Pósfacio," in Graciliano Ramos, *Angústia* (Rio de Janeiro: Record, 2003).

10. See Sartre, "Collectivities."

11. In a 1939 issue of *Revista Acadêmica, Angústia* is widely represented on various lists of the best Brazilian novel. Cf. *Revista Acadêmica*, no. 47 (November 1939): l.

12. Consider the titles of contemporaneous texts by Freud (*Civilization and Its Discontents*, 1930) and Sartre (*Nausea*, 1938); despite their differences, they share a late modernist affect of exhaustion or saturation. I consider the problem of narrative development in *Anguish* in "Graciliano, Historiador do Presente," *Miscelânea* 10 (July–December 2011): 23–41.

13. Examples included Leopoldo Torres Ríos's film *La vuelta al nido* (Return to the Nest [Argentina, 1938]) and Roberto Arlt's *La isla desierta* (Deserted Island [Argentina, 1937]).

14. Massumi, *Parables for the Virtual*, 236.

15. See Kittler, *Discourse Networks, 1800/1900*, 193. On the Anglo-American contexts, see Margery W. Davies, *A Woman's Place Is at the Typewriter: Office Work and Office Workers, 1870–1930* (Philadelphia: Temple University Press, 1982); Leah Price and Pamela Thurswell, eds., *Literary Secretaries/Secretarial Culture* (Aldershot: Ashgate, 2005).

16. In Kittler, *Gramophone, Film, Typewriter*, 198, 199.

17. Caroline Jones, "Senses," in *Critical Terms for Media Studies*, ed. W. J. T. Mitchell and Mark Hansen (Chicago: University of Chicago Press, 2010), 89.

18. Massumi, *Parables for the Virtual*, 59, 11.

19. Estalinho, "Ideologia Criminosa," O *Homem do povo*, no. 7 (April 9, 1931): 5), in *O homem do povo*, 57. The Portuguese word *pena* means both "pain" and "pen," a play on words that also signals the difficulty of authorship during a time of political and economic strife. (Note the psuedonym, "Little Stalin.")

20. Álvaro Yunque, "Limaduras," *Contra* 5, originally published in September 1933; reprinted in the facsimile edition: Sylvia Saítta, ed., *Contra: La*

revista de los franco-tiradores (Buenos Aires: Universidad de Quilmes Editorial, 2005), 439. Vicky Unruh's recent work on Cuba and labor makes for a fruitful comparison to Brazil in particular. See Unruh, "Modernity's Labors in Latin America: The Cultural Work of Cuba's Avant-Gardes," in *The Oxford Handbook to Global Modernisms*, ed. Mark Wollaeger (Oxford: Oxford University Press, 2012), 341–66.

21. I wish to thank Ed Dimendberg for suggesting the parallel with Kafka here.

22. Ramos, *Cartas inéditas*, 28.

23. Even after his unexplained imprisonment at the hands of the regime in 1936, Graciliano would work in the following decade for its cultural organs, including the journal *Cultura e política*, demonstrating the extent to which Brazilian modernist artists and intellectuals were successfully incorporated into the state in the 1930s.

24. Like the United States, Brazil was overwhelmingly agrarian throughout the nineteenth century and through the first decades of the twentieth; and, like the United States, during the 1930s writers who claimed to speak for "peripheral" parts of the country (the Brazilian Northeast and the U.S. South, respectively) acquired prowess in the cultural centers of their respective countries. See Sérgio Miceli, *Intelectuais y classe dirigente no Brasil (1920–1945)* (São Paulo: DIFEL, 1979); Bueno, *Uma história do romance de 30*; Johnson, *Literature, Culture and Authoritarianism in Brazil.* As Johnson shows, this Boom was paradoxically dependent on the centralization of the Brazilian publishing industry in Rio de Janeiro (in southern Brazil), as well as the Brazilian state under the Vargas regime (13).

25. See Flora Süssekind, *Tal Brasil, Qual Romance? Uma ideologia estética e sua história: O naturalismo* (Rio de Janeiro: Achiamé, 1984), 151–56.

26. Mário de Andrade, "Elegia de Abril" (1941), in *Aspectos da literatura brasileira* (São Paulo: Livraria Martins Editora, 1972), 190, my translation. For other examples, see Renato Almeida, "A literatura em 1934," *Lanterna Verde* 3 (February 1935): 103; or José Lins do Rego's northeastern novel, *Bangüe* (1934). For a scholarly account, see Luís Bueno, "Uma Figura-Síntese: O Fracassado" (*Uma história do romance de 30*, 74–80).

27. I cite from the draft of "Decadência do modernismo brasileiro," in the archives of the Instituto de Estudos Brasileros in São Paulo. A version is reprinted in José Carlos Garbuglio, Alfredo Bosi, and Valentim Facioli, *Graciliano Ramos: Antologia e estudos* (São Paulo: Editora Atica, 1987), 20–24. See also Graciliano Ramos, *Linhas tortas* (São Paulo: Editora Record, 1989), 144; Homero Senna, "Revisão do Modernismo," in *Graciliano Ramos: Coletânea*, ed. Sonia Brayner (Rio de Janeiro: Civilização Brasileira, 1978), 50–51.

28. Wilson Martins, *The Modernist Idea: A Critical Survey of Brazilian Writing in the Twentieth Century*, trans. Jack Tomlins (New York: New York University Press, 1970), 303.

29. See Jameson, "Seriality and Modern Literature," 74.

30. Graciliano's approach to words here approximates Michael Denning's reading of Dos Passos and his critique of the "word technicians" of the period. (See *The Cultural Front*, 176–80.) But in Graciliano, as in Brazilian late

modernism more broadly, the state is a much more instrumental force than the market. Luís's "jingles" and melancholic word games, in other words, are more likely to be linked to what he calls "the government" than to advertising or other industries, or anything like an autonomous sphere of technicians.

31. On homeopathy, see Jameson, "Seriality and Modern Literature," 73–74. On Luís's language games as meta-reflections on *Anguish* itself, see Lúcia Helena Carvalho, *A ponto do novelo: Uma interpretação de "Angústia," de Graciliano Ramos* (São Paulo: Editora Atica, 1983). Carvalho locates in the entangled knot or skein (*novelo*) a figure for the novel itself.

32. Lispector would express admiration for Graciliano as a writer who created a new "content-form" (*fundo-forma*) for northeastern Brazilian literature. See Clarice Lispector, *Outros escritos*, ed. Teresa Montero Lícia Manzo (Rio de Janeiro: Rocco, 2005), 104.

33. Following the sociological and regionalist turn of 1930s novelists like Graciliano, the 1940s witnessed the literary experimentalism of the postwar years, with Lispector herself a major figure. Her first novel, *Near to the Wild Heart*, was published in 1943; along with João Guimarães Rosa's *Sagarana* in 1946, it was hailed as a breakthrough in Brazilian literature. The novel and short story have a special role in this later experimentalism; poetry was the dominant idiom of the earlier avant-gardes. Lispector is frequently compared by writers outside of Brazil to Woolf and Joyce, the latter particularly present in *The Hour of the Star*'s ending, with its Molly Bloomian *yes*. Yet she often bristled at the suggestion that she was influenced by them. For a detailed account of Lispector's career, see Benjamin Moser's lovely *Why This World: A Biography of Clarice Lispector*, the only English-language biography of the writer (New York: Oxford University Press, 2009).

34. Süssekind, *Tal Brasil, Qual Romance*, 105–7, 182–88.

35. Ítalo Moriconi, "The Hour of the Star, or Clarice Lispector's Trash Hour," trans. Paulo Henriques Britto, *Portuguese Literary and Cultural Studies* 4/5 (Spring/Fall 2000): 218.

36. Moser translates this as "cheap tear jerker," which gets at the lack of capital implicit in the phrase, if not its material culture history (*Why This World*, 1). Lidia Santos offers an inspired analysis of Macabéa through mass culture's reappropriation of the *literatura de cordel*: see *Kitsch Tropical: Los medios en la literatura y el arte en América Latina* (Madrid: Iberoamericana, 2004), 194–205.

37. Clarice Lispector, *The Hour of the Star*, trans. Benjamin Moser (New York: New Directions, 2011), 45. Unless otherwise indicated, I use Moser's translation throughout. *Cinema poeira* is the term for a working-class or second-rate cinema, where the popular classes congregate; Lispector spells "Marilyn" incorrectly here in a nod to Macabéa's spelling difficulties and the way in which orality structures her approach to mass culture loanwords.

38. On these transformations, see, especially, Ortiz, "O Silêncio," in *A Moderna Tradicão Brasileira*, 38–50; Marcos Napolitano, *Cultura Brasileira: Utopia e massificação (1950–1980)* (São Paulo: Editora Contexto, 2001); Mattelart, *Networking the World*, especially 65–66.

39. Santiago, "Literature and Mass Culture," 120.

40. "Gratitude to the Machine," my translation. Clarice Lispector, "Gratidão à máquina," in *A descoberta do mundo: Crônicas* (Rio de Janeiro: Rocco, 1999), 69–70.

41. Sarte, "Collectivities," 256.

42. Storni, "La perfecta dactilógrafa," 910.

43. See Moser, *Why This World*, 325–26. See also Marta Peixoto, "Fatos são pedras duras: Urban Poverty in Clarice Lispector," in *Closer to the Wild Heart: Essays on Clarice Lispector*, ed. Cláudia Pazos Alonso and Claire Williams (Oxford: Legenda, 2002), 106–7.

44. See Moser, *Why This World*, 190–209. On this moment in Brazilian mass culture, see Ortiz, *A Moderna Tradicão Brasileira*; Napolitano, *Cultura Brasileira*. A franchise system of periodicals, including *Cosmopolitan* and *Good Housekeeping*, "networked" the feminine world, per Mattelart; *Cosmo* appeared in Latin America eight years before it appeared in France (*Networking the World*, 65–66).

45. Lispector, *Outros escritos*, 31. On Lispector's journalistic sketches from this period, see especially Debra A. Castillo, "Lispector, cronista," in *Clarice Lispector: Novos aportes críticos*, ed. Cristina Ferreira-Pinto Bailey and Regina Zilgerman (Pittsburgh: University of Pittsburgh Press, 2007), 95–108, and Peixoto, "Fatos são pedras duras."

46. Clarice Lispector, "Para a mulher que trabalha," in *Só para mulheres: Conceitos, receitas e segredos*, ed. Aparecida Maria Nunes (Rio de Janeiro: Rocco, 2006), 14, my translation.

47. As cited in Moser, *Why This World*, 286.

48. Clarice Lispector, *Selected Crônicas*, trans. Giovanni Ponteiro (New York: New Directions, 1996), 177–79.

49. Lispector, *A descoberta do mundo*, 137, my translation. Ponteiro offers the equally effective "racing against the typewriter." Lispector, *Selected Crônicas*, 103. Castillo notes that the sketches from this period more generally make frequent reference to the body as it is positioned in writing, as when she describes to her readers pausing to light a cigarette as she drafts what they are reading ("Lispector, cronista," 101).

50. Lispector, *A descoberta do mundo*, 232, my translation.

51. Macabéa's love interest, Olímpico, for example, resembles to the point of parody the deterministic naturalism that undergirds many historical approaches to the impoverished northeasterner and the subgenre of drought literature (*literatura da seca*) in Brazil: "He'd been born more charred and hard than a dry tree branch or a rock in the sun" (48).

52. Glauber Rocha, "An Esthetic of Hunger," in Randal Johnson and Robert Stam, *Brazilian Cinema* (New York: Columbia University Press, 1995), 68–72. On hunger in Lispector's journalistic sketches, see also Peixoto, "Fatos são pedras duras," 108–9.

53. Kittler, *Discourse Networks, 1800/1900*, 16.

54. See Victoria Olwell, "The Body Types: Corporeal Documents and Body Politics circa 1900," in *Literary Secretaries/Secretarial Culture*, ed. Leah Price and Pamela Thurswell (Aldershot: Ashgate, 2005), 48–49. On the relationship between media and embodiment, see Bernadette Wegenstein, "Body," in

Critical Terms for Media Studies, ed. W. J. T. Mitchell and Mark Hansen (Chicago: University of Chicago Press, 2010), 19–34. On gender, embodiment, and computer technology, see especially N. Katherine Hayles, *How We Became Posthuman: Virtual Bodies in Cybernetics, Literature, and Informatics* (Chicago: University of Chicago Press, 1999).

55. See Olwell, "The Body Types," 50.

56. Lispector, *A descoberta do mundo*, 404, my translation.

57. Ibid., 59, my translation.

58. Lispector also shared with Borges an interest in word play, mystical numbers, and hidden names, in particular the Kabbalah.

59. De Certeau, *The Practice of Everyday Life*, 25.

60. Süssekind, *Cinematograph of Words*, 105, 107.

61. In the archives of the Moreira Salles Institute in Rio de Janeiro, you can touch (with gloves) Lispector's last handwritten notes just before her death in 1979. The handwriting is shaky, often just shy of legible.

62. Hayles, *Writing Machines*, 22, 25.

63. I wish to thank Hannah Freed-Thall for her suggestions here.

64. Kittler, *Discourse Networks, 1800/1900*, 352.

65. At the very beginning of her career, the eminent critic Álvaro Lins published one of few negative reviews of her first novel, *Close to the Wild Heart* (1942), accusing it of betraying a feminine weakness, an inability to disguise her own subjectivity. Literary creation for Lins is a distancing and suppressing of the self, a creation ex nihilo. (There is more than a little bit of womb envy in his acerbic critique.) See Moser, *Why This World*, 134–35.

66. Huyssen notes the tendency of modernist male writers to identify women with mass culture in order to shore up their own elite status (*After the Great Divide*, 44–64).

67. For two powerful approaches to gender in Lispector, see Hélène Cixous, *Reading with Clarice Lispector* (Minneapolis: University of Minnesota Press, 1990) and Marta Peixoto, *Passionate Fictions: Gender, Narrative, and Violence in Clarice Lispector* (Minneapolis: University of Minnesota Press, 1992).

CHAPTER 4

1. Hernández, *Nadie encendía las lámparas*, 103, my translation.

2. In the early sketch "Gangster Philosophy": "I will ask you to interrupt your reading of this book as many times as possible" (x).

3. On the shifting hierarchies of the senses in the West from the Classical period to the present, including the often peripheral role of touch, see Robert Jütte, *A History of the Senses: From Antiquity to Cyberspace* (Cambridge: Polity, 2005).

4. For a history of cinema in Uruguay, see Saratsola, *Función completa, por favor*; Mario Raimondo Souto and Carlos Scavino, *Una historia del cine en Uruguay: Memorias compartidas* (Montevideo: Planeta, 2010).

5. Per Paul Willemen, cinephilia was born in France in the 1920s through the concept of *photogénie* but becomes consolidated in the 1960s. Willemen, *Looks*

and Frictions: Essays in Cultural Studies and Film Theory (Bloomington: Indiana University Press, 1994), especially 124–33. On 1960s cinephilia in Argentina, see David Oubiña, "Del sueño tecnológico a la escritura audiovisual: Literatura y Cine (1920–1960)," in *Historia crítica de la literatura argentina*, vol. 7, *Rupturas*, ed. Celina Manzoni (Buenos Aires: Emecé, 2009). On Western Europe, see Francesco Casetti and Mariagrazia Fanchi, "Cinephilia/Telephilia," *Framework* 45.2 (Fall 2004): 36–41; Thomas Elsaesser, "Cinephilia, or the Uses of Disenchantment," in *Cinephilia: Movies, Love and Memory*, ed. Marijke De Valck and Malte Hagener (Amsterdam: Amsterdam University Press, 2005), 27–44.

6. SODRE was founded in 1930 and initially focused on radio and theater. See Mariana Amieva, "*Cine Arte* del Sodre en la conformación de un campo audiovisual en Uruguay: Políticas públicas y acciones individuales," *Cine Documental* 6 (2012), http://revista.cinedocumental.com.ar/6/articulos_01.html. Also noteworthy is the cinema criticism found in the important late modernist journal *Marcha* (Montevideo, 1939–74).

7. See Elsaesser, "Cinephilia," 27, 32; Casetti and Fanchi, "Cinephilia/Telephilia," 40.

8. Dudley Andrew, "Time Zones and Jetlag: The Flows and Phases of World Cinema," in *World Cinemas, Transnational Perspectives*, ed. Nataša Durovicová and Kathleen Newman (New York: Routledge, 2010), 59–89.

9. Elsaesser, "Cinephilia," 29. On cinephilia and the fetishism of the detail, see especially Willemen, *Looks and Frictions*, 227, 235–40; Casetti and Fanchi, "Cinephilia/Telephilia,"36.

10. Ramón Goméz de la Serna, "Plantas y tranvías: Gran sonatista de los recuerdos y las quintas," http://www.felisberto.org.uy/critica.html; see also Blas Matamoro, "La música, ese perseguidor," *Cuadernos hispanoamericanos* 625 (2002): 129–38.

11. See the Felisberto Hernández Special Collection in the American University archive, box 4.

12. Luis Harss's English translations of his works under the title *Piano Stories* underscore this dimension.

13. See the Felisberto Hernández Special Collection in the American University archive, box 2, p. 108.

14. Hernández, "Around the Time of Clemente Colling," 13, my emphasis. Typically, the body becomes dismembered as synecdoche in Hernández's writings—mouths, for example, become "machines to produce words," per Jaime Concha. See "Los empleados del cielo: En torno a Felisberto Hernández," in *Felisberto Hernández ante la crítica actual*, ed. Alain Sicard (Caracas: Monte Ávila Editores, 1977), 67–68.

15. Hernández, *Piano Stories*, 18. The passage appears in the story "The Stray Horse."

16. Ibid., 127. This passage appears in "My First Concert," a short piece published posthumously in different formats.

17. Hernández, *Piano Stories*, 42; see also 93, 28.

18. For a phenomenological approach to Hernández, see Stephanie Merrim, "Felisberto Hernández's Aesthetic of 'lo otro': The Writing of Indeterminacy," *Revista Canadiense de Estudios Hispánicos* 11.3 (Spring 1987): 521–40.

19. Translations of each of these can be found in the collection *Piano Stories*, trans. Luis Harss.

20. In addition, they recall Roland Barthes's understanding that "play" has both ludic and musical dimensions ("From Work to Text," 63).

21. Massumi, *Parables for the Virtual*, 58.

22. See Laura Marks, *Touch: Sensuous Theory and Multisensory Media* (Minneapolis: University of Minnesota Press, 2002), 18. On the relationship between the haptic and the beholder, see also Jennifer Barker, *The Tactile Eye: Touch and the Cinematic Experience* (Berkeley: University of California Press, 2009), 1–2; Jennifer Fisher, "Relational Sense: Towards a Haptic Aesthetic," *Parachute* 87 (1997): 4–11; Sobchack, *Carnal Thoughts*, especially "What My Fingers Knew: The Cinesthetic Subject, or Vision in the Flesh," 53–84. Watching certain tactile experiences on a screen activates the same cortical centers as experiencing them "in the flesh." See David J. Linden, *Touch: The Science of Hand, Heart, and Mind* (New York: Penguin, 2015), 90–91.

23. Benjamin, "The Work of Art in the Age of Its Technological Reproducibility," 39–41; Massumi, *Parables for the Virtual*, 158; Lauren Rabinovitz, "More than the Movies: A History of Somatic Visual Culture through *Hale's Tours*, Imax, and Motion Simulation Rides," in *Memory Bytes: History, Technology, and Digital Culture*, ed. Lauren Rabinovitz and Abraham Geil (Durham, N.C.: Duke University Press, 2004), 99–125.

24. See especially Tom Gunning, "Cinema of Attractions: Early Film, Its Spectator, and the Avant-Garde," *Wide Angle* 8.3–4 (Fall 1986): 63–70; Miriam Hansen, "Early Cinema, Late Cinema: Transformations of the Public Sphere," in *Viewing Positions: Ways of Seeing Film*, ed. Linda Williams (New Brunswick, N.J.: Rutgers University Press, 1997), 134–54.

25. On the film spectator in 1970s film theory, see especially Jean-Louis Baudry, "Ideological Effects of the Basic Cinematographic Apparatus," in *Narrative, Apparatus, Ideology: A Film Theory Reader*, ed. Philip Rosen (New York: Columbia University Press, 1986), 286–98. On the skin of things, see Marks, *Touch*; Taussig, *Mimesis and Alterity*, 44.

26. Jacques Polet, "Early Cinematographic Spectacles: The Role of Sound Accompaniment in the Reception of Moving Images," in *The Sounds of Early Cinema*, ed. Richard Abel and Rick Altman (Bloomington: Indiana University Press, 2001), 193; see also Norman King, "The Sound of Silents," in *Silent Film*, ed. Richard Abel (London: Anthlone Press, 1999), 31–44. On the piano and improvisation, see also Jody Berland, "The Musicking Machine," in *Residual Media*, ed. Charles Acland (Minneapolis: University of Minnesota Press, 2007).

27. Noël Burch, *Life to These Shadows*, in Polet, "Early Cinematographic Spectacles," 193.

28. See, for example, Lisa Block de Behar, "Familiaridad y extrañeza: La repetición-fragmentación narrativa de Felisberto Hernández," *Lectura crítica de la literatura americana* 3 (1996–97): 210; Enriqueta Morillas Ventura, "Felisberto y el cine," *Anales de literatura hispanoamericana* 32 (2003): 83–88; Teresa Porzecanski, "Felisberto Hernández: Un estudio del régimen de la mirada," *Cuadernos Hispanoamericanos* 625 (2002): 81–86.

29. Felisberto Hernández, "En el cine," in *Obras Completas*, vol. 3 (Buenos Aires: Siglo XXI, 2005), 232, my translation.

30. Hernández, "Around the Time of Clemente Colling," 22. On a resonant relationship to the cinema in French surrealism, see Paul Hammond, "Available Light," in *The Shadow and Its Shadow: Surrealist Writings on the Cinema* (San Francisco: City Lights, 2000).

31. Laura Mulvey, "Visual Pleasure and Narrative Cinema," in *Film Theory and Criticism: Introductory Readings*, ed. Leo Braudy and Marshall Cohen (New York: Oxford University Press, 1999), 833–44. On voyeurism in Hernández, see Patrick O'Connor's compelling reading, "The Moving Target of Fixated Desire: Felisberto's Paper Dolls," in *Latin American Fiction and Narratives of the Perverse: Paper Dolls and Spider Woman* (New York: Palgrave, 2004), especially 88.

32. See Williams, "Dominant, Residual, and Emergent." On obsolescence as critique, see Joel Burges, "Adorno's Mimeograph: The Uses of Obsolescence in *Minima Moralia*," *New German Critique* 40.118 (Winter 2013): 65–92; John Davis, "Going Analogue: Vinylphiles and the Consumption of the 'Obsolete,'" in *Residual Media*, ed. Charles Acland (Minneapolis: University of Minnesota Press, 2007), 231.

33. F. T. Marinetti, "The Manifesto of Tactilism," January 11, 1921, http://peripheralfocus.net/poems-told-by-touch/manifesto_of_tactilism.html.

34. On games and rules, see Roger Caillois, *Man, Play, and Games*, trans. Meyer Barash (Urbana: University of Illinois Press, 2001), especially 3–10. On the ritual in Hernández, see Merrim, "Felisberto Hernández's Aesthetic of 'lo otro,'" especially 536.

35. "Yo me inicié poniendo las manos." Felisberto Hernández, "Menos Julia," in *Narraciones incompletas* (Madrid: Ediciones Siruela, 1990), 163.

36. Maurice Merleau-Ponty, *Phenomenology of Perception* (New York: Routledge, 2012), 94.

37. Walter Benjamin, "One-Way Street," in *Reflections: Essays, Aphorisms, Autobiographical Writings*, ed. Peter Demetz (New York: Schocken Books, 1978), 66. On the surrealist glove, see Hal Foster, *Compulsive Beauty* (Cambridge, Mass.: MIT Press/October Books, 1993), 33–35.

38. They are also one of Merleau-Ponty's examples of the chiasm, the reversible interface of the membrane between inner and outer. See Barker, *The Tactile Eye*, 58–59.

39. See Walter Benjamin, "Surrealism: The Last Snapshot of the European Intelligentsia," in *Reflections: Essays, Aphorisms, Autobiographical Writings*, ed. Peter Demetz (New York: Schocken Books, 1978), 177–92; Margaret Cohen, *Profane Illumination: Walter Benjamin and the Paris of Surrealist Revolution* (Berkeley: University of California Press, 1995). Hernández's own politics were far from Benjamin's Marxism; like another Hispanophone surrealist, Salvador Dalí, he flirted with fascism.

40. On the encounter in the Latin American historical avant-gardes, see Unruh, *Latin American Vanguards*, especially "Introduction: Contentious Encounters in Art and Life," 1–31.

41. It recalls the surrealist game of "one in the other," the openness to free association and chance, the possibility for the marvelous. See Mary

Ann Caws, *Surrealism* (New York: Phaidon Press, 2008), 11–16; Hammond, "Available Light," 9. Yet, in contrast to the surrealists, the rules are strictly delimited from the outset; the game of chance is somehow rigged. In a very different realm, scientific experiments conducted in the United States during the 1920s sought to isolate and explain the tactile sensations of clamminess, wetness, greasiness, and others (Linden, *Touch*, 193–94).

42. Hernández dedicated this text to María Luisa de Las Heras—also known as África de Las Heras, the nom de guerre of a beautiful KGB spy from Spain, coordinator of the organ's Latin American wing in Montevideo. Some suspect that he was aware of her activities, and this awareness is ciphered within the story: she is the gorgeous "doll" who in fact is pulling the strings.

43. Indeed, the novella at times seems to evoke an even earlier era, as though it were a nineteenth-century fairy tale in the vein of E. T. A. Hoffman. Its anachronic tone is highlighted in the first, very limited edition of *Hortensias*, an unbound paper copy with *naïf* illustrations by Olimpia Torres. *Las Hortensias* (Montevideo: Talleres Gráficos "Gaceta Comercial," 1949).

44. Anne Friedberg, *Window Shopping: Cinema and the Postmodern* (Berkeley: University of California Press, 1994), 68. For a paradigmatic example in South America, see José Asunción Silva's window-shop poem, "Anuncio del Almacén Bohemia" (1895), in *De Sobremesa* (Madrid: Cátedra, 2006), 277–79.

45. Huyssen, *After the Great Divide*; Doane, "Technophilia."

46. See Natalia Sucre, "Distracting Art: Reading Shock in Felisberto Hernández's 'Las Hortensias,'" *Hispania* 86.3 (September 2003): 482–92. Sucre's compelling analysis shows how the emphasis lies not on aesthetic *production* but on what a user "does with what is made for him through modern technology" (483).

47. Mark Goble's *Beautiful Circuits: Modernism and the Mediated Life* is a brilliant analysis of the desire to become part of circuits in U.S. modernist texts.

48. Bellmer's *Games of the Doll* of the mid-1930s anticipates Hernández's interest in subject-object mimesis through the uncanny figure of the mannequin. On the surrealist understanding of the mannequin as "the very image of capitalist reification," see Foster, *Compulsive Beauty*, 21, 126; on Bellmer as a desublimating force in surrealism, see pp. 101–9, 114–21.

49. As Anne Friedberg shows in *Window Shopping: Cinema and the Postmodern*.

50. Frank Graziano, *The Lust of Seeing: Themes of the Gaze and Sexual Rituals in the Fiction of Felisberto Hernández* (Bucknell, Pa.: Bucknell University Press, 1997). Luis Harss translates the phrase, which comes from "The Usher," as the "craving to see (*Piano Stories*, 76).

51. I take the term "anti-flâneur" from Michelle Clayton's exploration of César Vallejo's Parisian experiences during the 1920s–1930s. See *Poetry in Pieces: César Vallejo and Lyric Modernity* (Berkeley: University of California Press, 2011), 20.

52. Among Hernández's contemporaries in dialogue with surrealism (if only to reject it) are key writers such as César Vallejo, Pablo Neruda, Adolfo Bioy Casares, and Alejo Carpentier. The surrealist imprint can also be found

in later writers such as Mario Vargas Llosa, Alejandra Pizarnik, and Julio Cortázar.

53. Caillois was in dialogue not only with Hernández but also with Victoria Ocampo, editor of *Sur*, and was an early and perceptive international reader of Borges, mediating his first reception in France.

54. For example, the surrealist *hasard objectif* and its openness to chance or coincidence, as in Breton's *Nadja* (1928), or its reinscription in Julio Cortázar's *Hopscotch* (*Rayuela*, 1963). On the uncanny return of outmoded objects in European surrealism, see Foster, *Compulsive Beauty*, 126–36, 157–91. In Hernández, however, it is less the objects themselves that are outmoded than the practices that seemed embedded in them, activated through the ritual. Beyond Foster, the following scholarly works on surrealism have also proven useful to me: Hammond, "Available Light"; Caws, *Surrealism*; Linda Williams, *Figures of Desire: A Theory and Analysis of Surrealist Film* (Urbana: University of Illinois Press, 1981), especially 3–52. In many ways, his proliferating, tangential, and associative way of narrating recalls the non-representational dimensions of surrealist filmmaking.

55. In a dazzling analysis, Josefina Ludmer shows that Hernández's works posit two situations: either the poverty of the artist and the impossibility of consumption or the poverty of a market for his art: the impossibility of selling them. See Ludmer, "La tragedia cómica," *Escritura: Revista de Teoría y Crítica Literaria* 7.13–14 (1982): 111–18.

56. See Roger Caillois, *The Edge of Surrealism: A Roger Caillois Reader*, ed. Claudine Frank (Durham, N.C.: Duke University Press, 2003). Esther Allen also compares Hernández to Magritte in her prologue to her translation of *Lands of Memory* (x). Reinaldo Laddaga provides a reading of the way in which Hernández's earlier texts depart from Breton's surrealism. See *Literaturas indigentes y placeres bajos* (Rosario, Argentina: Beatriz Viterbo, 2000), especially 46–47. For an elucidation of the differences between Bataille and Breton, see Foster, *Compulsive Beauty*.

57. Epstein, "On Certain Characteristics of *Photogénie*," 53.

58. Marks, *Touch*, 18, 8.

59. "El acomodador," in Hernández, *Nadie encendía las lámparas*, 35–36, my translation.

60. See especially Rosario Ferré, *El acomodador: Una lectura fantástica de Felisberto Hernández* (Mexico City: Fondo de Cultura Económica, 1986).

61. On Hernández's early work, see Pablo Rocca, "Cruces y límites de la vanguardia uruguaya (campo, ciudad, letras, imágenes)," in *Las vanguardias literarias en Argentina, Uruguay y Paraguay*, ed. Carlos García and Dieter Reichardt (Madrid: Iberoamericana, 2004), 415–26.

62. See Rosario Ferré, "Felisberto Hernández: La vanguardia de un hombre solo," *La Gaceta del Fondo de Cultura Económica* 185 (1986): 17–19. Hernández would count Boom and post-Boom writers such as Ferré, Caillois, Julio Cortázar, Gabriel García Márquez, and Italo Calvino among his admirers and disciples. See Ítalo Calvino, introduction to *Piano Stories*, trans. Luis Harss (New York: New Directions, 2014), xx. Hernández's own definition

of his writing is similarly slippery; see "How Not to Explain My Stories," in *Piano Stories*, 3–4.

63. Hernández, "Around the Time of Clemente Colling," 6.

64. Marks, *Touch*, xiii. For other examples, see Sobchack, *Carnal Thoughts*; Barker, *The Tactile Eye*; Anne Cheng, "Skin, Tattoos and Susceptibility," *Representations* 108.1 (Fall 2009): 98–119; Heather Love, "Close, But Not Deep: Literary Ethics and the Descriptive Turn," *New Literary History* 41.2 (Spring 2010): 371–91; Stephen Best and Sharon Marcus, "Surface Reading: An Introduction," *Representations* 108.1 (Fall 2009): 1–21; Massumi, *Parables for the Virtual*, 12–13. Cheng argues for reading surfaces as a "mutual pedagogy of erotics" (102); Barker emphasizes the "intimacy" between spectator and film, both of which have bodies (surfaces and depths) (2) and expands on Marks in her section on eroticism in the chapter "Skin" (34–39). On the "ethics of making" as opposed to critique, see N. Katherine Hayles and Jessica Pressman, *Comparative Textual Media: Transforming the Humanities in the Postprint Era* (Minneapolis: University of Minnesota Press, 2013).

65. See *The Piano Tuner of Earthquakes* and their work in progress, *Unmistaken Hands: Ex-Voto F.H.*

CHAPTER 5

The epigraph comes from Adolfo Bioy Casares, *La invención de Morel* (New York: Penguin, 1989), 69, my translation. Unless otherwise indicated, I employ the following translation: Adolfo Bioy Casares, *The Invention of Morel*, trans. Ruth L. C. Simms (New York: Penguin, 2003).

1. The phrase "symbolic victories" appears in Borge, *Latin American Writers and the Rise of Hollywood Cinema*, 20–21. See Horacio Quiroga, "El Vampiro," in *Todos los cuentos* (Paris: Colección Archivos, 1996), 717–31; Clemente Palma, *XYZ: Una novela grotesca* (Madrid: La Tinta del Calamar Ediciones, 2010).

2. On media archaeology, the following have been useful to me: Parikka, *What Is Media Archaeology?*; Erkki Huhtamo and Jussi Parikka, eds., *Media Archaeology: Approaches, Applications, and Implications* (Berkeley: University of California Press, 2011); Wolfgang Ernst, "Dis/continuities: Does the Archive Become Metaphorical in Multi-Media Space?" in *New Media, Old Media: A History and Theory Reader*, ed. Wendy Hui Kyong Chun and Thomas Keenan (New York: Routledge, 2004), 105–23.

3. Eric Kluitenberg, "On the Archaeology of Imaginary Media," in *Media Archaeology: Approaches, Applications, and Implications*, ed. Erkki Huhtamo and Jussi Parikka (Berkeley: University of California Press, 2011), 54. See also Jussi Parikka, "Imaginary Media: Mapping Weird Objects," in *What Is Media Archaeology?* (Cambridge: Polity, 2012), 50; Eric Kluitenberg, ed., *The Book of Imaginary Media: Excavating the Dream of the Ultimate Communication Medium* (Rotterdam: NAi Publishers, 2006). In the context of Latin American literary history, the category of "imaginary media" has the advantage of trumping less-than-useful distinctions between "hard" and "soft" science fiction, or between science fiction and fantasy.

4. Media archaeology has focused almost exclusively on the Euro-American context, especially in regard to the modern period. More recently, some media archaeologies have begun to look beyond the West in order to expand their definitions, including Zielinski's "Variantologies of the South" project and Bruce Sterling's Dead Media Project, which begins with the *quipu*, the medium for "a society without ink." The medieval Islamic context has drawn particular interest. See Parikka, *What Is Media Archaeology?* 172–73.

5. Vilém Flusser, *Into the Universe of Technical Images*, trans. Nancy Ann Roth (Minneapolis: University of Minnesota Press, 2011).

6. On the narrator and his relationship to spatial/visual arts, see Margaret L. Snook, "The Narrator as Creator and Critic in 'The Invention of Morel,'" *Latin American Literary Review* 7.14 (Spring 1979): 45–51. See also Edmundo Paz Soldán, "La imágen fotográfica, entre el aura y el cuestionamiento de la identidad: Una lectura de 'La Paraguaya' y *La invención de Morel*," *Revista Iberoamericana* 73.221 (October–December 2007): 759–70.

7. Bioy Casares, *La invención de Morel*, 67, my translation.

8. On immediacy versus hypermediacy, see Bolter and Grusin, *Remediation*, especially 20–51.

9. Bioy Casares, *La invención de Morel*, 69, 75, my translation.

10. Harald Szeemann, ed., *Le Macchine Celebi/The Bachelor Machines* (New York: Rizzoli, 1975), 20. The term "bachelor" or "celibate machines" originated with Duchamp and was first elaborated by Michel Carrouges, before Deleuze and Guattari's theorization. See Gilles Deleuze and Félix Guattari, *Anti-Oedipus: Capitalism and Schizophrenia* (New York: Penguin, 2009), especially 18–22.

11. See Siegfried Zielinski, "Modelling Media for Ignatius Loyola: A Case Study on Athanasius Kircher's World of Apparatus between the Imaginary and the Real," in *The Book of Imaginary Media: Excavating the Dream of the Ultimate Communication Medium*, ed. Eric Kluitenberg (Rotterdam: NAi Publishers, 2006), 43.

12. Latour, *Pandora's Hope*, 304. On the process of media becoming authoritative, see especially Gitelman, *Always Already New*, 6–7.

13. See Josefina Ludmer, "Tricks of the Weak" (*tretas del débil*), in *Feminist Perspectives on Sor Juan Inés de la Cruz*, ed. Stephanie Merrim (Detroit: Wayne State University Press, 1991); de Certeau, *The Practice of Everyday Life*.

14. See Alf Seegert, "The Mistress of Sp[l]ices: Technovirtual Liaisons in Adolfo Bioy Casares's *The Invention of Morel*," *Journal of the Fantastic in the Arts* 23.2 (2012): 197–214.

15. In fact, Morel's desire for a more complete transmission and storage medium begets, seemingly inevitably, the narrator's own fantasies. He begins to sketch out his own imaginary medium, more virtual than realized, a "more complete apparatus" that would include affect and consciousness.

16. See Vilém Flusser, *Does Writing Have a Future?* trans. Nancy Ann Roth (Minneapolis: University of Minnesota Press, 2011), 5–14. In contrast,

Lydia Liu finds writing's origins in the Phoenician word for counting, *spr.* ("Writing," in *Critical Terms for Media Studies*, ed. W. J. T. Mitchell and Mark Hansen [Chicago: University of Chicago Press, 2010], 315).

17. On "The Readies," see North, *Camera Works*, 73–79.

18. Jorge Luis Borges, "The Aleph," in *Borges: A Personal Anthology*, trans. Anthony Kerrigan (New York: Grove Press, 1967), 147. Unless otherwise indicated, I employ this translation.

19. See especially the essay "History of Eternity" (1936), in which Borges explores different manifestations of eternity as ways to "secretly to staunch [*restañar*] in some way the course of the hours." The verb *restañar* suggests the necessity of fiction to interrupt the terrifying flux of time. Jorge Luis Borges, *Historia de la eternidad* (Madrid: Alianza Editorial, 1995), 36, my translation.

20. See Erkki Huhtamo, "The Pleasures of the Peephole: An Archaeological Exploration of Peep Media," in *The Book of Imaginary Media: Excavating the Dream of the Ultimate Communication Medium*, ed. Eric Kluitenberg (Rotterdam: NAi Publishers, 2006), 104.

21. My slight variation of the English, 112–13. This description recalls Kittler on the gramophone's recording of the Lacanian real with all its noise, as well as the archival desire that undergirds moving images. See Kittler, *Discourse Networks, 1800/1900*, especially 245–46; Doane, *The Emergence of Cinematic Time*, 33–68; Paula Amad, *Counter-Archive: Film, the Everyday, and Albert Kahn's Archives de la Planète* (New York: Columbia University Press, 2010).

22. Borges wrote only one poem during the 1930s, "Insomnia" (1937), emblematic of late modernist exhaustion. Here, the poetic "I" encounters the horror of having seen too much, of being unable to abstract, narrate, or otherwise master the vicissitudes of experience. Funes, Borges writes in the prologue to *Ficciones*, is a metaphor for insomnia. Like Funes's world, the world of "Insomnia" constitutes a nightmare of infinite repetition; the poetic voice only has access to what he has already seen. "Insomnio," *Sur* 27 (1937): 71. On exhaustion in Borges, see also Cascardi, "Mimesis and Modernism"; Barth, "The Literature of Exhaustion."

23. See Cascardi, "Mimesis and Modernism." Jorge Ruffinelli has suggested that "Funes" could have been influenced by "Mr. Memory" in Hitchcock's *39 Steps*. See Ruffinelli, "Leer a Borges Ver Cine," *Texto Crítico* 6.11 (July 2002): 43.

24. Doane, *The Emergence of Cinematic Time*, 66.

25. On Funes as literary realism, see Beatriz Sarlo, "Una poética de la ficción," in *Historia crítica de la literatura argentina: El oficio se afirma*, ed. Sylvia Saítta (Buenos Aires: Emecé, 2004), 19–38, and Isabel Stratta, "Documentos por una poética del relato," in *Historia crítica de la literatura argentina: El oficio se afirma*, ed. Sylvia Saítta (Buenos Aires: Emecé 2004), 39–63.

26. Jorge Luis Borges, "Funes, el memorioso," in *Obras Completas*, vol. 1 (Buenos Aires: Emecé Editores, 2005), 522, my translation.

27. Jorge Luis Borges, "El Aleph," in *Obras Completas*, vol. 1 (Buenos Aires: Emecé Editores, 2005), 666, my translation.

28. On the importance of the *orillas* to Borges, see Beatriz Sarlo, *Jorge Luis Borges: A Writer on the Edge*, trans. John King (London: Verso, 1993).

29. Susan Stewart, *On Longing: Narrative of the Miniature, the Gigantic, the Souvenir, the Collection* (Baltimore: Johns Hopkins University Press, 1984), 46–47. For Stewart, the miniature also shifts away from "lived historical time," tending instead "toward tableau"; it is spatial, rather than temporal, "a world of arrested time" (65–67). Stewart references "The Aleph" in her exploration of the miniature but focuses on the figure of Daneri rather than the narrator or the Aleph itself (52).

30. See Bernard Stiegler, "Memory," in *Critical Terms for Media Studies*, ed. W. J. T. Mitchell and Mark Hansen (Chicago: University of Chicago Press, 2010). See also Liu, "Writing," 310.

31. Stiegler, "Memory," 67–68. It is not memory's instrumentalization that Stiegler objects to—instrumentalizing is part of the "deep time" of humans as media users—but this particular outsourcing that divorces the reader from embodied memory.

32. Roland Christ analyzes the importance of brevity and concision for Borges, and ascribes to memory an important function in this respect (*The Narrow Act*, 8–12). Christ notes in particular the verbs *abbrevitate* and *cifrar* ("to abridge, to encompass" [11]). However, he argues that Borges "aims to condense the universe in a verbal or narrative abbreviation" (ibid.), whereas I argue that Borges questions such attempts.

33. Virgilio Piñera, "Nota sobre la literatura argentina de hoy," in *Órbita de Virgilio Piñera*, ed. David Leyva González (Havana: Ediciones Unión, 2011), 197, my translation. The Spanish verb *gozar*, and the noun *goce*, are similar to the French *jouissance*, a term difficult to translate into English; the milder "enjoy" (*disfrutar*) does not quite get at the pleasure Piñera attributes to the author here.

34. Jorge Luis Borges, "Prólogo," in *Ficciones* (Madrid: Alianza, 1997), 12, my translation.

35. For example, on the imaginary planet of "Tlön, Uqbar, Orbis Tertius," "Works of fiction are based on a single plot, which runs through every imaginable permutation." In Jorge Luis Borges, *Ficciones*, trans. Anthony Kerrigan (New York: Grove Press, 1962), 28. See also Adolfo Bioy Casares, "Prólogo," in *Antología de la literatura fantástica*, ed. Adolfo Bioy Casares, Jorge Luis Borges, and Silvina Ocampo (Barcelona: EdHasa Sudamericana, 1977), 7.

36. See Caillois, *Man, Play, and Games*. In the prologue to *Morel*, Borges will also explicitly reject modernist literature's *informe* tendency (6).

37. Bioy Casares, *The Invention of Morel*, 6.

38. See the introduction, note 10.

39. Nineteen forty was a watershed year for a particularly Argentine variant of fantastic fiction. In addition to the publication of *The Invention of Morel* and the *Anthology of Fantastic Fiction* he coauthored with Bioy, Borges also published "Tlön, Uqbar, Orbis Tertius" and "The Circular Ruins" in *Sur*. This new fantastic is already outlined in Borges's prologue

to *Morel* and anticipated in his review of Bioy's earlier *Luis Greve, Muerto* (1937).

40. See Adriana Mancini, *Bioy Casares va al cine* (Buenos Aires: Libraria, 2014), xiv–xxi. In Claude-Jean Bonnardot's filmic adaptation of *Morel*, this inheritance is cleverly referenced in the opening scene through a brief pan over Morel's library, which contains books by both Breton and Borges.

41. For good measure, Borges throws in a parody of Spanish American *modernismo* (not to be confused with modernism), and in particular of the work of both Rubén Darío and the Argentine Leopoldo Lugones, through Daneri's explosion of excessive, ornate synonyms for the adjective blue (662).

42. My translation, which admittedly misses the rhyme and near-rhyme that add to the catalog's pomposity.

43. Jorge Luis Borges, "The Argentine Writer and Tradition," in *Labyrinths: Selected Stories and Other Writings*, trans. James E. Irby (New York: New Directions, 1964), 181.

44. Borges, "El Aleph," 661, my translation. On Borges and Schopenhauer, see Chapter 1.

45. Zielinski, *Deep Time of the Media*, 7. See also Zielinski, "Modelling Media for Ignatius Loyola," 38.

46. Markus Krajewski, *World Projects: Global Information before World War I* (Minneapolis: University of Minnesota Press, 2014), 25, 30.

47. See Susan Sontag, *Regarding the Pain of Others* (New York: Picador, 2003); Paul Virilio, *War and Cinema: The Logistics of Perception*, trans. Patrick Camiller (New York: Verso, 1989).

48. A similar enthusiasm greeted the arrival of the World Wide Web, before morphing into anxieties over the dominance of channels located in the Global North.

49. In *Networking the World*, Mattelart details how a few countries used communication technologies to "underdevelop" the Global South during the late nineteenth and early twentieth centuries. See also Salvatore, "Imperial Mechanics," especially 663–64.

50. "Panel, Radiobroadcasting 1933," Donald Dohner, designer, Wolfsonian-Florida International University Museum (Miami, Florida).

51. Later, the role of Disney in refashioning these very old tropes will also become the object of urgent and extensive anti-imperialist critiques, most prominently in Ariel Dorfman and Armand Mattelart's *Para leer al pato Donald: Comunicación de masa y imperialismo* (1972), translated as *How to Read Donald Duck: Imperialist Ideology in the Disney Comic*, trans. David Kunzle (New York: International General, 1975).

52. See Mattelart, *Networking the World*, 33–34; John Rieder, *Colonialism and the Emergence of Science Fiction* (Middletown, Conn.: Wesleyan University Press, 2008). In *The Emergence of Latin American Science Fiction* (Middletown, Conn.: Wesleyan University Press, 2011), Rachel Haywood Ferreira shows how nineteenth-century Latin American science fiction began to respond to these fantasies. Bioy draws out a dimension of Wells's *The Island of Dr. Moreau*, which also posited the desert island as ostensibly disconnected from the world, only to bring back in the colonial trade networks that make possible Moreau's terrifying

experiments. On Wells and colonialism, see Payal Taneja, "The Tropical Empire: Exotic Animals and Beastly Men in *The Island of Dr. Moreau*," *English Studies in Canada* 39.2–3 (June/September 2013): 139–59. Luís Cano argues that Latin American science fiction tends to favor spatialization over futurity. See Cano, *Intermitente Recurrencia: La ciencia ficción y el canon literario hispanoamericano* (Buenos Aires: Corregidor, 2006), 65–69. In contrast, contemporaneous Euro-American science fiction is rife with anxieties about the dangers of planned obsolescence under an unrestrained future capitalism, most notably in Huxley's *Brave New World* (1932), with its mapping of U.S./U.K. planetary domination onto technological inefficiency of the primitive native.

53. See Geoffrey Kantaris, "Holograms and Simulacra: Bioy Casares, Subiela, Piglia," in *Science and the Creative Imagination in Latin America*, ed. Evelyn Fishburn and Eduardo L. Ortiz (London: Institute for the Study of the Americas, 2005), 175–89.

54. Borges, "Funes, el memorioso," 524, my translation. The *arrabal*, mythologized in Argentine popular music and poetry as the city's outskirts, is a key term for Borges. Kerrigan's translation of "farmhouse" does not do it justice.

55. See Lev Manovich, "New Media from Borges to HTML," in *The New Media Reader*, vol. 1, ed. Noah Wardrip-Fruin and Nick Montfort (Cambridge, Mass.: MIT Press, 2003); Stefan Herbrechter and Ivan Callus, eds., *Cy-Borges: Memories of the Posthuman in the Work of Jorge Luis Borges* (Lewisburg, Pa.: Bucknell University Press, 2009); Jay David Bolter, *Writing Space: The Computer, Hypertext, and the History of Writing* (Hillsdale, N.J.: Lawrence Erlbaum, 1991), 137–39; Hayles, *How We Became Posthuman*, 197; N. Katherine Hayles, *My Mother Was a Computer: Digital Subjects and Literary Texts* (Urbana: University of Chicago Press, 2010), 89, 114–16.

56. See Kantaris, "Holograms and Simulacra"; Teresa López Pellisa, "Virtualidades distópicas en la ficción analógica: *La invención de Morel*, de Adolfo Bioy-Casares," *Revista Iberoamericana* 78.238–39 (January–June 2012): 73–89. Bioy is also the only non-Euro-American author to be considered in the mammoth compendium *Bachelor Machines*, ed. Harald Szeemann.

57. Morel's wish to be "more than the movies" continues a dream present in cinema since its inception, to expand into different sensorial and perceptual realms, heightening its immediacy, abolishing its distinction from life offscreen. See Rabinovitz, "More than the Movies"; Thomas Elsaesser, "Early Film History and Multi-Media: An Archaeology of Possible Futures?" in *New Media, Old Media: A History and Theory Reader*, ed. Wendy Hui Kyong Chun and Thomas Keenan (New York: Routledge, 2004), 13–25; David Rodowick, *The Virtual Life of Film* (Cambridge, Mass.: Harvard University Press, 2007), 22.

58. See Jean Clair, "The Last Machine/Notes on L'Invention de Morel," in *Le Macchine Celebi/The Bachelor Machines*, ed. Harald Szeemann (New York: Rizzoli, 1975), 180–92. Scholars debate the extent to which Resnais's *Last Year at Marienbad* was directly inspired by *The Invention of Morel*.

59. While Borges and Bioy loved to denigrate Horacio Quiroga as a kind of second-rate Kipling, for example, he is a clear precursor to their own media laboratories.

60. Leon Trotsky, *Literature and Revolution* (Ann Arbor: University of Michigan Press, 1968), 126–27; Jorge Luis Borges, *Evaristo Carriego*, trans. Norman Thomas Di Giovanni (New York: E. P. Dutton, 1984), 19. On the semiperiphery and the avant-garde, see Harsha Ram, "Futurist Geographies: Uneven Modernities and the Struggle for Aesthetic Autonomy: Paris, Italy, Russia, 1909–1914," in *The Oxford Handbook to Global Modernisms*, ed. Mark Wollaeger (Oxford: Oxford University Press, 2012), 318. Manovich suggests that the velocity of U.S. capitalism "invisibilizes" new media and inhibits its theorizing in its initial stages, thereby calling for a more global approach ("New Media from Borges to HTML," 13).

61. Josefina Ludmer, *The Corpus Delicti: A Manual of Argentine Fictions*, trans. Glen Close (Pittsburgh: University of Pittsburgh Press, 2004), 335.

62. See especially Lidia Santos's influential *Kitsch Tropical*; Jean Franco, "Autor, narrador, superestrella: La narrativa latinoamericana en la época de la cultura de masas," *Revista Iberoamericana* 47.114–15 (January–June 1981): 129–48.

63. Graciliano reappears in Nelson Pereira dos Santos's seminal *Vidas secas* (1963), *Memórias do Cárcere* (1984), and a series of shorts based on the short stories in the collection *Insônio* (1980), and in Leon Hirszman's adaptation of *São Bernardo* (1973).

64. Latin American intellectuals and artists would begin to read the Frankfurt School in sustained fashion beginning in the 1960s.

65. See Hans Magnus Enzensberger, "The Aporias of the Avant-Gardes," in *Modern Occasions*, ed. Philip Rahv (New York: Farrar, Straus and Giroux, 1966), 100, 94.

66. Schwarz, "The Cart, the Tram, and the Modernist Poet," 109. Schwarz's understanding of modernism resonates with Jameson's definition of the *ideology of modernism* of the postwar period in *A Singular Modernity*. Other important revisionist accounts of modernism from the post-1968 period include Peter Bürger, *Theory of the Avant-Garde* (1974; English translation by Michael Shaw: Minneapolis: University of Minnesota Press, 1984); Cândido, "Literature and Underdevelopment" (originally published in 1970); Rama, "Las dos vanguardias latinoamericanas" (originally published in 1973); Jameson, "Seriality and Modern Literature"; and Silviano Santiago, "O intellectual modernista revisitado" (1987), in *Nas malhas da letra* (São Paulo: Companhia das Letras, 1989), 165–75.

67. For Martín-Barbero, mass culture during the 1960s ceases to become part of a political negotiation between the elites and the masses and becomes a node of economic control of the former over the latter.

68. Examples of the homages to Galvão that emerge in this moment include the Tropicalista song "Parque Industrial" and the first full-length study of her work, Campos, *Pagu-Vida-Obra*.

69. When Vargas Llosa returns to the transnational circulation of radio dramas in South America in *Aunt Julia and the Scriptwriter*, he does so, unlike Puig, to reassert authorship's privilege over mass culture. On the figure of the author in *Aunt Julia and the Scriptwriter*, see Anke Birkenmaier, "Transparencia del subconsciente: Escritura Automática, Melodrama y la Radio en *La*

Tía Julia y el escribidor," *Revista Iberoamericana* 74.224 (July–September 2008): 685–701. On the reemergence of the auratic in authors of the Boom, see Franco, "Autor, narrador, superestrella"; David Viñas, ed., *Más allá del Boom: Literatura y mercado* (Mexico City: Marcha Editores, 1981); Idelber Avelar, *The Untimely Present: Postdictatorial Latin American Fiction and the Task of Mourning* (Durham, N.C.: Duke University Press, 1999), especially 11–13.

EPILOGUE

1. César Aira, *Fragmentos de un diario en los Alpes* (Rosario, Argentina: Beatriz Viterbo, 2004), my translation throughout.

2. Not coincidentally, the thaumatrope is one of the many "gamelike toys of the pre-cinematic era" that have been particularly attractive to media archaeologists (Parikka, *What Is Media Archaeology?* 28). Jonathan Crary analyzes this "philosophical toy" in his *Techniques of the Observer: On Vision and Modernity in the Nineteenth Century* (Cambridge, Mass.: MIT Press, 1992), 105–6.

Bibliography

Aaron, Michele. *Spectatorship: The Power of Looking On*. London: Wallflower, 2007.

Acland, Charles. Introduction to *Residual Media*, ed. Charles Acland, xiii–xxvii. Minneapolis: University of Minnesota Press, 2007.

Adorno, Theodor W., and Anson G. Rabinbach. "Culture Industry Reconsidered." *New German Critique* 6 (Autumn 1975): 12–19.

Aguilar, Gonzalo. "El motor y el cachivache (La vanguardia martinfierrista y las transformaciones tecnológicas)." In *Episodios cosmopolitas en la cultura argentina*, 59–84. Buenos Aires: Santiago Arcos, 2009.

Aguilar, Gonzalo, and Emiliano Jelicié. *Borges va al cine*. Buenos Aires: Libraria, 2010.

Aira, César. *Fragmentos de un diario en los Alpes*. Rosario, Argentina: Beatriz Viterbo, 2004.

Aizenberg, Edna. "Borges, Postcolonial Precursor." *World Literature Today* 66.1 (Winter 1992): 21–26.

Alazraki, Jaime. "Génesis de un Estilo: *Historia Universal de la Infamia*." *Revista Iberoamericana* 123–24 (April–September 1983): 247–61.

Almeida, Renato. "A literatura em 1934." *Lanterna Verde* 3 (February 1935): 99–103.

Altman, Rick. *Silent Film Sound*. New York: Columbia University Press, 2004.

———. "Moving Lips: Cinema as Ventriloquism." *Yale French Studies* 60 (1980): 67–79.

Amad, Paula. *Counter-Archive: Film, the Everyday, and Albert Kahn's Archives de la Planète*. New York: Columbia University Press, 2010.

———. "*Visual Riposte*: Reconsidering the Return of the Gaze as Postcolonial Theory's Gift to Film Studies." *Cinema Journal* 52.3 (Spring 2013): 49–74.

Amado, Jorge. "Apontamentos sobre o moderno romance brasileiro." *Lanterna Verde* 2 (1933): 48–51.

Amieva, Mariana. "*Cine Arte* del Sodre en la conformación de un campo audiovisual en Uruguay: Políticas públicas y acciones individuales." *Cine Documental* 6 (2012). http://revista.cinedocumental.com.ar/6/articulos_01.html.

Amoroso Lima, Alceu (Tristão Athayde). "Idade Nova." *Lanterna Verde* 3 (February 1935): 97–102.

Anderson, Perry. "Modernity and Revolution." *New Left Review* 144 (March–April 1984): 96–113.

Anderson, Thomas. *Everything in Its Place: The Life and Works of Virgilio Piñera*. Lewisburg, Pa.: Bucknell University Press, 2006.

Andrade, Mario de. *O empalhador de passarinho*. São Paulo: Livraria Martins Editôra, 1972.

———. "O movimento modernista." In *Aspectos da literatura brasileira*, 21–46. São Paulo: Livraria Martins Editora, 1972.

———. *Taxi e crônicas no Diário nacional*. Ed. Telê Porto Ancona Lopez. São Paulo: Livraria Duas Cidades, Secretaria da Cultura, Ciência e Tecnologia, 1976.

Andrade, Oswald de. *Seraphim Grosse Point*. Trans. K. David Jackson and Albert Bork. Austin: New Latin Quarter Editions, 1979.

Andrew, Dudley. "Time Zones and Jetlag: The Flows and Phases of World Cinema." In *World Cinemas, Transnational Perspectives*, ed. Nataša Durovicová and Kathleen Newman, 59–89. New York: Routledge, 2010.

Antelo, Raul. "Gilberto Freyre: Alteração e iteração." In *Gilberto Freyre e os estudos latino-americanos*, ed. Joshua Lund and Malcolm McNee, 53–97. Pittsburgh: Instituto Internacional de Literatura Iberoamericana, 2006.

———. *Na ilha de Marapatá: Mário de Andrade lê os hispano-americanos*. São Paulo: Editora HUCITEC, 1986.

Arlt, Roberto. *Aguafuertes porteñas: Buenos Aires, vida cotidiana*. Buenos Aires: Losada, 1999.

———. "Recordando el Eclesiastés." In *Notas sobre el cinematógrafo*, 18–22. Buenos Aires: Ediciones Simurg, 1997.

Armstrong, Tim. "Film Finds a Tongue." In *Modernism, Technology and the Body: A Cultural Study*, 220–48. Cambridge: Cambridge University Press, 1998.

Arnheim, Rudolf. "A New Laocoön: Artistic Composites and the Talking Film." In *Film as Art*, 199–230. Berkeley: University of California Press, 1957.

Asunción Silva, José. "Anuncio del Almacén Bohemia." In *De Sobremesa*, 277–79. Madrid: Cátedra, 2006.

Athayde, Tristão de. "Síntese." *Lanterna Verde* 4 (November 1936): 89–95.

Avelar, Idelber. *The Untimely Present: Postdictatorial Latin American Fiction and the Task of Mourning*. Durham, N.C.: Duke University Press, 1999.

Bakhtin, Mikhail. "Discourse in the Novel." In *The Dialogic Imagination:*

Four Essays. Trans. Michael Holquist. Austin: University of Texas Press, 1982.

Balderston, Daniel. *Out of Context: Historical Reference and the Representation of Reality in Borges*. Durham, N.C.: Duke University Press, 1993.

Barker, Jennifer. *The Tactile Eye: Touch and the Cinematic Experience*. Berkeley: University of California Press, 2009.

Barnard, Timothy, and Peter Rist. *South American Cinema: A Critical Filmography*. Austin: University of Texas Press, 1999.

Barnard, Rita. *The Great Depression and the Culture of Abundance: Kenneth Fearing, Nathanael West, and Mass Culture in the 1930s*. Cambridge: Cambridge University Press, 1995.

Barth, John. "The Literature of Exhaustion." In *The Friday Book: Essays and Other Non-Fiction*, 62–76. Baltimore: Johns Hopkins University Press, 1984.

Barthes, Roland. "The Face of Garbo." In *Mythologies*, 56–57. London: Vintage, 1993.

———. "From Work to Text." In *The Rustle of Language*, trans. Richard Howard, 56–64. New York: Hill and Wang, 1987.

———. "The Grain of the Voice." In *Image-Music-Text*, trans. Stephen Heath, 179–89. New York: Hill and Wang, 1978.

———. "The Structure of the *Fait-Divers*." In *Critical Essays*, trans. Richard Howard, 187–96. Evanston, Ill.: Northwestern University Press, 1972.

Baudry, Jean-Louis. "Ideological Effects of the Basic Cinematographic Apparatus." In *Narrative, Apparatus, Ideology: A Film Theory Reader*, ed. Philip Rosen, 286–98. New York: Columbia University Press, 1986.

Bauer, Arnold J. *Goods, Power, History: Latin America's Material Culture*. Cambridge: Cambridge University Press, 2001.

Benjamin, Walter. "The Author as Producer." In *Reflections: Essays, Aphorisms, Autobiographical Writings*, ed. Peter Demetz, 220–38. New York: Schocken Books, 1978.

———. "One-Way Street." In *Reflections: Essays, Aphorisms, Autobiographical Writings*, ed. Peter Demetz, 61–95. New York: Schocken Books, 1978.

———. "Reflections on Radio." In *The Work of Art in the Age of Its Technological Reproducibility and Other Writings on Media*, ed. Michael W. Jennings, Brigid Doherty, and Thomas Y. Levin, 391–93. Cambridge, Mass.: Harvard University Press, 2008.

———. "Surrealism." In *Reflections: Essays, Aphorisms, Autobiographical Writings*, ed. Peter Demetz, 177–92. New York: Schocken Books, 1978.

———. "The Work of Art in the Age of Its Technological Reproducibility." In *The Work of Art in the Age of Its Technological Reproducibility and Other Writings on Media*, ed. Michael W. Jennings, Brigid Doherty, and Thomas Y. Levin, 19–55. Cambridge, Mass.: Harvard University Press, 2008.

Bergero, Adriana J. *Intersecting Tango: Cultural Geographies of Buenos Aires*. Pittsburgh: University of Pittsburgh Press, 2008.

Berland, Jody. "The Musicking Machine." In *Residual Media*, ed. Charles Acland, 303–28. Minneapolis: University of Minnesota Press, 2007.

Best, Stephen, and Sharon Marcus. "Surface Reading: An Introduction." *Representations* 108.1 (Fall 2009): 1–21.

Bioy Casares, Adolfo. *La invención de Morel*. New York: Penguin, 1989.

———. *The Invention of Morel*. Trans. Ruth L. C. Simms. New York: Penguin, 2003.

———. "Prólogo." In *Antología de la literatura fantástica*, ed. Adolfo Bioy Casares, Jorge Luis Borges, and Silvina Ocampo. Barcelona: EdHasa Sudamericana, 1977.

Birkenmaier, Anke. *Alejo Carpentier y la cultura del surrealismo en América Latina*. Madrid: Vervuert-Iberoamericana, 2006.

———. "Transparencia del subconsciente: Escritura Automática, Melodrama y la Radio en *La Tía Julia y el escribidor*." *Revista Iberoamericana* 74.224 (July–September 2008): 685–701.

Blanco Aguinaga, Carlos. "On Modernism from the Periphery." In *Modernism and Its Margins: Reinscribing Cultural Modernity from Spain and Latin America*, ed. Anthony L. Geist and José B. Monleón, 3–16. New York: Garland, 1999.

Block de Behar, Lisa. "Familiaridad y extrañeza: La repetición-fragmentación narrativa de Felisberto Hernández." *Lectura crítica de la literatura americana* 3 (1996–97): 205–24.

Bolter, Jay David. *Writing Space: The Computer, Hypertext, and the History of Writing*. Hillsdale, N.J.: Lawrence Erlbaum, 1991.

Bolter, Jay David, and Richard Grusin. *Remediation: Understanding New Media*. Cambridge, Mass.: MIT Press, 2000.

Bordwell, David. *The Cinema of Eisenstein*. Cambridge, Mass.: Harvard University Press, 1993.

Borge, Dain. "Review Essay: Brazilian Social Thought of the 1930s." *Luso-Brazilian Review* 31.2 (1994): 137–50.

Borge, Jason. *Avances de Hollywood: Crítica cinematográfica en Latinoamérica*. Rosario, Argentina: Beatriz Viterbo, 2005.

———. *Latin American Writers and the Rise of Hollywood Cinema*. New York: Routledge, 2008.

Borges, Jorge Luis. "The Aleph." In *Borges: A Personal Anthology*. Trans. Anthony Kerrigan, 138–54. New York: Grove Press, 1967.

———. "El Aleph." In *Obras Completas*. Vol. 1, 658–69. Buenos Aires: Emecé Editores, 2005.

———. "The Argentine Writer and Tradition." In *Labyrinths: Selected Stories and Other Writings*, 177–87. Trans. James E. Irby. New York: New Directions, 1964.

———. "Dos Films." *Sur* 103 (April 1943): 103–4.

———. *Evaristo Carriego*. Trans. Norman Thomas Di Giovanni. New York: E. P. Dutton, 1984.

———. *Ficciones*. Trans. Anthony Kerrigan. New York: Grove Press, 1962.

———. "Funes, el memorioso." In *Obras Completas*. Vol. 1, 519–25. Buenos Aires: Emecé Editores, 2005.

———. "Historia de la eternidad." In *Obras Completas*. Vol. 2, 11–42. Buenos Aires: Emecé Editores, 2005.

———. *Historia universal de la infamia.* Buenos Aires: Alianza Emecé, 1971.

———. "Insomnio." *Sur* 27 (1937): 71–72.

———. "Nueva refutación del tiempo." In *Obras Completas.* Vol. 3, 235–57. Buenos Aires: Emecé Editores, 2005.

———. "Prólogo." In *Ficciones*, 11–12. Madrid: Alianza, 1997.

———. "Street Scene." *Sur* 5 (Summer 1932): 198–200.

———. *A Universal History of Iniquity.* Trans. Andrew Hurley. New York: Penguin Classics, 2004.

Borges, Vavy Pacheco. "Anos trinta e política: Conceitos, imagens e temas." *Luso-Brazilian Review* 36.2 (Winter 1999): 109–26.

Bosi, Alfredo. *Céu, inferno: Ensaios de crítica literária e ideológica.* São Paulo: Editora Atica, 1988.

Brantlinger, Patrick. *Bread and Circuses: Theories of Mass Culture as Social Decay.* Ithaca, N.Y.: Cornell University Press, 1983.

Brecht, Bertolt. "The Radio as a Communications Apparatus." In *Bertolt Brecht on Film and Radio*, ed. Marc Silberman, 41–46. London: Methuen, 2000.

Brito, Mário da Silva. "O Alegre Combate de Klaxon." Fascimile edition of *Klaxon—Mensário de Arte Moderna.* São Paulo: Martins; Secretaria da Cultura, Ciência e Tecnologia do Estado de São Paulo, 1976.

Brown, Marshall. "Introduction." *Modern Language Quarterly* (December 2001): 309–16.

Buck-Morss, Susan. "Aesthetics and Anaesthetics: Walter Benjamin's Artwork Essay Reconsidered." *October* 62 (Autumn 1992): 3–41.

———. *Dreamworld and Catastrophe: The Passing of Mass Utopia in East and West.* Cambridge, Mass.: MIT Press, 2000.

Bueno, Luís. *Uma história do romance de 30.* São Paulo: EDUSP, 2006.

Bürger, Peter. *Theory of the Avant-Garde.* Trans. Michael Shaw. Minneapolis: University of Minnesota Press, 1984.

Burges, Joel. "Adorno's Mimeograph: The Uses of Obsolescence in *Minima Moralia.*" *New German Critique* 40.118 (Winter 2013): 65–92.

Caillois, Roger. *The Edge of Surrealism: A Roger Caillois Reader.* Ed. Claudine Frank. Durham, N.C.: Duke University Press, 2003.

———. *Man, Play, and Games.* Trans. Meyer Barash. Urbana: University of Illinois Press, 2001.

Calabre, Lia. "Políticas públicas culturais de 1924 a 1945: O rádio em destaque." *Estudos históricos* 31 (2003): 1–21.

Calinescu, Matei. *Five Faces of Modernity: Modernism, Avant-Garde, Decadence, Kitsch, Postmodernism.* Durham, N.C.: Duke University Press, 1987.

Calistro, Mariano. *Reportaje al cine argentino: Los pioneros del sonoro.* Buenos Aires: ANESA, 1978.

Calvino, Italo. Introduction to Felisberto Hernández, *Piano Stories*, trans. Luis Harss, xvii–xxi. New York: New Directions, 2014.

Campos, Augusto de. *Pagu-Vida-Obra.* São Paulo: Brasiliense, 1982.

Cândido, António. *On Literature and Society.* Princeton, N.J.: Princeton University Press, 1995.

———. "A Revolução de 1930 e a cultura." In *A educação pela noite*, 181–98. São Paulo: Editora Atica, 1987.

Câdido, António, and José Aderaldo Castello. *Presença da literatura brasileira: Modernismo*. São Paulo: Difel, 1982.

Cano, Luís. *Intermitente Recurrencia: La ciencia ficción y el canon literario hispanoamericano*. Buenos Aires: Corregidor, 2006.

Corbone, Rocco. "Erdosain entre Yrigoyen y Uriburu: *Los siete locos* y *Los lanzallamas* entre la república radical y el autoritarismo." In *La década infame y los escritores suicidas (1930–1943)*, ed. David Viñas, Gabriela García Cedro, and María Pía López, 65–79. Buenos Aires: Paradiso Ediciones, Fundación Crónica General, 2007.

Carvalho, Lúcia Helena. *A ponto do novelo: Uma interpretação de "Angústia," de Graciliano Ramos*. São Paulo: Editora Atica, 1983.

Cascardi, A. J. "Mimesis and Modernism: The Case of Jorge Luis Borges." In *Literary Philosophers: Borges, Calvino, Eco*, 100–128. New York: Routledge, 2002.

Casetti, Francesco. *The Eye of the Century: Film, Experience, Modernity*. New York: Columbia University Press, 2008.

———. *Inside the Gaze: The Fiction Film and Its Spectator*. Bloomington: Indiana University Press, 1998.

Casetti, Francesco, and Mariagrazia Fanchi. "Cinephilia/Telephilia." *Framework* 45.2 (Fall 2004): 36–41.

Castillo, Debra A. "Lispector, cronista." In *Clarice Lispector: Novos aportes críticos*, ed. Cristina Ferreira-Pinto Bailey and Regina Zilgerman, 95–108. Pittsburgh: University of Pittsburgh Press, 2007.

Castro Gomes, Ângela Maria de. "A 'cultura histórica' do Estado Novo." *Luso-Brazilian Review* 36.2 (1999): 103–8.

Cattaruzza, Alejandro, ed. *Crisis económica, avance del estado e incertidumbre política (1930–1943): Nueva historia de la nación argentina*. Tomo IX. Buenos Aires: Planeta, 1999.

Caws, Mary Ann. *Manifesto: A Century of Isms*. Lincoln: University of Nebraska Press, 2000.

———. *Surrealism*. New York: Phaidon Press, 2008.

Charney, Leo, and Vanessa Schwartz, eds. *Cinema: The Invention of Modern Life*. Berkeley: University of California Press, 1995.

Chaves, Flávio Loureiro. "Pagu e a experiência da linguagem." In Patrícia Galvão, *Parque industrial*, 7–11. Porto Alegre: Mercado Aberto; São Paulo: Edufscar, 1994.

Cheng, Anne. "Skin, Tattoos and Susceptibility." *Representations* 108.1 (Fall 2009): 98–119.

Chion, Michel. *The Voice in Cinema*. Trans. Claudia Gorbman. New York: Columbia University Press, 1999.

Christ, Roland. *The Narrow Act: Borges' Art of Allusion*. New York: Lumen, 1995.

Cixous, Hélène. *Reading with Clarice Lispector*. Minneapolis: University of Minnesota Press, 1990.

Clair, Jean. "The Last Machine/Notes on L'Invention de Morel." In *Le*

Macchine Celebi/The Bachelor Machines, ed. Harald Szeemann, 180–92. New York: Rizzoli, 1975.
Clarke, Katerina. *The Fourth Rome: Stalinism, Cosmopolitanism, and the Evolution of Soviet Culture, 1931–1941*. Cambridge, Mass.: Harvard University Press, 2011.
Clayton, Michelle. *Poetry in Pieces: César Vallejo and Lyric Modernity*. Berkeley: University of California Press, 2011.
Cohen, Debra Rae, Michael Coyle, and Jane A. Lewty. *Broadcasting Modernism*. Gainesville: University Press of Florida, 2009.
Cohen, Margaret. *Profane Illumination: Walter Benjamin and the Paris of Surrealist Revolution*. Berkeley: University of California Press, 1995.
Concha, Jaime. "Los empleados del cielo: En torno a Felisberto Hernández." In *Felisberto Hernández ante la crítica actual*, ed. Alain Sicard, 61–83. Caracas: Monte Ávila Editores, 1977.
Conde, Maite. *Consuming Visions: Cinema, Writing, and Modernity in Rio de Janeiro*. Charlottesville: University of Virginia Press, 2012.
Conniff, Michael L., ed. *Populism in Latin America*. Tuscaloosa: University of Alabama Press, 2012.
Conor, Liz. *The Spectacular Modern Woman: Feminine Visibility in the 1920s*. Bloomington: Indiana University Press, 2006.
Cozarinsky, Edgardo. *Borges in/and/on Film*. Trans. Gloria Waldman and Roland Christ. New York: Lumen Books, 1988.
Crary, Jonathan. *Techniques of the Observer: On Vision and Modernity in the Nineteenth Century*. Cambridge, Mass.: MIT Press, 1992.
———. *24/7*. London: Verso, 2013.
Dámaso Martínez, Carlos. "Horacio Quiroga: La industria editorial, sus relatos y la literatura fantástica." In Horacio Quiroga, *Todos los cuentos*, 1293–1303. Madrid: Fondo de Cultura Económica, 1993.
Danius, Sara. *The Senses of Modernism: Technology, Perception, and Aesthetics*. Ithaca, N.Y.: Cornell University Press, 2002.
Darío, Rubén. "The Bourgeois King." Trans. Andrew Hurley. In *Selected Writings*, 221–25. New York: Penguin, 2005.
Davies, Margery W. *A Woman's Place Is at the Typewriter: Office Work and Office Workers, 1870–1930*. Philadelphia: Temple University Press, 1982.
Davis, John. "Going Analogue: Vinylphiles and the Consumption of the 'Obsolete.'" In *Residual Media*, ed. Charles Acland, 222–36. Minneapolis: University of Minnesota Press, 2007.
De Certeau, Michel. *The Practice of Everyday Life*. Berkeley: University of California Press, 1984.
Deleuze, Gilles, and Félix Guattari. *Anti-Oedipus: Capitalism and Schizophrenia*. New York: Penguin, 2009.
Denning, Michael. *The Cultural Front: The Laboring of American Culture in the Twentieth Century*. New York: Verso, 2011.
———. *Culture in the Age of Three Worlds*. London: Verso, 2004.
Dennison, Stephanie, and Lisa Shaw. *Popular Cinema in Brazil, 1930–2001*. New York: Palgrave, 2004.
Díaz, Emilio Daniel, César Maranghell, and Elina Mercedes Tranchini. *El*

cine argentino y su aporte a la identidad nacional. Buenos Aires: Federación Argentina de la Industria Gráfica y Afines, 1999.

Díaz, Hernán. *Borges: Between History and Eternity.* New York: Continuum, 2012.

Doane, Mary Ann. *The Emergence of Cinematic Time: Modernity, Contingency, and the Archive.* Cambridge, Mass.: Harvard University Press, 2002.

———. "Technophilia: Technology, Representation, and the Feminine." In *Liquid Metal: The Science Fiction Film Reader,* ed. Sean Redmond, 182–90. London: Wallflower Press, 2004.

Dolar, Mladen. *A Voice and Nothing More.* Cambridge, Mass.: MIT Press, 2006.

Duarte, Eduardo de Assis. "Patrícia Galvão: Comunismo e Feminismo nos Anos 30." In *Mulher: Cinco séculos de desenvolvimento na América: Capítulo Brasil,* ed. Sylvia Maria von Atzingen. Venturoli Aud. Belo Horizonte: Unicentro Newton Paiva, 1999.

Durovicová, Nataša. "Local Ghosts: Dubbing Bodies in Early Sound Cinema." In *Il film e I suoi multipli/Film and Its Multiples,* ed. Anna Antonini, 83–98. IX Convegno Internazionale di Studi sul Cinema. Forum: Udine, 2003.

Eburne, Jonathan P., and Rita Felski. "Introduction." *New Literary History* 41.4 (Autumn 2010): v–xv.

Eglash, Ron, et al., eds. *Appropriating Technology: Vernacular Science and Social Power.* Minneapolis: University of Minnesota Press, 2004.

Ehrick, Christine. "Radio Transvestism and the Gendered Soundscape in Buenos Aires, 1930s–1940s." In *Media, Sound, and Culture in Latin America and the Caribbean,* ed. Alejandra Brofman and Andrew Grant Wood, 18–36. Pittsburgh: University of Pittsburgh Press, 2012.

———. "'Savage Dissonance': Gender, Voice, and Women's Radio Speech in Argentina, 1930–1945." In *Radio and the Gendered Soundscape: Women and Broadcasting in Argentina and Uruguay, 1930–1950,* 69–91. Cambridge: Cambridge University Press, 2015.

Eisenstein, Sergei. "A Dialectical Approach to Film Form." In *Film Form and Film Sense,* trans. and ed. Jay Leyda, 45–63. New York: Meridian Books, 1963.

———. "Methods of Montage." In *Film Form and Film Sense,* trans. and ed. Jay Leyda, 72–83. New York: Meridian Books, 1963.

———. "Montage Is Conflict." In *The Cinematic,* ed. David Campany, 30–32. Cambridge, Mass.: MIT Press, 2007.

Elsaesser, Thomas. "Cinephilia, or the Uses of Disenchantment." In *Cinephilia: Movies, Love and Memory,* ed. Marijke De Valck and Malte Hagener, 27–44. Amsterdam: Amsterdam University Press, 2005.

———. "Early Film History and Multi-Media: An Archaeology of Possible Futures?" In *New Media, Old Media: A History and Theory Reader,* ed. Wendy Hui Kyong Chun and Thomas Keenan, 13–25. New York: Routledge, 2004.

Enzensberger, Hans Magnus. "The Aporias of the Avant-Gardes." In *Modern*

Occasions, ed. Philip Rahv, 72–101. New York: Farrar, Straus and Giroux, 1966.
Epplin, Craig. *Late Book Culture in Argentina*. London: Bloomsbury Academic, 2014.
Epstein, Jean. "On Certain Characteristics of *Photogénie*." In *Film Theory: Critical Concepts in Media and Cultural Studies*, vol. 1, ed. Philip Simpson, Andrew Utterson, and Karen Shepherdson, 52–56. London: Routledge, 2003.
———. *The Intelligence of a Machine*. Trans. Christophe Wall-Romana. Minneapolis: Univocal, 2014.
Ernst, Wolfgang. "Dis/continuities: Does the Archive Become Metaphorical in Multi-Media Space?" In *New Media, Old Media: A History and Theory Reader*, ed. Wendy Hui Kyong Chun and Thomas Keenan, 105–23. New York: Routledge, 2004.
Esty, Jed. *A Shrinking Island: Modernism and National Culture in England*. Princeton, N.J.: Princeton University Press, 2004.
Fária, Otávio de. "Mensagem post-modernista." *Lanterna Verde*, no. 4 (November 1936): 49–67.
Fausto, Boris. *A revolução de 1930: Historiografia e história*. São Paulo: Editôra Brasiliense, 1976.
Felski, Rita. "Context Stinks!" *New Literary History* 42.4 (Autumn 2011): 573–91.
Ferré, Rosario. *El acomodador: Una lectura fantástica de Felisberto Hernández*. Mexico City: Fondo de Cultura Económica, 1986.
———. "Felisberto Hernández: La vanguardia de un hombre solo." *La Gaceta del Fondo de Cultura Económica* 185 (1986): 17–19.
Fisher, Jennifer. "Relational Sense: Towards a Haptic Aesthetic." *Parachute* 87 (1997): 4–11.
Flusser, Vilém. *Does Writing Have a Future?* Trans. Nancy Ann Roth. Minneapolis: University of Minnesota Press, 2011.
———. *Into the Universe of Technical Images*. Trans. Nancy Ann Roth. Minneapolis: University of Minnesota Press, 2011.
Foot Hardman, Francisco. *Nem pátria, nem patrão! (Vida operária e cultura anarquista no Brasil)*. São Paulo: UNESP, 2002.
Foster, Hal. *Compulsive Beauty*. Cambridge, Mass.: MIT Press/October Books, 1993.
Franco, Jean. "Autor, narrador, superestrella: La narrativa latinoamericana en la época de la cultura de masas." *Revista Iberoamericana* 47.114–15 (January–June 1981): 129–48.
———. "Vallejo and the Crisis of the Thirties." *Hispania* 72 (March 1989): 42–48.
Franco, Luis. "América Inicial." *La vida literaria* (October 4, 1931): 33–34.
Freed-Thall, Hannah. *Spoiled Distinctions: Aesthetics and the Ordinary in French Modernism*. Oxford: Oxford University Press, 2015.
Friedberg, Anne. "Reading *Close Up*, 1927–1933." In *Close Up: Cinema and Modernism*, ed. James Donald, Anne Friedberg, and Laura Marcus, 1–34. London: Bloomsbury, 2001.

———. *Window Shopping: Cinema and the Postmodern.* Berkeley: University of California Press, 1994.

Gabara, Ester. *Errant Modernism: The Ethos of Photography in Brazil and Mexico.* Durham, N.C.: Duke University Press, 2008.

Gallo, Rubén. *Mexican Modernity: The Avant-garde and the Technical Revolution.* Cambridge, Mass.: MIT Press, 2010.

Galvão, Patrícia. *Industrial Park.* Trans. Elizabeth Jackson and K. David Jackson. Lincoln: University of Nebraska Press, 1993.

———. *Paixão Pagu: A autobiografia precoce de Patrícia Galvão.* Rio de Janeiro: Agir, 2005.

Galvão Ferraz, Geraldo. "A *pulp fiction* de Patrícia Galvão." In Patrícia Galvão, *Safra macabra: Contos policias.* Rio de Janeiro: José Olympio Editora, 1998.

Garbuglio, José Carlos, Alfredo Bosi, and Valentim Facioli. *Graciliano Ramos: Antologia e estudos.* São Paulo: Editora Atica, 1987.

García Canclini, Néstor. *Hybrid Cultures: Strategies for Entering and Leaving Modernity.* Minneapolis: University of Minnesota Press, 2005.

Gardner, William. *Advertising Tower: Japanese Modernism and Modernity in the 1920s.* Cambridge, Mass.: Harvard University Press, 2006.

Garramuño, Florencia. *Primitive Modernities: Tango, Samba and Nation.* Trans. Anna Kazumi Stahl. Stanford, Calif.: Stanford University Press, 2011.

Gaudreault, André. "Showing and Telling: Image and Word in Early Cinema." In *Early Cinema: Space, Frame, Narrative,* ed. Thomas Elsaesser and Adam Barker, 68–75. London: BFI Publishing, 1990.

Giglin, Peter. "Aesthetics: History after Films." In *Mapping Benjamin: The Work of Art in the Digital Age,* ed. Hans Ulrich Gumbrecht and Michael Marrinan, 53–62. Stanford, Calif.: Stanford University Press, 2003.

Gitelman, Lisa. *Always Already New: Media, History, and the Data of Culture.* Cambridge, Mass.: MIT Press, 2008.

Giucci, Guillermo. "Gilberto Freyre e o (Pós) Modernismo." In *Arquivos literários,* org. Eneida Maria de Souza and Wander Melo Miranda, 167–82. Minas Gerais: Universidade Federal de Minas Gerais, Centro de Estudos Literários, 2003.

Goble, Mark. *Beautiful Circuits: Modernism and the Mediated Life.* New York: Columbia University Press, 2010.

Goldgel, Víctor. *Cuando lo nuevo conquistó América: Literatura, prensa y moda en el siglo XIX.* Buenos Aires: Siglo XXI, 2013.

Goméz de la Serna, Ramón. "Plantas y tranvías: Gran sonatista de los recuerdos y las quintas." http://www.felisberto.org.uy/critica.html.

González, José Eduardo. *Borges and the Politics of Form.* New York: Garland, 1988.

Grandin, Greg. *Fordlandia: The Rise and Fall of Henry Ford's Forgotten Jungle City.* New York: Picador, 2010.

Graziano, Frank. *The Lust of Seeing: Themes of the Gaze and Sexual Rituals in the Fiction of Felisberto Hernández.* Lewisburg, Pa: Bucknell University Press, 1997.

Grieveson, Lee. "The Work of Film in the Age of Fordist Mechanization." *Cinema Journal* 51.3 (Spring 2012): 25–51.

Groys, Boris. *The Total Art of Stalinism: Avant-Garde, Aesthetic Dictatorship and Beyond*. New York: Verso, 2011.

Guedes, Thelma. *Pagu: Literatura e revolução. Um estudo sobre o romance "Parque industrial."* São Paulo: Nankin Editorial, 2003.

Guha, Ranajit. *History at the Limit of World-History*. New York: Columbia University Press, 2000.

Guilherme, Olympio. "Questão de gosto . . . ," *Cinearte* 202 (January 8, 1930): 10.

Gumbrecht, Hans. *In 1926: Living on the Edge of Time*. Cambridge, Mass.: Harvard University Press, 2006.

Gunning, Tom. "Cinema of Attractions: Early Film, Its Spectator, and the Avant-Garde." *Wide Angle* 8.3–4 (Fall 1986): 63–70.

Halperin Donghi, Tulio. *The Contemporary History of Latin America*. Durham, N.C.: Duke University Press, 1993.

———. *La república imposible (1930–1945)*. Buenos Aires: Ariel, 2004.

Hamilton, James. "Unearthing Radio Broadcasting in the Anglophone World." In *Residual Media*, ed. Charles Acland, 283–300. Minneapolis: University of Minnesota Press, 2007.

Hammond, Paul. "Available Light." In *The Shadow and Its Shadow: Surrealist Writings on the Cinema*, 1–43. San Francisco: City Lights, 2000.

Hansen, Miriam. *Cinema and Experience: Siegfried Kracauer, Walter Benjamin, and Theodor W. Adorno*. Berkeley: University of California Press, 2011.

———. "Early Cinema, Late Cinema: Transformations of the Public Sphere." In *Viewing Positions: Ways of Seeing Film*, ed. Linda Williams, 134–54. New Brunswick, N.J.: Rutgers University Press, 1997.

———. "The Mass Production of the Senses: Classical Cinema as Vernacular Modernism." *Modernism/Modernity* 6.2 (1999): 59–77.

———. "Vernacular Modernism: Tracking Cinema on a Global Scale." In *World Cinemas, Transnational Perspectives*, ed. Nataša Durovicová and Kathleen Newman, 287–314. New York: Routledge, 2010.

Hayles, N. Katherine. *How We Became Posthuman: Virtual Bodies in Cybernetics, Literature, and Informatics*. Chicago: University of Chicago Press, 1999.

———. *My Mother Was a Computer: Digital Subjects and Literary Texts*. Chicago: University of Chicago, 2010.

———. *Writing Machines*. Cambridge, Mass.: MIT Press, 2002.

Hayles, N. Katherine, and Jessica Pressman. *Comparative Textual Media: Transforming the Humanities in the Postprint Era*. Minneapolis: University of Minnesota Press, 2013.

Hayot, Eric. "Against Periodization; or, On Institutional Time." *New Literary History* 42.4 (Autumn 2011): 739–56.

Haywood, Rachel. *The Emergence of Latin American Science Fiction*. Middletown, Conn.: Wesleyan University Press, 2011.

Hegel, G. W. F. *Lectures on the Philosophy of World History*. New York: Cambridge University Press, 1975.

Helft, Nicolás, ed. *Crítica: Revista multicolor de los sábados, 1933–1934*. Buenos Aires: Fondo Nacional de las Artes, 1999.

Henning, Michelle. "New Lamps for Old: Photography, Obsolescence, and Social Change." In *Residual Media*, ed. Charles Acland, 48–65. Minneapolis: University of Minnesota Press, 2007.

Herbrechter, Stefan, and Ivan Callus, eds. *Cy-Borges: Memories of the Posthuman in the Work of Jorge Luis Borges*. Lewisburg, Pa.: Bucknell University Press, 2009.

Hernández, Felisberto. "Around the Time of Clemente Colling." In *Lands of Memory*, trans. Esther Allen, 3–59. New York: New Directions, 2002.

———. "The Daisy Dolls." In *Piano Stories*, trans. Luis Harss, 173–228. New York: New Directions, 2014.

———. "En el cine." In *Obras Completas*. Vol. 3. Buenos Aires: Siglo XXI, 2005.

———. "Except Julia." In *Piano Stories*, trans. Luis Harss, 87–106. New York: New Directions, 2014.

———. *Las Hortensias*. Montevideo: Talleres Gráficos "Gaceta Comercial," 1949.

———. "Menos Julia." In *Narraciones incompletas*, 158–71. Madrid: Ediciones Siruela, 1990.

———. *Nadie encendía las lámparas*. Montevideo: Arca, 1967.

———. *Piano Stories*. Trans. Luis Harss. New York: New Directions, 2014.

———. "The Usher." In *Piano Stories*, trans. Luis Harss, 69–86. New York: New Directions, 2014.

Huhtamo, Erkki. "The Pleasures of the Peephole: An Archaeological Exploration of Peep Media." In *The Book of Imaginary Media: Excavating the Dream of the Ultimate Communication Medium*, ed. Eric Kluitenberg, 74–155. Rotterdam: NAi Publishers, 2006.

Huhtamo, Erkki, and Jussi Parikka, eds. *Media Archaeology: Approaches, Applications, and Implications*. Berkeley: University of California Press, 2011.

Hurtado, Leopoldo. "Acción y Reacción." *La vida literaria*, August 2, 1931, 2.

———. "Celuloide." *Martín Fierro* (November 1926). In Jason Borge, *Avances de Hollywood: Crítica cinematográfica en Latinoamérica*, 68–70. Rosario, Argentina: Beatriz Viterbo, 2005.

Huyssen, Andreas. *After the Great Divide: Modernism, Mass Culture, Postmodernism*. Bloomington: Indiana University Press, 1986.

Jackson, K. David, and Elizabeth Jackson. Afterword to Patrícia Galvão, *Industrial Park*, 140–54. Trans. Elizabeth Jackson and K. David Jackson. Lincoln: University of Nebraska Press, 1993.

Jameson, Fredric. "In the Mirror of Alternate Modernities." In *The Modernist Papers*, 281–93. London: Verso, 2007.

———. "Periodizing the 1960s." *Social Text* 9/10 (Spring 1984): 178–209.

———. *Postmodernism, or the Cultural Logic of Late Capitalism*. Durham, N.C.: Duke University Press, 1991.

———. "Seriality and Modern Literature." *Bucknell Review* 18.1 (Spring 1970): 63–80.

———. *A Singular Modernity: Essay on the Ontology of the Present*. London: Verso, 2013.

Jenemann, David. "Flying Solo: The Charms of the Radio Body." In *Broadcasting Modernism*, ed. Debra Rae Cohen, Michael Coyle, and Jane A. Lewty, 89–103. Gainesville: University Press of Florida, 2009.

Jenkins, Henry. *Fans, Bloggers, and Gamers: Exploring Participatory Culture*. New York: New York University Press, 2006.

Johnson, Randal. *The Film Industry in Brazil: Culture and the State*. Pittsburgh: University of Pittsburgh Press, 1987.

———. *Literature, Culture and Authoritarianism in Brazil, 1930–1945*. Washington, D.C.: Latin American Program, The Wilson Center, 1989.

Johnson, Randal, and Robert Stam. *Brazilian Cinema*. New York: Columbia University Press, 1995.

Jones, Caroline. "Senses." In *Critical Terms for Media Studies*, ed. W. J. T. Mitchell and Mark Hansen, 88–100. Chicago: University of Chicago Press, 2010.

Juan-Navarro, Santiago. "Hiperrealidad y simulacro: La crisis de la modernidad en 'El Muñeco,' de Virgilio Piñera." In *Virgilio Piñera: El artificio del miedo*, ed. Humberto López Cruz, 149–78. Madrid: Editorial Hispano Cubana, 2012.

Junco, Alfonso. "El cinematógrafo y la invasión pacífica." *El Universal*, June 1, 1929. In Jason Borge, *Avances de Hollywood: Crítica cinematográfica en Latinoamérica*, 115–19. Rosario, Argentina: Beatriz Viterbo, 2005.

Jurema, Abelardo de Araújo. "O Paraíso Norte Americano." *Momento*, no. 3 (March 1934): 14–15.

———. "Sobre os campos do noite." *Revista Acadêmica* 10 (April 1935): 3.

Jütte, Robert. *A History of the Senses: From Antiquity to Cyberspace*. Cambridge: Polity, 2005.

Kahn, Douglas. *Noise Water Meat: A History of Sound in the Arts*. Cambridge, Mass.: MIT Press, 2001.

Kantaris, Geoffrey. "Holograms and Simulacra: Bioy Casares, Subiela, Piglia." In *Science and the Creative Imagination in Latin America*, ed. Evelyn Fishburn and Eduardo L. Ortiz, 175–89. London: Institute for the Study of the Americas, 2005.

Karush, Matthew. *The Culture of Class: Radio and Cinema in the Making of a Divided Argentina*. Durham, N.C.: Duke University Press, 2012.

Keyserling, Conde. "Perspectivas sudamericanas." *Sur* 2 (1931): 3–12.

King, John. *Magical Reels*. London: Verso, 2000.

King, Norman. "The Sound of Silents." In *Silent Film*, ed. Richard Abel, 31–44. London: Anthlone Press, 1999.

Kittler, Friedrich A. *Discourse Networks, 1800/1900*. Stanford, Calif.: Stanford University Press, 1990.

———. *Gramophone, Film, Typewriter*. Trans. Geoffrey Winthrop-Young and Michael Wutz. Stanford, Calif.: Stanford University Press, 1999.

Kluitenberg, Eric. "On the Archaeology of Imaginary Media." In *Media Archaeology: Approaches, Applications, and Implications*, ed. Erkki Huhtamo and Jussi Parikka, 48–69. Berkeley: University of California Press, 2011.

———, ed. *The Book of Imaginary Media: Excavating the Dream of the Ultimate Communication Medium*. Rotterdam: NAi Publishers, 2006.

Kracauer, Siegfried. *The Mass Ornament: Weimar Essays*. Cambridge, Mass.: Harvard University Press, 2005.

———. *Theory of Film*. Princeton, N.J.: Princeton University Press, 1997.

Krajewski, Markus. *World Projects: Global Information before World War I*. Minneapolis: University of Minnesota Press, 2014.

Krauss, Rosalind. *The Originality of the Avant-Gardes and Other Modernist Myths*. Cambridge, Mass.: MIT Press, 1985.

Kronfeld, Chana. *On the Margins of Modernism*. Berkeley: University of California Press, 1996.

Laddaga, Reinaldo. *Literaturas indigentes y placeres bajos*. Rosario, Argentina: Beatriz Viterbo, 2000.

Lafetá, João Luíz. *1930, a crítica, e o modernismo*. São Paulo: Livraria Duas Cidades, 1974.

Latour, Bruno. *Pandora's Hope: Essays on the Reality of Science Studies*. Cambridge, Mass.: Harvard University Press, 1999.

Lee, Leo. *Shanghai Modern: The Flowering of a New Urban Culture in China, 1930–1945*. Cambridge, Mass.: Harvard University Press, 1999.

Leyda, Jay. *Kino: A History of the Russian and Soviet Film*. Princeton, N.J.: Princeton University Press, 1983.

Linden, David J. *Touch: The Science of Hand, Heart, and Mind*. New York: Penguin, 2015.

Lippit, Seiji. *Topographies of Japanese Modernism*. New York: Columbia University Press, 2002.

Lispector, Clarice. *A descoberta do mundo: Crônicas*. Rio de Janeiro: Rocco, 1999.

———. *The Hour of the Star*. Trans. Benjamin Moser. New York: New Directions, 2011.

———. *Outros escritos*. Ed. Teresa Montero Lícia Manzo. Rio de Janeiro: Rocco, 2005.

———. "Para a mulher que trabalha." In *Só para mulheres: Conceitos, receitas e segredos*, ed. Aparecida Maria Nunes, 14. Rio de Janeiro: Rocco, 2006.

———. *Selected Crônicas*. Trans. Giovanni Ponteiro. New York: New Directions, 1996.

Liu, Lydia H. "Writing." In *Critical Terms for Media Studies*, ed. W. J. T. Mitchell and Mark Hansen, 310–26. Chicago: University of Chicago Press, 2010.

López, Ana. "Early Cinema and Modernity in Latin America." *Cinema Journal* 40.1 (Fall 2000): 48–78.

López, María Pía. "30/43: Historia, Ensayo y Literatura." In *La década infame y los escritores suicidas (1930–1943)*, ed. David Viñas, Gabriela García Cedro, and María Pía López, 11–39. Buenos Aires: Paradiso Ediciones, Fundación Crónica General, 2007.

López Pellisa, Teresa. "Virtualidades distópicas en la ficción analógica: *La invención de Morel*, de Adolfo Bioy Casares." *Revista Iberoamericana* 78.238–39 (January June 2012): 73–89.

Love, Heather. "Close, But Not Deep: Literary Ethics and the Descriptive Turn." *New Literary History* 41.2 (Spring 2010): 371–91.

Loviglio, Jason. *Intimate Publics: Network Broadcasting and Mass-Mediated Democracy*. Minneapolis: University of Minnesota Press, 2005.

Ludmer, Josefina. *The Corpus Delicti: A Manual of Argentine Fictions*. Trans. Glen Close. Pittsburgh: University of Pittsburgh Press, 2004.

———. "La tragedia cómica." *Escritura: Revista de Teoría y Crítica Literaria* 7.13–14 (1982): 111–18.

———. "Tricks of the Weak." In *Feminist Perspectives on Sor Juan Inés de la Cruz*, ed. Stephanie Merrim, 86–93. Detroit: Wayne State University Press, 1991.

Madureira, Luís. *Cannibal Modernities: Postcoloniality and the Avant-Garde in Caribbean and Brazilian Literature*. Charlottesville: University of Virginia Press, 2005.

Magalhães Junior, R. "O romance proletário." *Correio da Manhã* (November 3, 1934): 6.

Mahieux, Viviane. *Urban Chroniclers in Latin America: The Shared Intimacy of Everyday Life*. Austin: University of Texas Press, 2011.

Mallea, Enrique. "La crisis y el hombre actual." *Megáfono*, no. 11 (August 1933): 1–6.

Mancini, Adriana. *Bioy Casares va al cine*. Buenos Aires: Libraria, 2014.

Manovich, Lev. "New Media from Borges to HTML." In *The New Media Reader*, vol. 1, ed. Noah Wardrip-Fruin and Nick Montfort, 13–25. Cambridge, Mass.: MIT Press, 2003.

Marcus, Laura. "Film." In *A Companion to Modernist Literature and Culture*, ed. David Bradshaw and Kevin J. H. Dettmar, 250–57. London: Blackwell, 2006.

Marinetti, Filippo Tommaso. "Drama of Distances" (1931). In "Radio Syntheses." *Modernism/Modernity* 16.2 (Spring 2010): 415–20.

Marks, Laura. *The Skin of the Film: Intercultural Cinema, Embodiment, and the Senses*. Durham, N.C.: Duke University Press, 2000.

———. *Touch: Sensuous Theory and Multisensory Media*. Minneapolis: University of Minnesota Press, 2002.

Martín-Barbero, Jesús. *De los medios a las mediaciones: Comunicación, cultura, hegemonía*. Mexico City: Ediciones G. Gili, 1987.

Martín Peña, Fernando. "Amigos del Cine." In *Amigos del Arte, 1924–1942*, ed. Patrícia Artundo and Marcelo Eduardo Pacheco. Buenos Aires: MALBA, 2008.

———. *Cien años de cine argentino*. Buenos Aires: Editorial Biblios, 2012.

Martins, Wilson. *The Modernist Idea: A Critical Survey of Brazilian Writing in the Twentieth Century*. Trans. Jack Tomlins. New York: New York University Press, 1970.

Marturano, Jorge. "Nuestro hombre en Buenos Aires: Una lectura cubana del peronismo a través de Virgilio Piñera." *MLN* 126.2 (March 2011): 323–43.

Masiello, Francine. *Between Civilization and Barbarism: Women, Nation, and Culture in Modern Argentina*. Lincoln: University of Nebraska Press, 1992.

———. *Lenguaje e ideología: Las escuelas argentinas de vanguardia*. Buenos Aires: Hachette, 1986.

Massumi, Brian. *Parables for the Virtual: Movement, Affect, Sensation*. Durham, N.C.: Duke University Press, 2002.

Matamoro, Blas. "La música, ese perseguidor." *Cuadernos hispanoamericanos* 625 (2002): 129–38.

Mattelart, Armand. *Networking the World: 1794–2000*. Trans. Liz Carey-Libbrecht and James A. Cohen. Minneapolis: University of Minnesota Press, 2000.

Mauro, Humberto. "Cinema falado no Brasil." *Cinearte* 324 (May 11, 1932): 10.

McCann, Bryan. *Hello, Hello Brazil!: Popular Music in the Making of Modern Brazil*. Durham, N.C.: Duke University Press, 2004.

McEnaney, Tom. "No Transmitter: Clandestine Radio Listening Communities in Ricardo Piglia's *The Absent City*." *Cultural Critique* 91 (Fall 2015): 72–97.

McHale, Brian. *Postmodernist Fiction*. New York: Methuen, 1987.

McLuhan, Marshall. *Understanding Media: The Extensions of Man*. Cambridge, Mass.: MIT Press, 1999.

Mejías-López, Alejandro. *The Inverted Conquest: The Myth of Modernity and the Transatlantic Onset of Modernism*. Nashville: Vanderbilt University Press, 2010.

Mello Franco, Afonso Arinos de. "Poesia, 1936." *Lanterna Verde* 4 (November 1936): 4, 11–12.

Merleau-Ponty, Maurice. *Phenomenology of Perception*. New York: Routledge, 2012.

Merrim, Stephanie. "Felisberto Hernández's Aesthetic of 'lo otro': The Writing of Indeterminacy." *Revista Canadiense de Estudios Hispánicos* 11.3 (Spring 1987): 521–40.

Miceli, Sérgio. *Intelectuais y classe dirigente no Brasil (1920–1945)*. São Paulo: DIFEL, 1979.

Miller, Nicola. *Reinventing Modernity in Latin America: Intellectuals Imagine the Future, 1900–1930*. New York: Palgrave, 2007.

Miller, Tyrus. *Late Modernism: Politics, Fiction and the Arts between the World Wars*. Berkeley: University of California Press, 1999.

Mitchell, W. J. T. "There Are No Visual Media." *Journal of Visual Culture* 4.2 (2005): 257–66.

Mitchell, W. J. T., and Mark Hansen, eds. *Critical Terms for Media Studies*. Chicago: University of Chicago Press, 2010.

Molloy, Sylvia. *Las letras de Borges y otros ensayos*. Rosario, Argentina: Beatriz Viterbo Editora, 1999.

Montaldo, Graciela, ed. *Yrigoyen entre Borges y Arlt (1916–1930)*. Buenos Aires: Paradiso, 2006.

———. *Zonas Ciegas: Populismos y experimentos culturales en Argentina*. Buenos Aires: Fondo de Cultura Económica, 2010.

Moriconi, Ítalo. "The Hour of the Star, or Clarice Lispector's Trash Hour." Trans. Paulo Henriques Britto. *Portuguese Literary and Cultural Studies* 4/5 (Spring/Fall 2000): 213–21.

Morillas Ventura, Enriqueta. "Felisberto y el cine." *Anales de literatura hispanoamericana* 32 (2003): 83–88.

Moser, Benjamin. *Why This World: A Biography of Clarice Lispector*. New York: Oxford University Press, 2009.

Mulvey, Laura. "Visual Pleasure and Narrative Cinema." In *Film Theory and Criticism: Introductory Readings*, ed. Leo Braudy and Marshall Cohen, 833–44. New York: Oxford University Press, 1999.

Murphet, Julian. *Multimedia Modernism: Literature and the Anglo-American Avant-garde*. Cambridge: Cambridge University Press, 2009.

Naficy, Hamid. "Theorizing 'Third World' Film Spectatorship." *Wide Angle* 18.4 (1996): 3–26.

Napolitano, Marcos. *Cultura Brasileira: Utopia e massificação (1950–1980)*. São Paulo: Editora Contexto, 2001.

Nieland, Justus. *Feeling Modern: The Eccentricities of Public Life*. Urbana: University of Illinois Press, 2008.

North, Michael. *Camera Works*. Oxford: Oxford University Press, 2005.

———. "International Media, International Modernism, and the Problem of Sound." In *Literature and Visual Technologies: Writing after Cinema*, ed. J. Murphet and L. Rainford, 53–58. London: Palgrave, 2003.

———. *1922: A Return to the Scene of the Modern*. New York: Oxford University Press, 1999.

O homem do povo. São Paulo: Impr. Oficial do Estado, Divisão de Arquivo do Estado de São Paulo, 1985.

O'Connor, Patrick. "The Moving Target of Fixated Desire: Felisberto's Paper Dolls." In *Latin American Fiction and Narratives of the Perverse: Paper Dolls and Spider Woman*, 75–120. New York: Palgrave, 2004.

Olivari, Nicolás. *El hombre de la baraja y la puñalada y otros escritos sobre cine*. Buenos Aires: Adriana Hidalgo, 2000.

Olwell, Victoria. "The Body Types: Corporeal Documents and Body Politics circa 1900." In *Literary Secretaries/Secretarial Culture*, ed. Leah Price and Pamela Thurswell, 48–62. Aldershot: Ashgate, 2005.

Ong, Walter. *Orality and Literacy: The Technologizing of the Word*. New York: Routledge, 2002.

Ortiz, Renato. *A Moderna Tradicão Brasileira: Cultura brasileira e indústria cultural*. São Paulo: Editora Brasiliense, 1988.

———. "Popular Culture, Modernity and Nation." In *Through the Kaleidoscope: The Experience of Modernity in Latin America*, ed. Vivian Schelling, 127–47. London: Verso, 2000.

Oubiña, David. "Del sueño tecnológico a la escritura audiovisual: Literatura y Cine (1920–1960)." In *Historia crítica de la literatura argentina*, vol. 7, *Rupturas*, ed. Celina Manzoni, 343–68. Buenos Aires: Emecé, 2009.

Palma, Clemente. *XYZ: Una novela grotesca*. Madrid: La Tinta del Calamar Ediciones, 2010.

Parikka, Jussi. *What Is Media Archaeology?* Cambridge: Polity, 2012.

Pauls, Alan. *El factor Borges*. Barcelona: Editorial Anagrama, 2004.

Paz, Octavio. *Los hijos del limo: Del Romanticismo a la Vanguardia*. Barcelona: Seix Barral, 1974.

Paz Soldán, Edmundo. "La imágen fotográfica, entre el aura y el cuestamiento de la identidad: Una lectura de 'La Paraguaya' y *La invención de Morel.*" *Revista Iberoamericana* 73.221 (October–December 2007): 759–70.

Peixoto, Marta. *Passionate Fictions: Gender, Narrative, and Violence in Clarice Lispector.* Minneapolis: University of Minnesota Press, 1992.

———. "Fatos são pedras duras: Urban Poverty in Clarice Lispector." In *Closer to the Wild Heart: Essays on Clarice Lispector*, ed. Cláudia Pazos Alonso and Claire Williams, 106–25. Oxford: Legenda, 2002.

Petit de Murat, Ulyses. *Borges.* Buenos Aires: Municipalidad de la Ciudad de Buenos Aires, Secretaría de Cultura, 1980.

Picchia, Menotti del. "Arte Moderna." In *Vanguarda Europeia e Modernismo Brasileiro*, ed. Gilberto Mendonça Telles, 417–24. Rio de Janeiro: José Olympio, 2012.

Piñera, Virgilio. *Cold Tales.* Trans. Mark Schafer. Hygiene, Colo.: Eridanos Press; New York: Rizzoli International, 1988.

———. "Grafomanía." In *Cuentos fríos & El que vino a salvarme*, 293. Madrid: Cátedra, 2008.

———. "El muñeco." In *Cuentos fríos & El que vino a salvarme*, 255–87. Madrid: Cátedra, 2008.

———. "Nota sobre literatura argentina de hoy." In *Órbita de Virgilio Piñera*, ed. David Leyva González, 191–98. Havana: Ediciones Unión, 2011.

Podestá, José María. "La evolución cinegráfica angloamericana." *La Pluma* (October 1930): 33–36.

———. "El film hablado." *La Pluma* (June 1929): 33–36.

Polet, Jacques. "Early Cinematographic Spectacles: The Role of Sound Accompaniment in the Reception of Moving Images." In *The Sounds of Early Cinema*, ed. Richard Abel and Rick Altman, 192–97. Bloomington: Indiana University Press, 2001.

Poole, Janet. *When the Future Disappears: The Modernist Imagination in Late Colonial Korea.* New York: Columbia University Press, 2014.

Porzecanski, Teresa. "Felisberto Hernández: Un estudio del régimen de la mirada." *Cuadernos Hispanoamericanos* 625 (2002): 81–86.

Price, Leah, and Pamela Thurswell, eds. *Literary Secretaries/Secretarial Culture.* Aldershot: Ashgate, 2005.

Puchner, Martin. *Poetry of the Revolution: Marx, Manifestos, and the Avant-gardes.* Princeton, N.J.: Princeton University Press, 2006.

Quay, Stephen, and Timothy Quay. *Piano Tuner of Earthquakes.* Zeitgeist Films, 2007.

Quiroga, Horacio. "Espectros que hablan." In *Arte y lenguaje del cine*, ed. Carlos Dámaso Martínez, 363–69. Buenos Aires: Losada, 1997. Originally published in *La Nación*, March 17, 1929.

———. "El Vampiro." In *Todos los cuentos*, 717–31. Paris: Colección Archivos, 1996.

Rabinovitz, Lauren. "More than the Movies: A History of Somatic Visual Culture through *Hale's Tours*, Imax, and Motion Simulation Rides." In *Memory Bytes: History, Technology, and Digital Culture*, ed. Lauren

Rabinovitz and Abraham Geil, 99–125. Durham, N.C.: Duke University Press, 2004.

Ram, Harsha. "Futurist Geographies: Uneven Modernities and the Struggle for Aesthetic Autonomy: Paris, Italy, Russia, 1909–1914." In *The Oxford Handbook to Global Modernisms*, ed. Mark Wollaeger, 313–40. Oxford: Oxford University Press, 2012.

Rama, Ángel. *La ciudad letrada*. Hanover, N.H.: Ediciones del Norte, 1984.

———. "Las dos vanguardias latinoamericanas." In *La riesgosa navegación del escritor exiliado*, 135–48. Montevideo: Arca, 1993.

Ramos, Graciliano. *Angústia*. São Paulo: Editora Record, 1985.

———. *Cartas inéditas: De Graciliano Ramos a seus tradutores argentinos*. Ed. Pedro Moacir Maia and Fernando da Rocha Peres. Salvador: EDUFBA, 2008.

———. *Linhas tortas*. São Paulo: Editora Record, 1989.

———. *Memórias do Cárcere*. Vols. 1 and 2. São Paulo: Martins, 1965.

Ramos, Julio. *Desencuentros de la modernidad en América Latina*. Mexico City: Fondo de Cultura Económica, 2003.

Rancière, Jacques. *The Emancipated Spectator*. London: Verso, 2011.

Ricoeur, Paul. *Time and Narrative*. Vol. 1. Trans. Kathleen Blamey and David Pellauer. Chicago: University of Chicago Press, 1990.

Rieder, John. *Colonialism and the Emergence of Science Fiction*. Middletown, Conn.: Wesleyan University Press, 2008.

Rocca, Pablo. "Cruces y límites de la vanguardia uruguaya (campo, ciudad, letras, imágenes)." In *Las vanguardias literarias en Argentina, Uruguay y Paraguay*, ed. Carlos García and Dieter Reichardt, 415–26. Madrid: Iberoamericana, 2004.

Rocha, Glauber. "An Esthetic of Hunger." In Randal Johnson and Robert Stam, *Brazilian Cinema*, 68–72. New York: Columbia University Press, 1995.

Rodowick, David. *The Virtual Life of Film*. Cambridge, Mass.: Harvard University Press, 2007.

Rodriguez Monegal, Emir. *Jorge Luis Borges: A Literary Biography*. New York: Paragon House, 1988.

Romero, José Luis. *Latinoamérica: Las ciudades y las ideas*. Mexico City: Siglo Veintiuno Editores, 1986.

———. "Introducción a un sudamericanismo esencial." *Sur* 8 (1933): 131–40.

Rosenberg, Fernando. *The Avant-gardes and Geopolitics in Latin America*. Pittsburgh: University of Pittsburgh Press, 2006.

Ruffinelli, Jorge. "Leer a Borges Ver Cine." *Texto Crítico* 6.11 (July 2002): 13–52.

Saítta, Sylvia, ed. *Contra: La Revista de los franco-tiradores*. Buenos Aires: Universidad Nacional de Quilmes, 2005.

———. "Nuevo periodismo y literatura argentina." In *Historia crítica de la literatura argentina*, vol. 7, *Rupturas*, ed. Celina Manzoni, 239–62. Buenos Aires: Emecé, 2009.

Salazkina, Masha. *In Excess: Sergei Eisenstein's Mexico*. Chicago: University of Chicago Press, 2009.

Salvatore, Ricardo Donato. "Imperial Mechanics: South America's Hemispheric Integration in the Machine." *American Quarterly* 58.3 (September 2006): 662–91.

Sampião, Jack. "Cinema." *Boletim de Ariel*, no. 1 (October 1931): 16.

Santiago, Silviano. *O cosmopolitismo do pobre: Crítica literária e crítica cultural.* Belo Horizonte: Editora UFMG, 2004.

———. "O intellectual modernista revisitado." In *Nas malhas da letra*, 165–75. São Paulo: Companhia das Letras, 1989.

———. "Literature and Mass Culture." In *The Space In-Between: Essays on Latin American Culture*, ed. Ana Lúcia Gazzola, 119–32. Durham, N.C.: Duke University Press, 2001.

———. *Nas malhas da letra.* São Paulo: Companhia das Letras, 1989.

———. "Pósfacio." In Graciliano Ramos, *Angústia.* Rio de Janeiro: Record, 2003.

Santos, Lidia. *Kitsch Tropical: Los medios en la literatura y el arte en América Latina.* Madrid: Iberoamericana, 2004.

Saratsola, Owald. *Función completa, por favor: Un siglo de cine en Montevideo.* Montevideo: Ediciones Trilce, 2005.

Sarlo, Beatriz. *La imaginación técnica: Sueños modernos de la cultura argentina.* Buenos Aires: Nueva Visión, 1992.

———. *Jorge Luis Borges: A Writer on the Edge.* Trans. John King. London: Verso, 1993.

———. *Una modernidad periférica: Buenos Aires, 1920 y 1930.* Buenos Aires: Ediciones Nueva Visión, 1988.

———. "Una poética de la ficción." In *Historia crítica de la literatura argentina: El oficio se afirma*, ed. Sylvia Saítta, 19–38. Buenos Aires: Emecé, 2004.

———. *The Technical Imagination: Argentine Culture's Modern Dreams.* Trans. Xavier Callahan. Stanford, Calif.: Stanford University Press, 2008.

———. *Tiempo Presente: Notas sobre el cambio de una cultura.* Buenos Aires: Siglo XXI, 2001.

Sartre, Jean-Paul. "Collectivities." In *Critique of Dialectical Reason I: Theory of Practical Ensembles*, trans. Alan Sheridan-Smith, 256–344. London: NLB, 1976.

Schachter, Allison. *Diasporic Modernisms: Hebrew and Yiddish Literature in the Twentieth Century.* Oxford: Oxford University Press, 2014.

Schopenhauer, Arthur. *The World as Will and Representation*, vol. 2, trans. E. F. J. Payne. Clinton, Mass.: Falcon's Wing Press, 1958.

Schwartz, Jorge. "De lo estético a lo ideológico: *Klaxon* y *Revista de Antropofagia.*" In *La cultura de un siglo: América Latina en sus revistas*, ed. Saúl Sosnowski, 51–64. Buenos Aires: Alianza, 1999.

———. *Las vanguardias latinoamericanas: Textos programáticos y críticos.* Mexico City: Fondo de Cultura Económica, 2002.

Schwarz, Roberto. "A Carroça, o Bonde e o Poeta Modernista." In *Que horas são?* 11–21. São Paulo: Companhia das Letras, 1987.

———. "The Cart, the Tram, and the Modernist Poet." In *Misplaced Ideas:*

Essays on Brazilian Culture*, trans. John Gledson, 108–25. London: Verso, 1992.

———. *Misplaced Ideas: Essays on Brazilian Culture*. Trans. John Gledson. London: Verso, 1992.

Scott, Travers D. "The Postfeminist User: Feminism and Media Theory in Two Interactive Media Properties." *Feminist Media Studies* 10.4 (2010): 457–75.

Seegert, Alf. "The Mistress of Sp[l]ices: Technovirtual Liaisons in Adolfo Bioy Casares's *The Invention of Morel*." *Journal of the Fantastic in the Arts* 23.2 (2012): 197–214.

Senna, Homero. "Revisão do Modernismo." In *Graciliano Ramos: Coletânea*, ed. Sonia Brayner, 50–51. Rio de Janeiro: Civilização Brasileira, 1978.

Sevcenko, Nicolau. *Orfeu Extático na Metrópole: São Paulo, cultura e sociedade nos frementes anos 20*. São Paulo: Companhia das Letras, 1992.

Shih, Shu-mei. *The Lure of the Modern: Writing Modernism in Semi-Colonial China, 1917–1937*. Berkeley: University of California Press, 2001.

Shohat, Ella, and Robert Stam. *Unthinking Eurocentrism: Multiculturalism and the Media*. New York: Routledge, 1994.

Silverman, Kaja. *The Acoustic Mirror: The Female Voice in Psychoanalysis and Cinema*. Bloomington: Indiana University Press, 1988.

Simis, Anita. "Movies and Moviemakers under Vargas." *Latin American Perspectives* 29.1 (January 2002): 106–14.

Snook, Margaret L. "The Narrator as Creator and Critic in 'The Invention of More.'" *Latin American Literary Review* 7.14 (Spring 1979): 45–51.

Sobchack, Vivian. *Carnal Thoughts*. Berkeley: University of California Press, 2004.

Sontag, Susan. *Regarding the Pain of Others*. New York: Picador, 2003.

Souto, Mario Raimondo, and Carlos Scavino. *Una historia del cine en Uruguay: Memorias compartidas*. Montevideo: Planeta, 2010.

Staiger, Janet. *Perverse Spectators: The Practices of Film Reception*. New York: New York University Press, 2000.

Stanford Friedman, Susan. "Definitional Excursions: The Meanings of Modern/Modernity/ Modernism." *Modernism/Modernity* 8.3 (2001): 493–513.

———. "Periodizing Modernism: Postcolonial Modernities and the Space/Time Borders of Modernist Studies." *Modernism/Modernity* 13.3 (2006): 425–43.

Sterling, Bruce. "Media Paleontology." In *The Book of Imaginary Media: Excavating the Dream of the Ultimate Communication Medium*, ed. Eric Kluitenberg, 56–73. Rotterdam: NAi Publishers, 2006.

Sterne, Jonathan. "Out with the Trash." In *Residual Media*, ed. Charles Acland, 16–31. Minneapolis: University of Minnesota Press, 2007.

Stewart, Susan. *On Longing: Narrative of the Miniature, the Gigantic, the Souvenir, the Collection*. Baltimore: Johns Hopkins University Press, 1984.

Stiegler, Bernard. "Memory." In *Critical Terms for Media Studies*, ed. W. J.

T. Mitchell and Mark Hansen, 64–87. Chicago: University of Chicago Press, 2010.

Storni, Alfonsina. "La perfecta dactilógrafa." In *Obras. Prosa. Narraciones, Periodismo, Teatro. Tomo II*, ed. Delfina Muschietti, 908–11. Buenos Aires: Losada, 2002.

Stratta, Isabel. "Documentos por una poética del relato." In *Historia crítica de la literatura argentina: El oficio se afirma*, ed. Sylvia Saítta, 39–63. Buenos Aires: Emecé, 2004.

Striphas, Ted. *The Late Age of Print: Everyday Book Culture from Consumerism to Control.* New York: Columbia University Press, 2011.

Sucre, Natalia. "Distracting Art: Reading Shock in Felisberto Hernández's 'Las Hortensias.'" *Hispania* 86.3 (September 2003): 482–92.

Süssekind, Flora. *Cinematograph of Words: Literature, Technique and Modernization in Brazil.* Trans. Paulo Henriques Britto. Stanford, Calif.: Stanford University Press, 1997.

———. *Tal Brasil, Qual Romance? Uma ideologia estética e sua história: O naturalismo.* Rio de Janeiro: Achiamé, 1984.

Suvin, Darko. "On the Poetics of the SF Genre." *College English* 34.3 (December 1972): 372–82.

Szeemann, Harald, ed. *Le Macchine Celebi/The Bachelor Machines.* New York: Rizzoli, 1975.

Taneja, Payal. "The Tropical Empire: Exotic Animals and Beastly Men in *The Island of Dr. Moreau.*" *English Studies in Canada* 39.2–3 (June/September 2013): 139–59.

Taussig, Michael. *Mimesis and Alterity: A Particular History of the Senses.* New York: Routledge, 1993.

Tew, H. P. "Cinema in the Argentine." *Close Up* 17.2 (February 1930): 140–45.

Todorov, Tzvetan. *The Fantastic: A Structural Approach to a Literary Genre.* Ithaca, N.Y.: Cornell University Press, 1975.

Tratner, Michael. *Crowd Scenes: Movies and Mass Politics.* New York: Fordham University Press, 2008.

Treadwell, Sophie. *Machinal.* London: Royal National Theater, 1995.

Trotsky, Leon. *Literature and Revolution.* Ann Arbor: University of Michigan Press, 1968.

Trotter, David. *Cinema and Modernism.* London: Wiley, 2007.

Ulanovsky, Carlos. *Paren las rotativas: Diarios, revistas, periodistas.* Buenos Aires: Emecé, 2005.

Unruh, Vicky. "Las ágiles musas de la modernidad: Patrícia Galvão y Norah Lange." *Revista Iberoamericana* 64.182–83 (January–June 1998): 271–86.

———. *Latin American Vanguards: The Art of Contentious Encounters.* Berkeley: University of California Press, 1994.

———. "Modernity's Labors in Latin America: The Cultural Work of Cuba's Avant-Gardes." In *The Oxford Handbook to Global Modernisms*, ed. Mark Wollaeger, 341–66. Oxford: Oxford University Press, 2012.

Valente, Luiz Fernando. "Canonizando Pagu." *Letras de hoje* 33.3 (1998): 27–38.

Vallejo, César. "Autopsia del superrealismo." In Jorge Schwartz, *Las vanguardias latinoamericanas: Textos programáticos y críticos*, 465–70. Mexico City: Fondo de Cultura Económica, 2002.

Veiroj, Federico. *La vida útil*. PAL, 2010.

Verani, Hugo. *Narrativa vanguardista hispanoamericana*. Mexico City: Manatí, 1996.

Viñas, David. "La historia excluida: Ubicación de Martínez Estrada." In *La década infame y los escritores suicidas (1930–1943)*, ed. David Viñas, Gabriela García Cedro, and María Pía López, 100–107. Buenos Aires: Paradiso Ediciones, Fundación Crónica General, 2007.

———, ed. *Más allá del Boom: Literatura y mercado*. Mexico City: Marcha Editores, 1981.

Virilio, Paul. *War and Cinema: The Logistics of Perception*. Trans. Patrick Camiller. New York: Verso, 1989.

Weber, Eugene. *The Hollow Years: France in the 1930s*. New York: W. W. Norton, 1994.

Wegenstein, Bernadette. "Body." In *Critical Terms for Media Studies*, ed. W. J. T. Mitchell and Mark Hansen, 19–34. Chicago: University of Chicago Press, 2010.

Wells, Sarah Ann. "Graciliano, Historiador do Presente." *Miscelânea* 10 (July–December 2011): 23–41.

——— ."Parallel Modernities? The First Reception of Soviet Cinema in Latin America." In *Cosmopolitan Film Cultures in Latin America, 1896–1960*, ed. Rielle Navitski and Nicholas Poppe. Bloomington: University of Indiana Press, 2017.

White, Hayden. "The Modernist Event." In *The Persistence of History: Cinema, Television, and the Modern Event*, ed. Vivian Sobchack, 17–38. New York: Routledge, 1996.

Wicke, Jennifer. "Appreciation, Depreciation: Modernism's Speculative Bubble." *Modernism/Modernity* 8.3 (September 2001): 389–403.

Willemen, Paul. *Looks and Frictions: Essays in Cultural Studies and Film Theory*. Bloomington: Indiana University Press, 1994.

Williams, Daryl. *Culture Wars in Brazil: The First Vargas Regime, 1930–1945*. Durham, N.C.: Duke University Press, 2001.

Williams, Linda. *Figures of Desire: A Theory and Analysis of Surrealist Film*. Urbana: University of Illinois Press, 1981.

Williams, Raymond. "Dominant, Residual, and Emergent." In *Marxism and Literature*, 121–27. Oxford: Oxford University Press, 1977.

———. *Key Words: A Vocabulary of Culture and Society*. Oxford: Oxford University Press, 1985.

———. *Television: Technology and Cultural Form*. New York: Schocken Books, 1975.

Wollaeger, Mark. Introduction to *The Oxford Handbook to Global Modernisms*, ed. Mark Wollaeger. Oxford: Oxford University Press, 2012.

Wollen, Peter. "Modern Times: Cinema/Americanism/The Robot." In *Raiding the Icebox: Reflections on Twentieth-Century Culture*, 35–71. Bloomington: Indiana University Press, 1993.

Yúdice, George. "Rethinking the Theory of the Avant-Garde from the Periphery." In *Modernism and Its Margins: Reinscribing Modernity from Spain and Latin America*, ed. Anthony Geist and José Monleón, 52–80. New York: Garland, 1999.

Yunque, Álvaro. "Limaduras." In *Contra: La revista de los franco-tiradores*, ed. Sylvia Saítta. Buenos Aires: Universidad de Quilmes Editorial, 2005.

Zielinski, Siegfried. *Deep Time of the Media: Towards an Archaeology of Seeing and Hearing by Technical Means*. Cambridge, Mass.: MIT Press, 2006.

———. "Modelling Media for Ignatius Loyola: A Case Study on Athanasius Kircher's World of Apparatus between the Imaginary and the Real." In *The Book of Imaginary Media: Excavating the Dream of the Ultimate Communication Medium*, ed. Eric Kluitenberg, 28–55. Rotterdam: NAi Publishers, 2006.

Index

FLASHPOINTS

1. *On Pain of Speech: Fantasies of the First Order and the Literary Rant,* Dina Al-Kassim
2. *Moses and Multiculturalism,* Barbara Johnson, with a foreword by Barbara Rietveld
3. *The Cosmic Time of Empire: Modern Britain and World Literature,* Adam Barrows
4. *Poetry in Pieces: César Vallejo and Lyric Modernity,* Michelle Clayton
5. *Disarming Words: Empire and the Seductions of Translation in Egypt,* Shaden M. Tageldin
6. *Wings for Our Courage: Gender, Erudition, and Republican Thought,* Stephanie H. Jed
7. *The Cultural Return,* Susan Hegeman
8. *English Heart, Hindi Heartland: The Political Life of Literature in India,* Rashmi Sadana
9. *The Cylinder: Kinematics of the Nineteenth Century,* Helmut Müller-Sievers
10. *Polymorphous Domesticities: Pets, Bodies, and Desire in Four Modern Writers,* Juliana Schiesari
11. *Flesh and Fish Blood: Postcolonialism, Translation, and the Vernacular,* S. Shankar
12. *The Fear of French Negroes: Transcolonial Collaboration in the Revolutionary Americas,* Sara E. Johnson
13. *Figurative Inquisitions: Conversion, Torture, and Truth in the Luso-Hispanic Atlantic,* Erin Graff Zivin
14. *Cosmopolitan Desires: Global Modernity and World Literature in Latin America,* Mariano Siskind
15. *Fiction Beyond Secularism,* Justin Neuman
16. *Periodizing Jameson: Dialectics, the University, and the Desire for Narrative,* Phillip E. Wegner
17. *The Practical Past,* Hayden White
18. *The Powers of the False: Reading, Writing, Thinking Beyond Truth and Fiction,* Doro Wiese
19. *The Object of the Atlantic: Concrete Aesthetics in Cuba, Brazil, and Spain, 1868–1968,* Rachel Price
20. *Epic and Exile: Novels of the German Popular Front, 1933–1945,* Hunter Bivens
21. *An Innocent Abroad: Lectures in China,* J. Hillis Miller
22. *Form and Instability: East Europe, Literature, Postimperial Difference,* Anita Starosta
23. *Bombay Modern: Arun Kolatkar and Bilingual Literary Culture,* Anjali Nerlekar
24. *Intimate Relations: Social Reform and the Late Nineteenth-Century South Asian Novel,* Krupa Shandilya
25. *Media Laboratories: Late Modernist Authorship in South America,* Sarah Ann Wells